No Safe Place

Toxic Waste,
Leukemia,
and Community Action

Phil Brown and
Edwin J. Mikkelsen

With a New Foreword by Jonathan Harr
and a New Preface by Phil Brown

UNIVERSITY OF CALIFORNIA PRESS
BERKELEY LOS ANGELES LONDON

University of California Press
Berkeley and Los Angeles, California

University of California Press, Ltd.
London, England

© 1990 by
The Regents of the University of California
First Paperback Printing 1992

Foreword and Preface (1997)
© 1997 by The Regents of the University of California

The Library of Congress has cataloged the previous printing
of this book as follows:

Library of Congress Cataloging-in-Publication Data

Brown, Phil.
    No safe place : toxic waste, leukemia, and community action / Phil
Brown and Edwin J. Mikkelsen.
        p. cm.
    Includes bibliographical references and index.
    ISBN 0-520-07034-8 (alk. paper)
    1. Leukemia in children—Massachusetts—Woburn. 2. Hazardous
wastes—Environmental aspects—Massachusetts—Woburn.
    I. Mikkelsen, Edwin J.   II. Title.
    RJ416.L4B76   1990
    618.92'99419'0097444—dc20   90-33991

ISBN 0-520-21248-7 (pbk. : alk. paper)

Printed in the United States of America

2 3 4 5 6 7 8 9

The paper used in this publication meets the minimum requirements of American National Standard for Information Sciences—Permanence of Paper for
Printed Library Materials, ANSI Z39.48-1984

In recognition of their suffering,
and as testimony to their importance
beyond the bounds of their community,
we dedicate this book
to the children of Woburn.

Contents

List of Tables and Maps

Maps

Tables

Foreword

I spent eight and a half years researching and writing my book *A Civil Action*, which recounts the saga of the Woburn case. During that time, as I spoke with the parents in Woburn whose children had been stricken with leukemia, and with Jan Schlichtmann, the lawyer who represented the families and who became the central figure in my book, I learned that there was another writer hard at work on the same subject. This was not, I admit, welcome news. Most writers I know are exceedingly, almost insanely, possessive of their subjects. The specter of someone else coming up behind you—and swiftly gaining ground at that—is ample cause for mental derangement.

This jealousy was, of course, a churlish reaction on my part. The Woburn story didn't belong to me. If it "belonged" to anyone, it was to the Woburn families, and they had made abundantly clear their desire to have the story told and disseminated as widely as possible.

I'd been working on my book for almost four years before I finally made Phil Brown's acquaintance. We shared some of our experiences—me as wary as a poker player and Phil, as far as I could tell, wonderfully open and engaging. It quickly became apparent to both of us that we were writing very different and yet entirely compatible books. I now regard them as brother and sister, as companions to each other. Together they give the fullest picture of what happened in the Woburn toxic waste case.

My narrative strategy was to use the tragic events in Woburn as the germ from which the lawsuit against Beatrice Foods and W. R. Grace sprang, and to examine in detail the inner workings of the law. Phil and his co-author, Edwin Mikkelson, chose to keep their focus largely on Woburn—on the families and their efforts to cope with personal tragedy and to organize a concerted response.

I confess that in some ways I regard *No Safe Place* as a more important book than my own. It provides a virtual blueprint for community action by offering a detailed, lucid, and highly readable analysis of the significance of Woburn for countless other communities across America. By using examples taken from other contaminated communities, as well as from Woburn, it develops the concept of "popular epidemiology," which explains how laypeople can gather information to make a case for deleterious environmental health effects.

The Woburn families exhibited incredible energy, courage, and resolve in their investigations, and *No Safe Place* does a wonderful job of telling that part of the story. It offers a clinical, yet compassionate glimpse into the minds of people for whom environmental contamination meant severe illness and often death. It traces the opposition the families faced from the polluting corporations and from the state and federal agencies that were supposed to protect them. And yet, despite the suffering and the difficulties it documents, *No Safe Place* holds out the hope that through communal support and political action we can make the world a safer place.

Jonathan Harr
Northampton, MA
March 1997

Preface (1997)

As you read this preface, the Woburn case will have been going on for one-quarter of a century, since Jimmy Anderson was diagnosed with leukemia in 1972. For the 1997 printing of *No Safe Place* I am taking this opportunity to update some material: the incidence of leukemia, the litigation, the Department of Public Health reanalyses of data, the cleanup, and the larger impact of the Woburn case. Richard Clapp and Gretchen Latowsky have been very helpful in this task.

Leukemia Incidence

Only two new cases of childhood leukemia were diagnosed in Woburn from 1985 to the 1990s; this incidence is slightly lower than what would be expected by chance (that is, lower than the background rate) and represents a significantly smaller number of cases than was recorded when Wells G and H were operating. This additional piece of data, available in retrospect, provides evidence that the closure of the contaminated wells removed the cause of the leukemia cluster.

The Litigation

The book ends with the rejection of an appeal of the case against Beatrice by a three-judge panel of the appellate court. Following that, the full Court of Appeals turned the case away. Jan Schlictmann asked the Massachusetts Superior Court for depositions and a bill of discovery from Mary Ryan, who had been involved in withholding Riley tannery documents. Taking the case to its final possible location, Schlictmann sought a hearing at the U.S. Supreme Court but was turned down.

Department of Public Health Reanalyses

The Department of Public Health reanalyzed the Woburn Environment & Birth Study (WEBS) but then kept the record under wraps for several years. In 1994 the DPH reported only on reproductive disorders and birth defects and said it was still working on the leukemia reanalysis. The officials claimed they found no excess of reproductive disorders and birth defects for Woburn. However, the FACE activists, Harvard biostatisticians, and various scholars in the natural, life, and social sciences examined the DPH report. They found that the most intensive study period for the DPH was a prospective study for 1989–1991—long after the wells were closed. As a result, the citizens and their supporters believe the state continues to deny the health effects of Woburn's past contamination. They are working to obtain the DPH's data set and conduct a new reanalysis themselves.

In May 1996 the DPH released the report that detailed their reanalysis of the leukemia data: "Woburn Childhood Leukemia Follow-Up Study." The officials concurred with the Woburn activists that there was a significant dose-response relationship ($p < .05$) between leukemia and mothers' drinking contaminated water (from Wells G and H) during pregnancy. Some family members wept on hearing the results, and the families were pleased and vindicated by this finding.

The Cleanup

Wells G and H are being cleaned up with an air stripper which creates droplets that vaporize and remove the volatile organic compounds (VOCs) from the water, a process that is expected to produce drinkable water from those wells in fifty years. Although EPA procedures call for a cleanup, it is not clear why producing potable water is a useful thing to do; the wells have been off line for a long time and suitable water is provided from other sources. At the Industriplex site, originally thought to be the contamination source, the contaminated area has been capped to develop the site as a commercial property. The EPA touts Industriplex as a model for its "brownfields" development program, which upsets Woburn activists because they don't believe Industriplex can be sufficiently cleaned up to be useful. In particular, the site continues to leach arsenic and chromium into the Aberjona River, which distributes these substances downstream to the Mystic Lakes. Activists are also upset that the upcoming Superfund reauthorization bill may remove third party liability at cleanups, making it impossible to hold the polluting firms responsible.

The Larger Impact of Woburn

The leukemia reanalysis provided a form of closure to FACE's major public presence. As an organization, FACE has basically reverted to a grassroots organization that meets in people's kitchens. Leaders are still called by the

DPH to review materials and other citizen groups call each week to seek advice, but FACE does not have the public presence it once did. Donna Robbins, one of the leaders, received an award from the Massachusetts Public Health Association in 1996 for her many years of hard work on the Woburn case. Gretchen Latowsky is frequently called upon to lecture on Woburn.

Even if Woburn activists are not still in the trenches, thousands of communities around the country are fighting similar battles. In many cases, they know of Woburn and are inspired by the efforts of the residents, their lawyers, and their supporters. The toxic waste movement has become a major force in American political culture. Arising from that, environmental justice activists have emphasized the inequalities of race and class in exposure to toxic hazards, in obtaining Superfund status, and in assessment of fines against polluters.

In 1995 Jonathan Harr published his book *A Civil Action*, which became a bestseller. The book has been on the New York Times Paperback Bestseller List for thirty-six weeks and is now in fourth place (June, 1997). Anyone interested in the history of the Woburn cluster will find this book an exciting, well-written approach to the complex legal issues in the case, a good snapshot of many personalities, and a remarkable insight into the daily actions and feelings of Jan Schlictmann, the families' lawyer. Robert Redford purchased the film rights and work is under way on a film version starring John Travolta as Jan Schlictmann. It is amazing that a book of this sort should grab so much public attention. The fine writing of the book certainly accounts in part for its success, but more important, the book's popularity signifies that an enormous number of people sympathize with the plight of the Woburn families and that many others face a similar plight in contaminated communities around the country.

Studying the Woburn case had a dramatic impact on me, causing me to shift my research focus substantially from the time of my first explorations of this topic in 1985. I have written a number of articles on the further developments of toxic activism (some based on additional interviews with FACE activists, subsequent to the book research), which are listed below as part of the Bibliography for the 1997 printing.

Phil Brown
May 1997

Bibliography

Additional Studies on Woburn

Harr, Jonathan. *A Civil Action.* New York: Random House, 1995.

Massachusetts Department of Public Health. "Woburn Environment & Birth Study—Synopsis." Massachusetts Department of Public Health, Bureau of Environmental Health Assessment. August 1994.

———. "Woburn Childhood Leukemia Follow-Up Study." Massachusetts Department of Public Health, Bureau of Environmental Health Assessment. May 1996.

Articles by Phil Brown on Woburn and Other Toxic Contamination Issues

Allen, Susan, and Phil Brown. "Public Reaction to Toxic Waste Contamination: Analysis of a Social Movement." *International Journal of Health Services,* 1990, 20:485–499.

Brown, Phil. "The Popular Epidemiology Approach to Toxic Waste Contamination." Pp. 133–155 in Stephen Robert Couch and J. Stephen Kroll-Smith, eds., *Communities at Risk: Collective Responses to Technological Hazards.* New York: Peter Lang Publishers, 1991.

———. "Toxic Waste Contamination and Popular Epidemiology: Lay and Professional Ways of Knowing." *Journal of Health and Social Behavior,* 1992, 33:267–281.

Brown, Phil, and Susan Masterson-Allen. "The Toxic Waste Movement: A New Kind of Activism." *Society and Natural Resources,* 1994, 7:269–286.

Brown, Phil, and Faith Ferguson. " 'Making a Big Stink': Women's Work, Women's Relationships, and Toxic Waste Activism." *Gender & Society,* 1995, 9:145–172.

Brown, Phil. "Popular Epidemiology, Toxic Wastes, and Social Movements." Pp. 91–112 in Jonathan Gabe, ed., *Medicine, Health and Risk: Sociological Perspectives.* Oxford, UK: Blackwell, 1995.

———. "Race, Class, and Environmental Health: A Review and Systematization of the Literature." *Environmental Research,* 1995, 69:15–30.

Brown, Phil, and Judith Kelly. "Physicians' Knowledge of and Actions Concerning Environmental Health Hazards: Analysis of Survey of Massachusetts Physicians." *Industrial and Environmental Crisis Quarterly,* 1996, 9:512–542.

Brown, Phil. "Popular Epidemiology Revisited." *Current Sociology,* 1997, 45:137–156.

Brown, Phil, Desiree Ciambrone, and Lori Hunter. "Does Green Mask Grey?: Environmental Equity Issues at the Metropolitan Level." *International Journal of Contemporary Sociology,* forthcoming.

Preface (1990)

Everybody is going to be poisoned,
even the people making the profits.
Woburn mother

There is a childhood leukemia cluster in the working-class
and lower-middle-class town of Woburn, a dozen miles
north of Boston. The decade of 1969–1979 brought
nineteen cases of the deadly disease to Woburn children;
only two children have survived.[1] Since 1983 nine more
children have contracted leukemia. This rate is monu-
mentally high, four times higher than would normally be
expected. Adult leukemia and renal cancer rates are high
as well, and many other health problems occur in Woburn at rates significantly greater than expected.

Through a process we term "popular epidemiology,"
the Woburn victims detected this cluster on their own.
This book is the story of the valiant efforts of victims,
their families, and community activists to investigate the
cluster and act on it. It is the story of over a decade of
struggle in which Woburn residents fought against corporations and grappled with local, state, and federal government. It is the story of how people linked their disease
to corporate pollution and came to a larger understanding of the destructive roles that both corporations and

xix

government play in environmental degradation. It is the story of ordinary citizens becoming remarkably informed and working with scientific experts. This book is also the story of other communities that have waged similar battles and of innumerable communities that still suffer in silence.

Although *No Safe Place* concerns the suffering experienced by everyone affected by toxic waste contamination, we see a special tragedy in the fact that children have been the chief victims. Children in contaminated communities may respond to their plight with a penetrating analysis or with deep emotion. Accordingly, we present two children's experiences with toxic waste.

In 1986 a Department of Energy (DOE) "siting specialist" visited Conway, New Hampshire, to speak about a possible nuclear waste dump site in nearby Hillsboro. A ten-year-old boy was among those raising serious questions:

Boy: What if it leaks? There'd be no more me.

DOE siting specialist: That wouldn't happen for hundreds of years.

Boy: Oh, don't you care about the future?

The DOE man told the audience that sometimes "personal sacrifices must be made" for the good of society.[2]

This interchange reveals many issues surrounding the hazardous waste issue. First, toxic wastes are prevalent in our society and represent a serious danger to human health and the environment. Second, despite clear evidence of the ravages, government officials cling to a narrow view of how to deal with hazardous waste. Third, government officials demand nebulous personal sacrifice for some undefined larger good. Those whom they ask to make the sacrifice learn the precise nature of neither the sacrifice nor the larger good. Fourth, government officials use public meetings and committees to bulldoze people with misinformation and deception. Fifth, even young children are aware of the problems involved and can see through the official deception.

Several hundred miles south of Conway, another child recently expressed dread in reaction to toxic waste contamination. In the Legler section of Jackson Township, New Jersey, residents had to have water delivered after pollution from a landfill made their well water dangerous. One parent recounted a frightening episode:

> We told the kids that there was poison in the water, that they couldn't even brush their teeth with it. One time our son forgot and drank some. He came out screaming, "I drank the bad water, I'm going to die now."[3]

Why should a child have to experience this dread? Toxic wastes create panic, not only among the adults who must fight the situation, but also among the children whose innocence and security are prematurely shattered.

These two American children have confronted a threat that is no longer rare or unexpected but is ever present in our culture. Indeed, it may have become the modern equivalent of the plague.[4] Unlike earlier plagues of infectious diseases, toxic waste contamination is a product of human design and can be remedied by concerted human action.

When a child in New Jersey experiences the dread of being poisoned by polluted water, it is possible for any of us to know such a dread. If the boy in New Hampshire can see through the deception of the DOE official, there is hope that large numbers of Americans can do the same.

In *No Safe Place* we point out the dangers of toxic waste contamination and show how community action offers the hope of overcoming it. These children and the children of Woburn represent the next generation and all future generations. We want the world to be a safe place for them.

Acknowledgments

This research began during the first author's two years of research at the Massachusetts Mental Health Center (MMHC), supported in part by Grant MH1426-10 from the National Institute of Mental Health. The two authors and their colleagues first discussed the Woburn case in the Program in Psychiatry and the Law at MMHC, a stimulating environment for working out some initial conceptions.

Brown University has supported this work in a number of ways. The Wayland Collegium provided release time and financial resources, as well as a faculty seminar through which a number of the ideas in the book were brought into sharper focus. Anne Fausto-Sterling, John Ladd, Toby Page, and Harold Ward were coparticipants in the seminar "Science, Democracy, and Knowledge: The Participation of an Informed Public in Social Applications of Science and Technology," and many interesting discussions came from that collaboration. A sabbatical leave in the fall of 1988 provided a much needed chunk of time for writing. The Faculty Development Fund furnished support for research supplies and transcriptions of interviews. The Brown University Small Grants Program and Biomedical Research Support Grant #5-27178 from the

National Institutes of Health, allocated by Brown University, gave funds for research assistants and supplies.

Elizabeth Cooksey and Carol Walker did a remarkable job of transcribing interviews from tapes that were often full of background noise. Carol Walker also helped in preparation of the manuscript. Robert Gay worked as a research assistant, organizing and managing data files, helping pick out extracts from the voluminous interview transcripts, and looking things up in the library. Miriam Blumenkrantz and Michelle Lesowski provided valuable research assistance in locating materials.

Jan Richard Schlichtmann, Kathleen A. Boyer, and Peggy Vecchione, of Schlictmann, Conway, Crowley, and Hugo, opened a huge archive of data on Woburn and other toxic waste cases. They provided extensive legal documents, answered many questions, helped in making connections with resource people, and heartily encouraged the book. Gretchen Latowsky of Woburn's For a Cleaner Environment (FACE) helped out with materials in the organization's files.

The people we interviewed all helped to make this book what it is. In particular, families of the leukemia victims opened their hearts to us and spurred us on. Members of FACE and public health researchers involved in the Woburn cluster likewise gave support.

Peter Conrad, Stephen R. Couch, Ann Dill, Sheldon Krimsky, J. Stephen Kroll-Smith, Donald Light, Ronnie Littenberg, Dorothy Nelkin, Alonzo Plough, and Irving K. Zola read drafts of journal articles based on some of this material and helped to shape that material for the book.

Other colleagues and friends read the entire manuscript and offered invaluable advice, suggestions, and corrections: Richard Clapp, a loyal friend and colleague, continually called attention to articles, data, and lectures that improved the book. He supported the book from its inception, and his reading contributed a public health and epidemiological orientation. Michael Edelstein and Nicholas Freudenberg have written important books in the field of community response to toxic waste contamination. Their groundwork in this area led to insightful readings of the manuscript from the public health and social science points of view. Gretchen Latowsky, Donna Robbins, and Richard Toomey have been longtime activists in Woburn. Their readings helped with the community perspective. Jan Schlictmann, who has represented the Woburn families for so many years, gave a careful reading from the legal point of view.

Naomi Schneider, editor at University of California Press, has given wise counsel and continued support. Marcia Yudkin's editorial pen has been of great assistance.

Ronnie Littenberg has been a consistent discussant of the issues in this book for many years. Articles and presentations drawn from this material, as well as the book itself, have been vastly improved as a result of her input.

Introduction

In the mid-1970s residents of Woburn, Massachusetts, began to realize that their children were contracting leukemia at exceedingly high rates. By their own efforts affected families discovered a leukemia cluster, which they attributed to carcinogens leached into their drinking-water supply from industrial waste. Families of the affected persons channeled their outrage into a civil suit against the corporate giants W. R. Grace and Beatrice Foods that eventually opened in Boston in March 1986. On July 28, 1986, a federal district court jury found that Grace had negligently dumped chemicals on its property, although it absolved Beatrice Foods.

In the next stage of the case families were required to prove that the chemicals had actually caused leukemia. During this second phase, the judge decided that the jury had not understood the hydrogeological data concerning water movement through the ground, which were crucial to the suit. On September 17, 1986, he ordered the case to be retried from the start. Because of this ruling, the families reached an out-of-court settlement with Grace on September 22, 1986, for a reported $8 million. In addition, the Woburn families appealed, seeking to reverse the prior finding that absolved Beatrice, on the grounds that Beatrice had withheld information. Three appellate judges rejected the request on March 26, 1990, and the families are appealing to the full court.

This case has brought much national attention to the Woburn cluster. Not only has Woburn focused public attention on corporate responsibility for toxic wastes and their health effects, but it has also highlighted the responsibility of local, state, and federal governments to deal with the problems of toxic waste sites when they are detected. For some time environmental, health, and civic activists have been organizing widespread opposition to the poisoning of America. The Woburn situation is a valuable case study that can help us understand, forecast, and catalyze similar efforts in the future.

From the Woburn case we know that the health effects of toxic wastes are not restricted to physical disease, but also include emotional problems. The Woburn families were one of the first groups of toxic waste plaintiffs to gather such evidence to introduce in court. The data expand what we know about the psychological effects of disasters and trauma generally.

Woburn also offers a valuable example of popular participation in health controversies surrounding toxic wastes as well as of the discovery and communication of health risks to scientific experts and government officials by laypersons. But Woburn residents made a more concerted effort than citizens elsewhere who had previously attempted to uncover hazards and report risks. In fact, toxic waste hazards are nearly always detected by ordinary individuals in affected communities. Wherever community members who are not scientists investigate disease patterns and causes and struggle with government agencies and professionals to ameliorate the situation, they are engaged in what we term "popular epidemiology."

No Safe Place addresses these issues by relating Woburn as a case study to other communities that have responded to toxic waste crises. The book tells the story of a group of leukemia victims and their families and how they dealt with their suffering. It describes the larger significance of one town's situation and places it in a social and political context. Like Love Canal in the 1970s, Woburn will become a model for community involvement in toxic waste problems and a code word for environmental struggles.

We emphasize several themes in this book:

1. Toxic waste contamination is disturbingly prevalent in this country and throughout the world, and it demands immediate attention and drastic remedies.
2. The corporate profit motive and government's implicit or explicit support of that motive have caused the toxic waste crisis and seriously hamper remedial action.
3. Toxic contamination produces extensive adverse health effects, both physical and mental.
4. The most significant force for detecting and ameliorating toxic disasters is the public that is affected by them. As in many other areas of medical knowledge, social movements play a crucial role in discovery and action.
5. We need a thorough revision of our concepts of lay-professional and lay-governmental communication and relations. Laypersons, government officials, and scientists must acknowledge the grave public health dangers of toxic chemicals.

We title this book *No Safe Place* for two reasons. First, the Woburn leukemia victims and their families who remained in Woburn—and most did—said they stayed because they felt that there were no truly safe places in America. The families were often asked the question "Why didn't you leave?" by friends, neighbors, relatives, and strangers. In fact, residents rarely leave toxic waste sites except when they are relocated by the government, as in

Times Beach, Missouri, and Love Canal, New York. Second, on a national—indeed, a global—scale, there *are* few if any safe places to live. An environmental crisis of inexplicable proportions exists and grows daily worse. The entire world is becoming an unsafe place.

We came to this project from two different but complementary backgrounds. One of us (Phil Brown), a medical sociologist, has studied and written about lay-professional communication in the mental health field and about social movements in health care. He has been particularly interested in Love Canal and other communities that developed a popular epidemiology. The other (Edwin Mikkelsen), a psychiatrist, acted as a psychiatric consultant to the plaintiffs in the Woburn suit against Beatrice Foods and W. R. Grace. During the course of this work he became more interested in the larger context surrounding the case. The two of us began to discuss our common interests in several meetings of the Program in Psychiatry and the Law at the Massachusetts Mental Health Center and found that we wanted to write a book to tell the Woburn story.

We had data from an earlier round of interviews in 1985 (by Mikkelsen) with the litigant families, conducted as part of the litigation. Since the partitioning of the case meant that the effects of the contamination would not be taken up until there was proof that the corporations had dumped wastes, these interviews never made it into open court. They focused largely on stress, coping, and emotional problems, although they touched also on physical problems and overall perceptions of the crisis. We returned in 1988 to the litigants' homes (except that of one family who did not wish to speak with us) to explore further some issues that had come up in the initial interviews. In the second round of interviews, we asked residents about their feelings concerning the long path of community organizing and activism, the settlement with Grace, the appeal against Beatrice, toxic waste issues, and government and corporate responsibility. We also spoke extensively with other persons involved in community organizing and environmental activism, public health officials who had dealt with the Woburn situation, public health researchers who had conducted the community health survey and others who criticized it, and the lawyers and their colleagues who represented the Woburn families. All the follow-up interviews were tape-recorded and transcribed. In order to link the Woburn case with other toxic waste sites, we incorporate material about people and groups elsewhere who have confronted similar problems and taken similar action.

To protect their privacy, we do not name the litigant families when we quote from them. All uncited quotes are from our interviews with the families. Because some articles about initial organizing efforts in Woburn have already been published, we mention some names when we discuss the history of the cluster detection, but only as public figures, not as persons responding to intimate questions.

We begin in chapter 1, "Town in Turmoil: History and Significance of the Woburn Cluster," with a description of the events in Woburn from the first suspicions that a leukemia cluster might exist through the litigation. In chapter 2, "The Formation of an Organized Community," we look at the obstacles to community organizing and how Woburn activists overcame them to create a case of national proportions. In chapter 3, "The Sickness Caused by 'Corporate America': Effects of the Woburn Cluster," we examine the physical, emotional, and psychosocial effects on the toxic waste victims and their families. In chapter 4, "Taking Control: Popular Epidemiology," we take an in-depth look at the components of popular epidemiology in Woburn and other places, developing a theoretical and practical model of this growing form of citizen involvement. We frame this model by discussing the general upsurge of popular participation in science and technology. We conclude in chapter 5, "Making It Safe: Securing Future Health," by focusing on deregulation and abdication of governmental responsibility in the Reagan era, and on corporate malfeasance, crime, and cover-up in toxic waste situations. We finish this chapter and the book by proposing a safe policy for toxic wastes and governmental and corporate responsibility.

Despite claims to the contrary, social science research can never be totally detached or value-free. Nevertheless, to the extent that any observations are objective, a social scientific approach to research can produce objective observations even if the researcher is an "interested" party. Indeed, all researchers are interested parties, even if they deny it or fail to realize it. Our approach to the details of the case has produced as objective an analysis as we believe possible, in that our observations are both valid and reliable.

But beyond that, we are convinced that the perceptions of the Woburn families and activists of their family and community problems are accurate and that the data they have gathered to make their case are solid and substantial. We are further convinced that toxic wastes are a significant menace to our society and that serious efforts are necessary to overcome corporate greed, government inaction, bureaucratic inefficiency, and public inertia.

1

Town in Turmoil

History and Significance of the Woburn Cluster

Woburn is a town of 37,000 people lying twelve miles north of Boston. Per capita income in this working-class and lower-middle-class community is $12,904; only 21.5 percent of adults are college graduates. In the mid-nineteenth century, Woburn was an important leather-tanning center. At the beginning of the present century it developed a large chemical industry. Among the products of Woburn's factories were arsenic-based insecticides, textiles, paper, and animal glues. The chemical industry remains, although the town is now dominated by other forms of manufacturing and by commercial firms. Woburn is typical of communities in which chemical contamination is a routine part of the production process. In view of what we now know about toxic waste exposure in industrial areas, Woburn is very much the sort of place one would expect to find toxic waste contamination.

Coming in the wake of the Love Canal disaster, the toxic waste contamination in Woburn drew national attention. This publicity was due to the arduous efforts of an inquisitive and courageous group of residents. Besides publicizing the case nationally, they acted as detectives, pressured the city, state, and federal governments to investigate and clean up, embarked on a major lawsuit, and helped survey the health of the local population. They continue to be involved in efforts to study Woburn's health further.

History of the Woburn Leukemia Cluster

The Woburn saga began in May 1979 with the chance discovery in Woburn of chemical barrels believed to contain toxic wastes. Builders found 184 fifty-five-gallon drums in a vacant lot along the Aberjona River. They called the police, who then called the state Department of Environmental Quality Engineering (DEQE) . Water samples from the contiguous wells G and H, the principal source of municipal water for East Woburn, showed large concentrations of organic compounds known to cause cancer in laboratory animals. Of particular concern were trichloroethylene (TCE) and tetrachloroethylene (PCE). The Environmental Protection Agency recommends that the concentration of TCE be zero parts per billion and sets a maximum of five parts per billion; well G had forty times that amount. The state ordered both wells closed because of their TCE and PCE levels.[1] Map 1 shows the contaminated wells and the nearby industrial contamination sites.

That was not the first time Woburn and Massachusetts officials and local corporations had learned of problems in Woburn's water supply. Since the 1930s, townspeople noticed that Lake Mishawum often took on a red coloring and emitted a nauseating odor.[2] In 1952 many houses in Woburn developed measle-like spots and a veneer of greenish brown, and residents reported being disturbed by odors. The Woburn Board of Health and the Massachusetts Department of Public Health (DPH) investigated the possibility that World War II chemical industries might have left pollution behind them, but they obtained no information because of inadequate records.[3] As early as 1956

Map 1. Contaminated Wells and Nearby Industrial
Contamination Sites

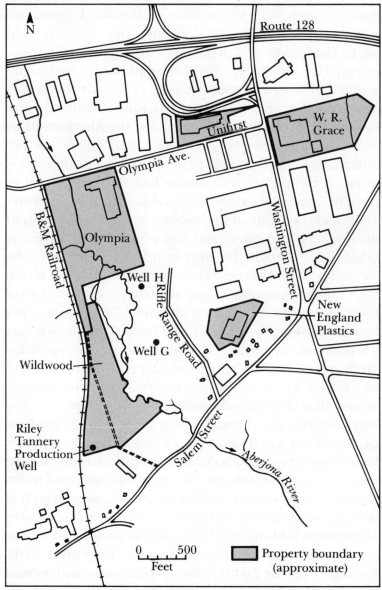

SOURCE: Environmental Protection Agency, "EPA Proposes Clean-Up Plan for Wells G and H Site" (Boston: Environmental Protection Agency Region I Office, February 1989), p. 6.

the DPH ordered Woburn's Riley tannery to clean up a sludge dump.[4] Workers there remembered calling the dump "Death Valley" because of the dead trees surrounding the site.[5] In 1964 an insurance company told W. R. Grace that TCE was highly toxic and that employees working around it should wear protective masks and goggles, although company managers did not follow that instruction.[6] In 1972 the Aberjona River Commission informed the Woburn City Council that the Aberjona River and most of its watershed were seriously polluted.[7] As with other such reports in that period, the information failed to reach the public. The nation had not yet learned to take the impending environmental catastrophe seriously.

Residents continued to complain about discoloration of dishwashers, bad odor, and bad taste, and in 1978 city officials commissioned a study by private consultants. The consulting firm, Dufresne-Henry, used an umbrella screen for organic compounds and reported a carbon-chloroform extract (CCE) concentration of 2.79 milligrams per liter. According to the firm, the limit of safety was just 0.1 milligrams per liter. The Dufresne-Henry report led Woburn water officials to ask the DPH if the town might be allowed to change its chlorination method: they assumed that chlorine was interacting with minerals. The DPH allowed the change, telling town officials on June 24, 1975, not to rely on wells G and H because of their high concentrations of salt and minerals. But the department did not mention another important piece of information it possessed: in 1975 a DEQE engineer, who had been applying a more stringent screening test to all wells in the state, told the DPH that wells G and H had higher concentrations of organic compounds than nearby wells. Retrospectively he said that the concentrations had seemed high but that "at the time I was doing research only on the method and nobody knew how serious water contamination problems could be."[8]

Information gathering in the community also predated the 1979 well closings. Anne Anderson, whose son Jimmy was diagnosed with acute lymphocytic leukemia in 1972, gathered information about other cases by word of mouth and by chance meetings with other victims at stores and at the hospital where Jimmy was being treated. In 1973 she began to suspect that the growing number of leukemia cases might have been caused by something carried in the water. She asked state officials to test the water but was told that testing could not be done at an individual's initiative. Anderson's husband did not support her in this effort and instead asked the family pastor to help her get her mind off what he felt to be an erroneous idea. Ironically, this request led the reverend Bruce Young to become a leading participant in the struggle to understand and alleviate Woburn's toxic waste problems.[9] As he later put it, "I set out to prove her wrong, that cancer and leukemia don't run in neighborhoods, but she was right."[10]

Another fortuitous circumstance occurred in June 1979, barely a month after the state ordered the wells shut down. On his way to work a DEQE engineer drove past the nearby Industri-Plex construction site (about two miles from the wells) and thought he spotted construction in violation of the Wetlands Act. He notified the Environmental Protection Agency (EPA), which dispatched the Army Corps of Engineers to investigate, since the Corps monitors wetlands violations for the federal government. The army engineers found violations. EPA scientists investigated as well and found dangerous levels of lead, arsenic, and chromium; yet they told neither the town officials nor the public. The public learned about the EPA findings only when the *Woburn Daily Times* broke the news

Map 2.   Twenty-eight Leukemia Cases, 1964–1989, Identified by FACE (For a Cleaner Environment)

SOURCE: Handout prepared by For a Cleaner Environment, 1989.

in September. Their findings convinced Bruce Young that Anne Anderson had been thinking along the right lines. He placed an ad in the newspaper, asking people who knew of childhood leukemia cases to respond. Young prepared a map and designed a questionnaire in consultation with Dr. John Truman, the physician treating Jimmy Anderson. Several days later, Anderson and Young plotted the cases (see Map 2). There were twelve, with six of them closely grouped within blocks of the Anderson house in East Woburn's Pine Street area. Alarmed by the results, Dr. Truman called the Centers for Disease Control (CDC) and requested a study of the cluster. Local activists spread the word through the press and persuaded the city council on December 19, 1979, formally to ask the CDC to investigate. In January 1980 Young, Anderson,

Map 3.   Twelve Leukemia Cases, 1969–1979, Identified by Massachusetts Department of Public Health

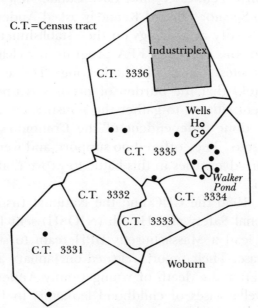

SOURCE: John L. Cutler, Gerald S. Parker, Sharon Rosen, Brad Prenney, Richard Healy, and Glyn G. Caldwell, "Childhood Leukemia in Woburn, Massachusetts," *Public Health Reports*, 1986, 101:204.

and twenty other people formed the citizens' group For a Cleaner Environment (FACE) to mobilize public concern about the leukemia cluster.[11]

Five days after the city council request to the CDC, the Massachusetts DPH issued a report that contradicted the Young-Anderson map model of the leukemia cluster. According to the DPH, there were eighteen cases among all ages for the period 1968–1979 when 10.9 were expected, but the DPH felt that the difference was not very large for a ten-year period. Further, the DPH denied the existence of a cluster pattern. Despite this blow, Woburn activists were buoyed by growing public awareness of the environmental hazards and popular epidemiological ef-

forts in other places, such as Legler, New Jersey; Hardeman County, Tennessee; and Love Canal, New York. In
June 1980 Senator Edward Kennedy asked Anderson and
Young to testify at hearings on the establishment of the
Superfund, the proposed EPA program for cleaning up
toxic waste sites. Young told the hearing: "For seven years
we were told that the burden of proof was upon us as
independent citizens to gather the statistics. . . . All our
work was done independent of the Commonwealth of
Massachusetts. They offered no support, and were in fact
one of our adversaries in this battle to prove that we had
a problem." [12]

In May 1980 the CDC and the National Institute for
Occupational Safety and Health (NIOSH) sent Dr. John
Cutler to lead a Massachusetts DPH team to study the
Woburn case. Their report, released on January 23, 1981,
five days after the death of young Jimmy Anderson, reported twelve cases of childhood leukemia in East Woburn, where 5.3 were expected (see Map 3 and Table 1).
They also found an elevated incidence of kidney cancer.
The DPH, however, believed the data were inconclusive.
They argued that the case-control method, matching such
features as age, class, and sex, failed to find environmental characteristics that differentiated victims from nonvic-
tims. Further, the state officials pointed to a lack of environmental data for earlier periods as an obstacle to a link
between disease and the water supply. [13] Were those objections valid? We believe that a case-control method was
not even appropriate to Woburn because of the small
number of leukemia cases there. [14] It is simply too difficult to show significant differences between two populations of so small a size. As for the lack of environmental
data, Woburn residents were soon to fill in the missing
information with facts and figures from the Harvard/FACE
health study.

Table 1.   *Characteristics of Childhood Leukemia Cases,*
1969–1979 (Identified by Department of Public Health)

Case Number	Sex	Date of Birth	Date of Diagnosis	Age at Diagnosis (Yrs)	Status	Length of Woburn Residence Prior to Diagnosis (Yrs)
1	M	7/68	1/72	3	Alive	3
2	M	12/63	3/78	14	Alive	14
3	M	10/70	6/73	2	Alive	2
4	M	3/72	10/76	4	Alive	4
5	M	6/69	8/79	10	Alive	10
	F	4/64	12/75	11	Alive	10
7	F	12/63	8/76	12	Died (2/78)	12
8	M	3/75	9/75	1	Died (11/75)	<1
9	M	5/64	11/69	5	Died (3/80)	<1
10	F	4/58	3/69	11	Died (7/70)	4
11	M	9/65	7/74	8	Died (6/77)	8
12	M	6/65	7/71	6	Died (2/74)	6

SOURCE: Gerald S. Parker and Sharon L. Rosen, "Woburn: Cancer Incidence and Environmental Hazards, 1969–1978" (Boston: Massachusetts Department of Public Health, January 23, 1981), p. 31.

Finding Allies

The conjunction of Jimmy Anderson's death and the report's failure to confirm the connection between the water and leukemia led the families and friends of the leukemia victims, along with their local allies, to question the nature of the scientific study. As Paula DiPerna puts it in her journalistic account, *Cluster Mystery,* "a layperson's approach to epidemiological science evolved."[15] Larry Brown from the Harvard School of Public Health (SPH) helped this development when he invited Anderson and Young to present their Woburn data to a seminar of the school's Community Health Improvement Program. Marvin Zelen, an SPH biostatistician, attended the seminar along with two colleagues, Steve Lagakos and Alec Walker. Afterward all three Harvard scientists took Young and Anderson upstairs and told them, "We may be able to help you with something,"

> and off the top of our heads we outlined the Woburn study. And the idea was, well, if there really was a problem, . . . whatever caused the cancer cluster obviously might have caused other health problems in the area. It might be real or it might not be real. But if it was real there might be other health problems.[16]

At this time, clusters of cancer and other diseases were being investigated around the United States, although the CDC did not inform Woburn residents of the heightened public and scientific interest in studies of cancer clusters like theirs. Moreover, the DPH issued a follow-up report in November 1981 that stated that the number of childhood leukemia deaths in Woburn had begun to rise in the period 1959–1963, before the contaminated wells G and H were drilled. Assuming an average latency period of two to five years between exposure and cancer, the DPH report argued that deaths should not have started to increase until 1969–1973, a period during which the rate was in fact lower than expected.[17]

The citizens group came up with figures that differed from the DPH's. When the suit was filed, five children from the litigant families had died, and two children and an adult were ill. The adult died while the case was being tried. Looking at the town as a whole rather than just at the litigants, FACE activists counted twenty-eight cases of childhood leukemia and sixteen deaths where the Department of Public Health counted only twenty cases and eleven deaths between 1965 and 1980. The DPH did not count some children who moved from Woburn and some nonresidents who were cared for by family members in the town.[18]

To gather more conclusive data, Zelen and Lagakos undertook a detailed study of Woburn residents' health status. They focused on birth defects and reproductive disorders, which were widely considered to be related to environmental conditions. The biostatisticians and the FACE activists teamed up in what was to become an important epidemiological study and a prototype of popular epidemiological alliances between citizen activists and sympathetic scientists. Coordinated by FACE, volunteers from Woburn and the SPH administered a telephone survey from April to September of 1982, designed to reach 70 percent of city residents who had phones.[19]

At the same time, the EPA contracted for a hydrogeological study of groundwater movement through Woburn, which found that the bedrock in the affected area sloped to the southwest and was bowl-shaped. Wells G and H were in the deepest part of the bowl. The EPA consultant's March 1982 report identified two plumes of contaminants but did not identify the sources. The families' attorneys, however, did: contrary to previous expectations, the source was not the Industri-Plex site but the sites of W. R. Grace's Cryovac Division and Beatrice Foods' Riley Tannery. Beatrice had bought the property from Riley in 1978 and sold it back to Riley in 1983, but retained legal liability.

Filing the Lawsuit

The hydrogeological report led thirty-three members of eight families of leukemia victims to file suit (*Anne Anderson et al. v. Cryovac et al.*, 96 F.R.D. 431 [D. Mass. 1983] [Anderson I]; later changed to *Anderson et al. v. W. R. Grace et al.*, 628 F. Supp. 1219 [D. Mass. 1986] [Anderson

II]) in May 1982 against Beatrice and Grace for poor waste disposal practices leading to groundwater contamination and hence to fatal disease. The families alleged wrongful death and sought compensation for medical expenses, financial losses, pain and suffering, possible future illness due to the chemicals, and mental anguish due to fear of future illness.[20]

The plaintiffs added a smaller company, Unifirst, to the suit in April 1985. Unifirst countersued the families in June, claiming that they had been libeled.[21] But Unifirst quickly settled before trial, on October 11, 1985, for a reported $1.05 million.[22] The first flush of victory greatly encouraged the families to pursue their claims against Beatrice and Grace. The case has cost $13 million to date.[23]

To that point, their struggle had seemed chancier than David's against Goliath. Jan R. Schlictmann, of Schlictmann, Conway, and Crowley, was the chief counsel. Charles R. Nesson, a Harvard Law School professor, assisted Schlictmann. Schlictmann's three-member law office faced two of the nation's largest and most prestigious corporate law firms, Hale and Dorr (for Beatrice) and Foley, Hoag, and Eliot (for Grace). Just as the Woburn families saw themselves as fighting two of the nation's largest corporations, so too did the small law firm see itself pitted against two giants.

The lawsuit employed some strikingly new approaches to toxic waste litigation. In addition to the evidence of groundwater movement, the families were relying on the logic of immunologist Dr. Alan Levin, who argued that TCE disrupted the immune system by altering lymphocytes (white blood cells) and that damaged lymphocytes were linked to acute lymphocytic leukemia (although there was no proven causal chain).[24] That was indeed a novel tack in toxic tort cases, as well as an innovative epidemiological approach.

Another unusual approach in the lawsuit, although some recent precedents existed, was the victims' demand for compensation for potential future conditions. In 1983 a court had awarded $17 million to ninety-seven families in Jackson Township, New Jersey. Residents of the Legler section of Jackson sued the township for failing to protect them from toxic chemicals in a landfill. The court awarded 399 plaintiffs $2 million for emotional distress, $8 million for medical surveillance (intensive annual screenings to protect against future illness), $5.4 million for diminished quality of life, and $200,000 to supply plaintiffs' houses with uncontaminated municipal water. Then, in 1986, the Velsicol Chemical Corporation was found guilty of pollution in Hardeman County, Tennessee. The court awarded the plaintiffs $12.7 million for damage to their immune systems, which damage was held responsible both for present and potential future diseases.[25]

After the Woburn suit was filed, both the Jackson Township and Hardeman County decisions were altered. A 1985 appeal reversed the awards for emotional distress and medical surveillance but upheld the rest. In 1987 the New Jersey Supreme Court reinstated the medical surveillance component, but upheld the appeals court's reversal of emotional distress on the ground that New Jersey forbade "pain and distress" awards against government.[26] On May 24, 1988, a federal appeals court reviewing the Velsicol suit eliminated the award based on increased risk of cancer, saying that a 30 percent chance of developing cancer "does not constitute a reasonable medical certainty" of a personal injury. The court also struck post traumatic stress syndrome damages, saying that consumption of contaminated water is not "the type of psychologically traumatic event that is a universal stressor." According to the appeals panel, fear of cancer could be calculated only for the period during which people were drinking the water (based on *Laxton v. Orkin Exterminating*). The appeals court eliminated $9 million in interest on the award and lowered the award for fear of cancer from $725,000 to $207,000.

In addition, the appeals court in Hardeman County, Tennessee, rejected damages against Velsicol based on immune system disorder. The court ruled that there was no general medical acceptance of the "clinical ecology" perspective, the viewpoint that environmental factors can produce immune system damage. The court specifically stated that there was no evidence that carbon tetrachloride or chloroform were linked to immune defects. On June 11 the plaintiffs asked for a rehearing, arguing that Velsicol had argued during the appeal but not at the trial against the acceptability of immune system disruption. They also charged that raising the issue of the general medical acceptance of any perspective was improper, since it relied on hearsay testimony. On the issue of the reasonable medical certainty of developing cancer, the victims argued that the appellate court was wrong to reject it on the basis of expert testimony that cancer was "most probably due to" immune damage or that it was only "the most likely reason." The same appeals court had ruled previously that medical experts did not have to use the "magic words" of "reasonable medical certainty." As to fear of cancer, the plaintiffs said the court incorrectly applied the Laxton case, in which the plaintiffs drank contaminated water for only a short period of time and contracted no known disease. On August 29, the appellate court released its reply to the request for a rehearing. It sustained the original appeals decision, with the minor exception of saying that although the "magic words" of "reasonable medical certainty" need not be used, nevertheless experts had to be more certain than they were.[27] In August 1989, Velsicol settled out of court for $10 million.

At the time the Woburn families filed their suit, however, those higher court decisions were not in existence, and the Woburn attorneys set their sights on the new legal frontiers created by the original Velsicol decision. The recent reversals may, however, portend more difficult times for future toxic waste litigation.

Another case was significant, even though it did not involve the same disease or etiology, since it concerned potential future suffering. In 1982, the Massachusetts case of *Payton v. Abbott Labs* held that women exposed to diethylstilbestrol (DES) could be compensated for anticipatory distress if they showed a demonstrable symptom that could form a reasonable basis for fear. The lawyers saw this ruling as another favorable indication for the outcome of the Woburn case.[28]

The Harvard School of Public Health/FACE Study

The SPH/FACE study was conducted about the same time as the litigation; they were separate projects that overlapped significantly. The survey data never made it into court because the trial never proceeded to the point of examining the effects of pollution from wells G and H. (That phase of the partitioned trial could not occur, since Beatrice was acquitted of the responsibility for dumping and Grace settled out of court after the judge ordered a retrial of the first part. However, if the appeal is successful, the data from the study may finally enter open court.) Nevertheless, the Woburn families and other activists continue to view the results of the health study as ammunition for their legal case and the larger social cause.

The health study incorporated information about twenty cases of childhood leukemia (in children ages nineteen and under) diagnosed between 1964 and 1983 and relied on the DEQE model of geographical and temporal distribution of water from wells G and H, as well as on the community health survey. Three hundred and one volunteers trained by the Harvard scientists asked 5,010 households—57 percent of Woburn residences with telephones—about adverse outcomes of pregnancy and childhood disorders.[29] Despite the lack of funding, the study gradually became a major project for the SPH scholars—and a major preoccupation for the families, as it promised needed data and dredged up painful memories.

Professors Zelen and Lagakos of the SPH had had no prior involvement with environmental health issues; but they found Woburn an intriguing problem, and they felt sympathy for the Woburn residents. Zelen recalls, "What impressed us the most was how the bureaucracy had shunted these people around." He and Lagakos located a small amount of money, $10,000, within the Department of Biostatistics and elsewhere in the SPH, which enabled the researchers to hire Barbara Wessen to manage the study. In addition, Lagakos and Zelen directed a computer facility at the nearby Dana-Farber Cancer Institute, which provided the computer time and the personnel necessary to analyze the survey results. The CDC had already rejected a request for funds to research the Woburn cluster; Zelen believes that rejection stemmed from difficulty in accepting such innovative research methods as those proposed for the project.[30] If the Woburn study had been funded by a typical research grant Lagakos estimates it would have cost between $500,000 and $750,000.[31]

Because of the immensity of the project and the reliance on a large group of volunteer interviewers, the study took longer than originally expected. The researchers had hoped to finish data collection by June 1982 but in fact finished a year later.[32] During that time, the SPH team refused to reveal any of the study findings to the Woburn residents, in order to preserve their view of scientific objectivity. Only the night before the public presentation of the findings did Woburn citizens learn what had been discovered.[33]

On February 8, 1984, Zelen and Lagakos publicly announced the Harvard SPH data. The study found that childhood leukemia was significantly associated with exposure to water from wells G and H, when exposure was viewed both cumulatively and on a none versus some basis. Children with leukemia had received, on average, 21.2 percent of their yearly water supply from the wells, in contrast to 9.5 percent for children without leukemia.[34]

The survey included data about 4,396 pregnancies that terminated between 1960 and 1982. Controlling for important risk factors in pregnancy (such as smoking, maternal age, pregnancy history), the investigators found that access to contaminated water was not associated with spontaneous abortions; low birth weight; perinatal deaths before 1970; or musculoskeletal, cardiovascular, or "other" birth anomalies (see Table 2). Exposure to contaminated water was, however, associated with perinatal deaths since 1970, eye/ear anomalies, and CNS/chromosomal/oral cleft anomalies. With regard to childhood disorders, contaminated water was associated with kidney/urinary tract and lung/respiratory problems but not with allergies, anemia, diabetes, heart/blood pressure, learning disability, neurologic/sensory, or "other" disorders.[35] If we look specifically at cases that were in utero when the mothers were exposed, the positive associations are even stronger.[36]

The researchers conducted extensive analyses to demonstrate that the data were not biased. They compared baseline rates of adverse health effects for West Woburn (never exposed to wells G and H water) and East Woburn (before the opening of the wells) and found no differ-

Table 2.   *Adverse Pregnancy Outcomes in Areas of High and Low Exposure before (1977–1979) and after (1980–1982) Closure of Wells G and H*

	1977–1979	1980–1982
Zones A–C (high exposure)		
Average G and H exposure (%)	58	0
Number of pregnancies	107	78
Perinatal deaths	4	0
Eye/Ear anomalies	1	0
CNS/Chromosomal/Oral cleft	2	0
Zones D–E (low exposure)		
Average G and H exposure (%)	.01	0
Number of pregnancies	436	397
Perinatal deaths	2	3
Eye/Ear anomalies	0	0
CNS/Chromosomal/Oral cleft	3	3

SOURCE: Steven Lagakos, Barbara J. Wessen, and Marvin Zelen, "An Analysis of Contaminated Well Water and Health Effects in Woburn, Massachusetts" (*Journal of the American Statistical Association*, 1986, 81: 583–596), p. 591.

NOTE: Average G and H exposure refers to average exposure scores corresponding to pregnancies.

ences. They tested whether population transiency rates were related to exposure and ruled out that possibility. Other tests ruled out a number of biases potentially attributable to the volunteer interviewers.[37]

The report met with criticism from many sources: the CDC, the American Cancer Society, the EPA, and even the Harvard SPH Department of Epidemiology. Some critics demonstrated straightforward scientific concerns, but others clearly revealed elitist attitudes and opposition to community involvement in scientific work. One straightforward concern was that researchers had grouped diseases into categories despite their different etiologies. In the same vein, some critics charged that the biostatisticians had grouped diverse birth defects under the broad heading "environmentally associated disease."[38] The researchers explained, however, that they grouped defects because separately the numbers of each defect would not reach statistical significance. Further, they claimed that their groupings were based on the literature about chemical causes of birth defects. In fact, if the groupings were incorrect, they would not have yielded positive results.[39]

Some critics questioned whether the computer model of the flow of water to affected households was precise enough and whether it was independently verified.[40] Because the DEQE officials failed to release the water data in a timely fashion, it was impossible to obtain other validation.[41] The DEQE now has a more refined model, commissioned from Paul Murphy at the University of Massachusetts. Although FACE and the SPH scientists had trouble obtaining funding to conduct new analyses, it now appears that there will be a DPH reanalysis of the study data that will include the new water model.

Critics of the study have also noted that there were elevated numbers of leukemia cases even after the wells were shut down, and that these new cases were more often found in West Woburn than in East Woburn. If wells G and H were the culprit, these critics ask, how likely is the existence of yet another independent cluster?[42] The response is that because of the rich chemical soup in Woburn, additional clusters are indeed plausible.

An industry research organization, the American Industrial Health Council, hired researchers to criticize the study. The SPH team learned about the industry critique from a television crew preparing a "Nova" special on Woburn when the crew gave the biostatisticians a copy of the critique. Zelen and Lagakos wrote the council's head scientist a letter pointing out misstatements of fact; as a result the scientist declined to be interviewed for "Nova."[43] It is interesting that one of the leading critics of the Wo-

burn study was Brian MacMahon, chairman of the SPH
Department of Epidemiology, and a longtime consultant
to chemical firms. He had originally agreed to serve on
the American Industrial Health Council panel, but later
withdrew for unspecified reasons.[44]

The most common objections to the study were directed against the very concept of public participation in
science. All the critics charged that the study was biased
because volunteers had conducted the health survey and
because the study had a political goal. In view of the poor
history of toxic waste studies and remediation, criticism
on those grounds, if it won out, would eliminate the only
existing avenue for affected citizens seeking knowledge
or action. Without popular epidemiology, cases such as
Woburn simply cannot come to trial and gain sufficient
public attention.

The Trial

In their suit, the affected families argued that Grace and
Beatrice, through their subsidiary companies, dumped
toxic chemicals that contaminated Woburn's municipal
water supply and led to fatal disease. The families sued
for wrongful death and requested an award for medical
expenses, financial losses, pain and suffering, mental anguish, and future possible illness.

Throughout the trial, the Woburn families faced a judge
who was extremely critical of their attorneys and who many
observers felt gave every possible advantage to the companies. The attitude of Judge Walter J. Skinner of the
U.S. District Court was revealed September 4, 1985, when
he placed a gag order on the participants, prohibiting them
from any public comment on the suit. That order obviously benefited the corporations, not the families. After
protests from the Massachusetts Civil Liberties Union, the

judge narrowed the gag order on October 3 so that it forbade only discussions of information obtained in test diggings or pretrial discovery. The gag order was lifted in its entirety in February 1986, thanks to a flurry of magazine articles and television specials on the Woburn case.[45]

The suit against W. R. Grace and Beatrice Foods opened in federal district court in Boston in February 1986. Judge Skinner ruled that there were to be three parts to the trial. The court would first consider the question whether the companies were responsible for dumping the chemicals. If the jury found that they were, the case would proceed to the second part, in which the jury would decide whether the chemicals had caused the victims' leukemia. If that were proved, the jury would then assess the damages. As it turned out, only the first phase of the trial was carried out.

In order to prove the companies' responsibility for the presence of the toxins, the families had to demonstrate what paths the chemicals took from the plants into the groundwater. One of the families' expert witnesses, John Drobinski from Weston Geophysical Corporation, offered evidence for the connection between well G and Beatrice's Riley Tannery property. When the EPA pumped water from that well in 1985, the water table under the Riley plant dropped two and a half feet. John J. Riley, former owner of the tannery, knew as early as 1968 that there was a relationship between the wells and the water table under his plant.[46] Such a relationship made it likely that the Riley discharges had made their way into the municipal water.

George Pinder, a hydrogeologist from Princeton University, was the leading expert witness for the families, since his water model seemed solidly to implicate Grace and Beatrice. Pinder showed evidence of water movement from the Grace and Beatrice sites to the wells, distances of 2,400 and 600 feet, respectively. Defense attorneys attempted to show that the wells drew water from the Aberjona River, an external source of pollution. But Pinder argued that the wells' aquifer was higher than the river, making such travel unlikely. Furthermore he stated, the river bottom was impermeable.[47]

As evidence of a chemical causeway from Grace's Cryovac and Beatrice's Riley plants to the victims' water supply grew, the companies turned their efforts to denying that they in fact had placed any chemicals in the ground. Grace and Beatrice claimed that they did not dump chemicals and that the many chemicals in the water could have come from other sites in Woburn. In response to the finding of TCE on their properties, the firms stated that trespassers had dumped it there, even though trial witnesses testified that they saw Riley workers dump toxic waste.[48] When John Riley testified that the tannery had not dumped chemicals, the families' lawyer produced a 1980 letter to Riley from the Massachusetts Division of Water Pollution Control, requesting that the tannery clean up its hazardous waste.[49]

Workers and executives from Grace's Cryovac plant testified that they had witnessed frequent dumping, specifically of TCE, by the company. Moreover, company officials knew at the time that improper use of TCE could cause injury to the heart, liver, and nervous system.[50] The man who managed the Cryovac facility from the early 1960s to 1984 had, in 1985, denied knowledge of any chemical use or disposal. Yet the families' lawyers brought into court a contractor who had been asked by that manager in 1974 to build a pit in which to bury chemical wastes.[51]

There was other evidence of dumping. In preparation for the trial, the plaintiffs hired Weston Geophysical Corporation to test for the presence of toxic waste at Grace's Cryovac plant. In tests run from July 1 to July 4, 1985, Weston Geophysical scientists found extensive evidence of dumping of TCE, PCE, toluene, and other industrial solvents. When FACE made the finding public on August 28, 1985, and accused Grace of withholding this information from the EPA, Grace denied the charges. Grace officials claimed that the plaintiffs were staging a "media circus," working to "manipulate the media in order to prejudice the public."[52] Grace's lying to the EPA about its chemical dumping later led to the company's conviction in federal court in 1988.

At that point in the trial there was evidence of pathways through the ground and of the presence of the toxic chemicals. Grace and Beatrice then argued that even if the toxic chemicals were present, none had been shown to be carcinogenic. They based this assertion on environmental epidemiological research that had so far tied leukemia only to benzene and radiation. But the families were basing their claim of injuries on a more indirect and longterm immunological effect whereby TCE altered the immune system and thus allowed a carcinogenic process to develop.

Although the Woburn families had produced a large amount of incriminating evidence, they faced a judge whose rulings had so far appeared to favor the defendants. As the first part of the trial was nearing its end, Judge Skinner ruled that Beatrice could be found guilty only of dumping that took place after 1968, since it was not until then that the Riley Tannery could have known of the relationship between the wells and the water table beneath the property. The judge dated Grace's responsibility to 1964, when the wells went on-line. Skinner ruled that Grace could be found guilty on standards of strict liability, that is, that their use of dangerous substances made them responsible regardless of actions they took or failed to take. Beatrice, on the other hand, could be found guilty only on standards of purposeful negligence, since there was no evidence that the tannery itself had dumped chemicals. Skinner told the jurors that they could not consider the possibility of Riley's role in the contamination of a nearby fifteen-acre parcel. The families' lawyers believed that parcel might have played a significant role in contamination. For the Woburn families, the impact was mixed. Although the judge had made it difficult to obtain a victory over Beatrice, his ruling on Grace was the first in a Massachusetts court to hold a firm accountable to strict liability.[53]

After seventy-seven days of trial, the jury decided on July 28, 1986, that W. R. Grace had negligently dumped chemicals on its property, although they found Beatrice Foods not guilty. The acquittal of Beatrice was due to the ruling that disallowed evidence concerning pre-1968 dumping. The case was to have proceeded to the second stage in which the plaintiffs would have to prove that the chemicals had caused leukemia. But as this stage began, Judge Skinner decided that the jury had not understood the hydrogeological data that constituted major evidence for the first phase of the case. Skinner based his belief on the jurors' confused written answers to his complex interrogatories, which he himself admitted were confusing. On September 17 he ordered the case retried from the start, that is, from the first phase of proving dumping. According to the families' legal team, the judge's move stemmed from his knowledge that an out-of-court settlement was near. Grace and the families in fact reached a settlement on September 22, 1986, for $8 million.[54]

The families filed an appeal in May 1987 (*Anderson et al. v. Beatrice Foods,* 862 F. 2d 910 [1st Cir. 1988]), seeking to reverse the finding that absolved Beatrice, on the grounds that the judge was wrong to rule out the dumping of chemicals and the existence of toxic waste before 1968.[55] The narrowness of the judge's ruling on evidence led the Massachusetts attorney general and the county district attorney to file an amicus curiae brief asserting that the ruling "could set precedent adverse to the effective enforcement of environmental laws by public authorities."[56]

On October 8, 1987, shortly after learning from an EPA official that Beatrice had withheld a 1983 report on toxic waste at the Riley site, Jan Schlictmann, the families' attorney, requested a new trial. Schlictmann had repeatedly requested copies of all investigations into the property and had never received the report in question. Commissioned by the Riley Tannery and executed by Yankee Environmental Engineering and Research Services, it offered new evidence and pointed up discrepancies in Beatrice's legal defense during the trial. The Yankee Report mentioned that tannery wastes were present, that TCE and other toxic wastes had been dumped, that the aquifer under Riley was more permeable than the litigants' expert witness, George Pinder, had argued, and that the Aberjona's river bottom was less permeable than Pinder had determined. The report thus contradicted Beatrice's earlier criticism of Pinder's view of the river's permeability. The impermeability of the river bottom made it more likely that pollutants from Riley entered wells G and H. Further, the report stated that toxic wastes could have flowed from the Riley well to the well on the adjoining fifteen-acre property, a site the judge had ruled irrelevant to the trial. To evade responsibility, Beatrice had played what Schlictmann terms a "corporate shell game" in which it sold the tannery back to Riley and made the fifteen-acre parcel a separate entity, which it also returned to Riley. Beatrice then used its concealment of ownership to claim that it

had no information about the Riley site and to convince
the judge to deny the Woburn plaintiffs access to that site
during pretrial discovery.[57]

If all this information had been available and allowed
in testimony, Schlictmann believes that Beatrice would have
been held to a strict liability standard. The routine discharge of toxic wastes to the fifteen-acre site would clearly
have been "ultrahazardous activity."[58] But on January 22,
1988, Judge Skinner ruled that the Yankee Report was
insufficient reason to allow a new trial. Three days later
the plaintiffs appealed that ruling. Then on February 4,
1988, the Appeals Court, on the plaintiffs' motion, con-
solidated the original appeal and the appeal of the motion for a new trial.[59] Thus the appeal heard in July 1988
included the issues of concealment of evidence in the
matter of the Yankee Report. On December 7, 1988, the
court denied the original appeal, in which the plaintiffs
argued that limitation on evidence of dumping before 1968
was unfair. The court agreed to allow a hearing, but not
a new trial, on the question whether Beatrice had withheld evidence. The three-judge panel did not say whether
the report was significant enough to have affected the trial,
but it issued strict guidelines for the trial court to follow
in determining that possibility. The appeals judges, on
December 14, 1988, ordered the trial judge, Judge Skinner, to ask whether Beatrice's suppression of evidence was
"misconduct" or merely a "lapse of judgment."[60]

The families felt hopeful, because the EPA had just released a 300-page technical document confirming that the
Beatrice site was the most polluted location in the well
area. Skinner ordered the hearing that began in January
1989 to focus narrowly on whether Beatrice intentionally
withheld evidence. The families' legal team also has reason to hope. After the Riley Tannery went out of business,

in December 1988, the workers became willing to confirm the withholding or suppression of test results. Schlictmann got the judge to order Beatrice to answer the original discovery questions again and to produce documents they should have produced the first time. Over the course of a two-month hearing, Beatrice produced many documents useful to the families, and there were many more that had not yet been searched.[61]

The court ruled that if Beatrice had knowingly and intentionally withheld evidence, then the company would have to prove by "clear and convincing evidence" (a high degree of proof) that the material was not important. If Beatrice withheld the evidence, but not knowingly and intentionally, then the families would have to prove by "a preponderance of the evidence" (a lower level of proof) that the material was important. After the hearing, Judge Skinner will make a recommendation to the First Circuit Court of Appeals, which will make the final decision. Because of numerous instances of legal misconduct by Beatrice's attorneys, Schlictmann made a motion on April 6, 1989, to default Beatrice, a procedure by which the judge finds the firm guilty and sends the case to a jury to assess damages.[62]

During the first several months of the hearing, witnesses testified that Riley directed them to remove toxic waste and to do so "quietly." Further testimony showed that environmental reports on sludge and groundwater were not revealed until after the trial.[63] The EPA has played a disruptive role in the appeals hearings. In February, Judge Skinner supported the agency's request to block the subpoena of EPA employee David Delaney, who the families argue witnessed important waste-removal activities in 1983.[64]

On July 7, 1989, Judge Skinner found that John Riley's

lawyer, Mary Ryan, led the plaintiff families to believe that there were no further relevant documents. In fact, the judge continued, Riley had commissioned two studies that it deliberately kept from the families. Although Skinner ruled that Riley's acts constituted "deliberate misconduct" that "substantially impaired [the plaintiffs'] preparation for trial," he nevertheless concluded that there was insufficient evidence that Beatrice's lawyers deliberately concealed evidence.[65] The next step of the hearing then began with Schlictmann seeking to prove the importance of the withheld reports. In a dramatic turn of events, on October 11, 1989, Riley's attorneys sought to protect themselves by filing an affidavit in court that Beatrice and its lawyers knew of the reports in 1984. The affidavit further states that the Riley attorneys were told to keep quiet about their knowledge, or else Beatrice and its lawyers would not defend Riley (most of the Riley defense costs have been borne by Beatrice). Schlictmann contends that the affidavit shows that Beatrice's attorneys Jerome Facher and Neil Jacobs lied in court about the importance of the reports. As a result, it seemed more likely that Beatrice would be held in default. Nevertheless, on December 16, 1989, Judge Skinner recommended that the Appeals Court not allow the families a new trial. At the same time, however, he denied Beatrice's motion to throw the case out.[66] Three appellate judges upheld Skinner's rejection of a new trial on March 26, 1990, and the families are appealing to the full court.

Like all toxic waste litigation, the Woburn suit has been protracted. It has been full of contradictory elements—some victories, some defeats, endless uncertainty. The greatest uncertainty is not the outcome of the suit, but the health effects of toxic waste exposure over a human lifetime. The families view their lawsuit as transcending their personal concerns: for them, it is an important part of a community and nationwide movement to combat the scourge of toxic waste.

The Aftermath and the Significance of the Woburn Case

In view of the larger significance of the case, there are developments outside the trial itself that the families and their attorneys consider worthwhile. A moment of vindication came after the original trial when W. R. Grace admitted in U.S. District Court that it had lied to the EPA. In 1982 the EPA had asked Grace about its chemical use and disposal practices, and Grace gave out false information. The plaintiffs' lawyers, in the course of their research, uncovered and forwarded to the EPA evidence of wrongful toxic waste disposal leading to a federal grand jury indictment on January 28, 1987.[67] On May 31, 1988, Grace bargained a plea of guilty to one of twelve charges for the maximum fine of $10,000 (a later amendment to the Federal Code increased the maximum fine to $500,000 for the same crime committed after 1984).[68] Woburn family members and their lawyers saw Grace's guilty plea as inextricably tied to their lawsuit. As Schlictmann put it:

> The important issue is the declaration that they violated the law, they didn't tell the truth about the use of chemicals and disposal practices, and that was our whole point. They were not truthful, they had not come clean, and the whole issue of the trial was their acknowledging the reality. Just like the settlement itself, it was the acknowledgment that they had done wrong and hurt the community and that gave us some satisfaction. It has been such a long struggle, we are now going into our eighth year; it is just an added

vindication, a message to the world that we were right and they were wrong. People stop me on the street and they know that I am not involved in the criminal [EPA] case, and some don't even know whether I have provided information, but they all congratulate me for this great victory. So in the public's mind it is one and the same issue. It is very satisfying.[69]

Nevertheless, Woburn remains a very toxic environment. Between 1982 and 1986 seven children were diagnosed with leukemia (nearly four times the state average), as were thirty-eight adults (more than twice the expected rate for men, and about one and one-half times the expected rate for women). The victims' residences were scattered throughout the city, although proportionately more were in the original cluster area.[70]

Despite the national attention paid to the Woburn case, late in 1989 the EPA had not started to clean up Woburn's two Superfund sites, wells G and H and the Industri-Plex site. The latter is designated by the EPA the worst toxic waste site in New England and the fifth highest priority of the 850 designated sites in the United States.[71] This neglect is ironic, since Woburn activists figured strongly in the Congressional hearings that resulted in the five-year, $9 billion extension of the Superfund in 1985.[72] Not until January 31, 1989, did a plan to clean up Industri-Plex emerge, with a pact between the EPA and thirty-four current or former landowners, including Stauffer Chemical Company, the Mark-Phillip Trust, Monsanto Company, and ICI Americas, who had polluted the 245-acre parcel for over a century. It is expected that the $24 million project will start in mid-1990 and take between two and two-and-a-half years to complete.[73]

In fact the fence around Industri-Plex long ago collapsed, and, as Woburn residents remark angrily, children ride dirt bikes over the toxic waste piles. With the fence down, in the spring of 1988 "midnight dumpers" apparently added new waste drums, discovered by members of FACE who were showing the site. When they called the state DEQE to inspect the new drums, the FACE members were shocked to learn that the regional staff person (in an office close to the site) did not know that the Industri-Plex location contained toxics.[74] Residents find it hard to give credence to a government agency for the environment that remains ignorant of a significant toxic waste site in its immediate vicinity.

Furthering their loss of trust in government, federal officials continued to thwart the Woburn residents' efforts to bring the truth to light. FACE discovered in May 1988 that the EPA had been conducting a secret investigation of the Woburn data since 1984, thereby denying the public access to important scientific information. FACE learned that a secret investigative panel existed only when panel members began to telephone state and university officials to ask for Woburn data. Despite the long involvement of Woburn residents and independent professionals in many investigations, the EPA deliberately withheld the knowledge that a separate study was being conducted. FACE activists feared that the aim of the panel was to discredit the Harvard/FACE study. After FACE officers and Senator Kennedy's office pressed EPA officials, they did admit there was a panel, although they denied it was secret. Yet if the group were not secret, why was its existence hidden? All researchers conducting reputable investigations at Woburn discuss their work with the Citizens Advisory Council (CAC), a body made up of FACE members as well as state and federal officials.[75] Citizens successfully pressured the EPA to call a meeting between

the CAC and William Farland, acting director of the EPA
Office of Health and Environmental Assessment, and to
provide copies of the secret report.

The report by what the EPA terms the Woburn Workgroup argues that the Harvard study failed to account
for all of the excess leukemia cases. The EPA report also
asserts that since the Harvard study used water data based
on households rather than individuals, the link between
water exposure and adverse reproductive outcomes was
tenuous. Further, the EPA workgroup criticized the data
collection on the grounds that interviewers were untrained and that proxy responses from husbands about
their wives could have provided inaccurate data. The TCE
and PCE threat is played down; research on benzene and
vinyl chloride, known leukemogens present in nearby wells
in high concentrations, is encouraged.[76]

The residents of Woburn agree that benzene and vinyl
chloride, along with many other components of the town's
chemical contamination, are worthy of study. But they have
been continually frustrated by the tendency of government investigators to stress the existence of all other carcinogens while belittling the role of TCE. Members of the
CAC were particularly upset by the failure of the EPA
workgroup either to use data gathered by David Ozonoff,
a key medical researcher in the Woburn case, or to give
Steven Lagakos of the School of Public Health a chance
to review its findings.[77]

The Massachusetts DPH has not changed its position
on the relationship between water and leukemia, prefer-
ring to state only that there is an unexplained excess of
cancer that requires further study. It is a tragic irony that
during the course of the trial the Woburn town engineer
who had testified for the companies that the water could
not have caused leukemia was diagnosed with the disease.[78] Just before the engineer died he told a litigant

family that he doubted the safety of the water he had earlier defended.

The activism of Woburn residents has prompted continuous research into pollution and health. The first phase of the DPH study in 1981 served as the major impetus for reestablishing the state cancer registry. A previous registry had been voluntary and had utilized data only from cooperating hospitals; the new registry was mandated to collect data about all tumors in the state, including those detected at clinics.[79] At present the DPH and the CDC are conducting a five-year study of reproductive outcomes in Woburn, utilizing both prospective and retrospective data. Citizens have had a large role in designing the research, although FACE was unsuccessful in its efforts to include in this study other diseases often attributed to environmental contamination, such as cardiac arrhythmias and lupus. Officials also rejected FACE's suggestion that the study conduct physical examinations of children for up to one year rather than use just the postnatal hospital exams. The DPH is conducting a more elaborate case-control study of leukemia in Woburn for the period 1969–1986 than it did originally, although it still does not include some leukemia cases FACE believes should be included. The newer Murphy water distribution model for wells G and H will be used in conjunction with the reproductive outcomes study and a reanalysis of the Harvard/FACE data.[80] In addition, scientists at the Massachusetts Institute for Technology (MIT) are embarking on a Woburn-inspired study of genetic mutations caused by TCE and other toxics found in the watershed.[81]

With input from the CAC, which advises on all Woburn research, the DPH requested funding from the Agency for Toxic Substances and Disease Registry, a federal body connected with the CDC, to supplement other funds in the planned reproductive health study. In January 1988 the funding request was turned down.[82]

Despite the frequent shortcomings of state and federal agencies, FACE works hard at maintaining good relations with EPA and the Massachusetts DPH. Deborah Prothrow-Stith, the DPH commissioner who took office in 1988, has asked for a more official relationship with FACE. After visiting the area of the leukemia cluster, Prothrow-Stith said that she was "struck with how epidemiology is dependent on the role the public plays in bringing these things to light."[83] Woburn activists welcome these signs of increased respect for the role of an informed and mobilized citizenry.

Citizen activism in Woburn has had important national effects as well. David Ozonoff, who prepared medical testimony for the trial, told a group of citizens and scientists in 1988: "In hazardous waste, three names come up—Love Canal, Times Beach, and Woburn. Woburn stands far and above them all in the amount of scientific knowledge produced. All over the country, Woburn has put its stamp on the science of hazardous waste studies."[84] Ozonoff cites in particular the TCE syndrome involving three major body systems—immune, cardiovascular, and neurological—that was discovered in Woburn and is increasingly being recognized at other TCE locations.

Woburn's problems, as reflected in the lawsuit, have become beacons for toxic waste law, and a victory for the residents of Woburn would light the way for a large number of other similar suits. Some lawyers for victims of pollution are already talking about a "Woburn strategy" that links toxic wastes to immune system defects.[85] The business community is particularly concerned about the potentially enormous costs of such suits.[86] Even though the original trial did not go forward to a victory for the plaintiffs, the attorneys and families still hope the appeal against

Beatrice will succeed. They are keenly aware that their action is part of a larger movement and that they are helping to guide that movement.

Anthony Roisman of Trial Lawyers for Public Justice, who helped the Woburn families develop their case, believes that the Woburn and Velsicol cases together create "a very important milestone in environmental law."[87] Roisman, former head of the Hazardous Waste Litigation Section of the Department of Justice, writes that until recently toxic tort cases required indirect evidence, which includes both epidemiological data showing a correlation between exposure and disease and experimentation on animals. Both types of data are difficult to obtain and may not show statistically significant relationships. The requirement of indirect evidence has kept lawyers from taking on many toxic tort cases, except those involving an injury unique to the exposure, such as asbestos and mesothelioma or vinyl chloride and angiosarcoma of the liver. Researchers can now learn a great deal from clinical data about the diseases and complaints people have after exposure that they did not have before. Moreover, new techniques of immune system testing (DTH skin tests, T-cell surface marker analysis, B-cell counts, non-T-cell peripheral lymphocytes, ratios between various T-cells, urinalysis) can show evidence of injury long before the appearance of full-fledged disease, which requires a long latency period. Roisman finds a growing trend toward accepting such evidence.[88] The appeals court decisions in Jackson Township, New Jersey, and Hardeman County, Tennessee, discussed earlier in this chapter, do present some problems for future cases. Nevertheless, we feel confident that the more we learn about the effects of environmental chemicals on the immune system, the greater the likelihood of success in suits against corporations such as Beatrice and Grace.

In a 1977 study, polybrominated biphenyls (PBBs), for example, used in fire retardants, were found to have altered immunological processes in 1,000 farm residents who ate PBB-contaminated food. Compared with a control group of Wisconsin farm families who were not exposed to PBBs, the study group showed an unusual number of neurological, behavioral, joint, and gastrointestinal problems. They had more and longer-lasting upper respiratory infections and their cuts healed more slowly. Blood tests of subsamples showed fewer and defective T-lymphocytes in PBB-exposed people. The findings suggest greater susceptibility to infections and perhaps to cancer.[89] Even though medical experts for Grace and Beatrice termed the immune theory ridiculous, some chemical companies may be taking it seriously; Monsanto Chemical was already testing its agricultural chemists for immune system defects as early as 1977.[90]

The new medical and legal area of toxic effects on the immune system promises to play a significant role in our future understanding of environmental contamination. Most of our present knowledge ultimately stems from popular epidemiological work in the affected communities. In Woburn, the litigant families and the FACE activists set in motion an extensive process that is a model for many communities contaminated by toxic wastes. They pioneered the detection of the leukemia cluster; they spurred government to investigate and clean up both the wells and the Industri-Plex site; they brought the contamination to national attention; they launched a lawsuit with many future ramifications; they were central actors in a major health survey; and they continue to be active in the continuing research effort.

2

The Formation of an Organized Community

Organizing a community contaminated by toxic wastes is extremely difficult and full of contradictions. The victims and their families, already suffering physical and emotional pain, must relive painful memories as they delve into the causes of their trouble. Indeed, the more ammunition they find for their case, the more reasons they have to be angry and afraid. To become activists, citizens must overcome an ingrained reluctance to challenge authority: they must shed their preconceptions about the role and function of government and about democratic participation. They must also develop a new outlook on the nature of scientific inquiry and the participation of the public in scientific controversy. Activists must learn how to mobilize and organize the public to challenge government successfully. Most of all, as the affected families and other activists in Woburn discovered, enormous patience and energy are required, because the struggle can continue for more than a decade.

Who Got Involved?

The Woburn community organized on a different pattern from most other toxic waste sites. Elsewhere we often

43

see either a single community organization (as in Legler, New Jersey) or competing community groups with separate memberships (as in Love Canal). Alternatively, we may see a group composed of persons who have suffered specific health problems (as in Hardeman County, Tennessee).

In Woburn we find a hybrid pattern. The eight families affected by leukemia who filed the lawsuit make up one group with a particular focus. A larger number of people in Woburn and surrounding communities belong to FACE, which pursues a broader range of activities. The two groups overlap somewhat, although not all the litigant families belong to FACE. The mothers in two families involved in the suit were also prime organizers of FACE and have continued their association with that group. Other litigants may be members but have not generally been active. For most, dealing with chronic and usually fatal disease was simply too draining. Adults had to succor ailing children, spend time and energy pursuing medical care, care for healthy children, participate in tests and interviews for the lawsuit, and frequently deal with marital problems that either arose from or were exacerbated by the disease. A FACE leader explained: "The people who are involved in the case became so wrapped up in what was involved in following through on the case that they didn't really have a lot of energy left over for the other issues."[1]

Within FACE there have been some disagreements, particularly about how militant the group should be. Most remaining members are willing to cooperate with state and federal officials. Some members preferred to focus on further health studies rather than expand to community and school educational activities (toxic waste garbage pickup, school modules on environmental issues, and so on). In fact, FACE continues to pursue both research and community education.[2]

The original organizers of FACE were by and large politically and environmentally inexperienced persons, and FACE was their first attempt at political action. Some newer members are more environmentally aware than longer-term members. FACE activists have chosen to keep distant from most national organizations. They have continued to be active at the state level, in such matters as lobbying for clean water legislation. They help other local groups with information and strategies and sometimes write or phone agencies and legislators on their behalf. But they do not see themselves as national activists: they see themselves as seriously affected by a local problem that they have sought to rectify by every means in their power.[3]

The leaders of FACE and of the litigant group are predominantly women, as in most toxic waste site organizations, and for similar reasons. The typical toxic contamination site is a poor working-class or lower-middle-class neighborhood, where many women are likely to be home with their children; women have community-based social networks to sustain the necessary communication and action; they are more likely to recognize their neighborhood's health problems; they are less likely than men to agree that disease is a necessary risk of economic growth.[4] One study of twenty-one Superfund sites found that the concern most frequently voiced was for the health of children;[5] and women generally take the primary responsibility for their children's health.

Despite a well-organized campaign, activist Woburn families and their allies were not able to recruit all the affected families for the lawsuit. Litigant families told us that some victims who worked for the city or for one of

the two corporations feared that their jobs would be jeop-
ardized. The family of another victim feared a loss of customers from their small business. Litigants remember
seeing reluctant parents in the hospital hallways and remember, too, that they stood apart. Some families dreaded
the added emotional burden of the suit. Other victims
worried about the publicity or simply did not see themselves as the kind of people who sued others.

The families who joined the suit did not really see
themselves as activists. Most said that they were not the
type to join organizations. Several family members who
testified at state and federal hearings on environmental
matters saw that action as a logical consequence of their
activities at home. Two persons from different families
expressed interest in helping out with research and measurement of toxic wastes. Even so, after years of active
involvement in the Woburn crisis, almost none of the
families expect to be involved in further political actions.
Only one woman explicitly stated a desire to be involved
in further political action, and that was around women's
issues.

The Making of a National Case

If the families who filed the lawsuit and the activists who
mobilized Woburn were not experienced political organizers, what accounts for Woburn's national prominence?
Despite the great prevalence of toxic waste contamination
in this country, relatively few sites have become the focus
of community organizing. Although public surveys show
a general awareness of toxic waste issues, and local toxic
waste activism has been growing, the fact remains that
most victims do not fight back. One study of twenty-five
cases of toxic contamination in residential communities
found that in the sixteen cases in which the victims un-

covered the problem, they still did surprisingly little on their own behalf.[6] Moreover, of communities where victims do organize, only a handful have attained national significance: Love Canal; Times Beach, Missouri; and Woburn. Each of them, like Woburn, presents a particular set of circumstances leading them to prominence.

Gretchen Latowsky, an organizer of FACE, tried to sum up why Woburn residents were willing to become so involved:

> It was all new, and I think this sounds kind of crazy, but there was a tremendous amount of excitement. As awful as that sounds, I think part of the reason people got so involved was that it was fascinating, the whole thing—the technology, the illness, the statistics, the government relations, the publicity, the media involvement—all of that.[7]

What exactly were the factors creating such excitement?

In other major toxic waste contaminations, people often noticed adverse health effects, but typically those effects did not include deaths. Residents near toxic waste sites sometimes attribute deaths to contamination in retrospect, but it is not usually a rash of deaths that alerts them to the problems.[8] Woburn is salient, Latowsky told us,

> because the children died. Sixteen children died in Woburn. I think it had to do with the fact that the children died of leukemia and some mothers got very involved. They tell a very unhappy story and I think people relate to that. It is a human tragedy.[9]

Families and activists also credit the coincidence of Woburn's crisis with the well-reported hearings on the reauthorization of the Superfund, which featured powerful testimony from Woburn victims. Having two Superfund sites in one small area—Industri-Plex and wells G and H—Woburn bore a particularly heavy toxic waste burden and thus appeared in sharp focus. News stories revealing government ineptitude and inaction in regard to a number of other toxic waste sites made the claims of Woburn residents more credible. The antagonism of the DPH to community involvement in many locations also contributed to the believability of Woburn victims.

The attention of the media—especially coverage on "Nova" and "60 Minutes"—fixed a national spotlight on Woburn. National media were in fact more supportive of the community effort than local media. Woburn families and FACE leaders note that the *Woburn Daily Times* provided a great deal of coverage but failed to be overtly critical of the city's inaction. During the trial, National Public Radio carried more coverage than the *Boston Globe,* the largest newspaper in the Woburn area. National media, especially the *New York Times,* play the major role in placing toxic waste problems on the public agenda.[10] Lack of coverage in local media, however, can sabotage community organizing around toxic hazards, as it did when an office building fire in Binghamton, New York, released polychlorinated biphenyls (PCBs). Local journalists failed to cover the work of the Citizen's Committee on the Binghamton Office Building, and activists lost a key ingredient in successful community organizing.[11]

Politicians such as Senator Edward Kennedy, Representative Edward Markey, state representative Nicholas Paleologos, and state senator Richard Krauss helped spread the word about the Woburn situation. Kennedy's involvement of Woburn residents in the Superfund reauthorization hearings was particularly significant. Sympathetic politicians, particularly members of Congress, have been important publicizers of specific instances of contamination at other toxic waste sites.

Legal and public health experts contributed much to

the Woburn effort as well. The Harvard biostatisticians gave both hard data and legitimacy, especially valuable because of the caution and opposition of other scientific groups and public health agencies. Medical experts chosen by the lawyers developed strong convictions about the case and added emotional support along with their technical expertise. Jan Schlictmann and his legal colleagues provided the victims with hope, energy, and resources beyond their original expectations. "The case kept picking up steam as more people got aboard," one litigant notes, "more scientific people and more attorneys . . . saying, 'Yes, there is something here, let's make something of this.' Otherwise this would have just withered, I think."

The larger environmental and toxic waste network also contributed to the attention focused on Woburn, as other nonlocal toxic waste groups began to speak about Woburn as a case on the order of Love Canal. Still, Woburn's ascent to national significance must eventually be credited to conscious organizing efforts by the victims and their neighbors. They took "favorable" circumstances, created more of their own, and wove events into a tight web. In most other contaminated communities, victims fail to counteract government stonewalling. Woburn victims and their supporters showed unusual courage and persistence in withstanding so much hostility, obstruction, inaction, and ineffective action.

Community Opposition

Community resistance to the efforts of the families and activists was strong. Woburn's identity as an industrial city goes back to its early years as a center for the tanning industry. Even today the high school football team calls itself the Woburn Tanners. The tanning industry itself left behind a considerable legacy of pollution in the form of mineral pits and large holes in which hides were buried. As the tanning industry died out the city administration actively courted new industry with significant concessions. It was a combination of the old industry (Beatrice's Riley Tannery site) and new industry (Grace's Cryovac plant) that fouled the city's wells. Woburn's long-standing industrial tradition made it hard for many city residents to stomach the charge by a small group of citizens that the city's well-established relationship with industry had brought with it sickness, misery, and death.

Community tensions grew as the Woburn litigants went forward with their suit. Early on, for example, cars of people attending an organizational meeting at the Trinity Episcopal church of which Young was pastor were ticketed, although the area had previously been ignored by police. City officials consistently denied that Woburn had a problem and sometimes obstructed the efforts of activists. Charles Ryan, the reporter who broke the story in the *Woburn Daily Times,* felt that "at first the reaction from most city officials was, 'Why are you writing that stuff? You will only frighten people.' People were more concerned about property values than any possible health effects." [12]

Mayor John Rabbitt (elected in 1983), was more supportive of the victims than his predecessor, Thomas M. Higgins, under whom the contamination was discovered; but he nevertheless expressed anger at the "Nova" television documentary, because "it put Woburn on trial rather than the companies." [13] Ironically, community opposition may have helped to give the group cohesion and purpose.

There were also snide comments and thinly veiled ridicule from neighbors and occasionally family members. A family member who was an early organizer told us:

People didn't appreciate what I was doing. Sometimes it surprised me because sometimes it was people who knew [her son] and knew how sick he was, and I thought they might have been a little more open to the possibility of it being caused by something. And knowing what kind of a life he had, they might want to prevent that from happening again. So that surprised me, people that I knew, that knew him fairly well. But I guess it was so difficult from the very beginning, I was getting so much negative feedback, that it was part of the whole issue with me anyway. It was all entwined, as soon as I started asking questions, as soon as I starting making noises I was getting a lot of negative response, so it was all part of it.

Another activist family member said:

We had fights with my own neighbor, of all people. I couldn't believe it. But we have also met people all over the city, you know, and all over the country who believed us, didn't we? Didn't we? I think people are afraid to believe that their back yard could be contaminated, that they could be killed by these chemicals. I think people are afraid.

As in other toxic waste sites, property values have been an issue. The father of a leukemia victim told us:

They are afraid that their property values will go down. Oh yes, there is a whole bunch of crap. I had more arguments with people. I used to dispatch a cab company, and I knew everybody in the city of Woburn. I had more arguments with people over that. I was telling them wait and see, wait and see. I said, "I can't tell you everything, wait and see when the trial comes out, with the medical, wait and see what they tell you. Then you will believe it." Most of them believe it now, don't they. And they are kind of glad that we did it because they are not a bad city. The property values went up because it is so watched, and we helped them more than everybody else in Woburn.

Similar community opposition has occurred at many toxic waste sites. When Donna Connelly of Waterford, New York, started Citizens for Safe Water in 1982, she was greeted by threats and hostility from many townspeople. General Electric's silicone plant employed 1,400 people in Waterford, and thus "their reaction was 'leave GE alone.'" General Electric was releasing a large amount of hazardous waste legally into the Hudson River, including 105 pounds of toluene and eight pounds of benzene every day. In addition, the company reported at least twenty spills in three years. The New York Department of Environmental Conservation and the local health department tested Waterford's water and declared it was safe, with a few exceptions. Some of those exceptions involved TCE. After it became clear that the local water was contaminated, Connelly said, "Now people are saying 'I don't want to hurt GE but I don't want to drink the water, either.'" In the wake of the Bhopal methyl isocyanate disaster, Waterford residents became wary of their town's large storage tanks of methyl chloride, which is extremely flammable and dangerous to humans. The area would have to be evacuated in the case of a release. But as Laura Cole, chairwoman of the Waterford Environmental Conservation Commission, told a *New York Times* reporter, "A lot of people are afraid to say we need an evacuation plan. It's an admission you are in danger."[14]

When the Friendly Hills Action Group in Colorado found increased leukemia, birth defects, and other diseases locally, they sued Martin Marietta Corporation and the Denver water board for contaminating their water supply. An influential local civic leader and a Martin Marietta employee complained that the publicity had depressed property values and that the group had "destroyed the peacefulness and harmony of the neighborhood over a bogeyman that doesn't exist."[15]

In communities such as Woburn, victims and their families must often bear stigmatization in addition to more direct opposition. When the one adult litigant who later died of leukemia first told his workmates that he was ill, they began to shy away from him. His wife reported that a townsperson "verbally attacked" her at a hockey game, saying that she was "against Woburn" and that her family was giving Woburn a bad name. Some siblings reported being teased about their ill brothers and sisters. One brother said,

> I got into a couple of fights around the neighborhood
> sticking up for him about his hair [which had fallen
> out as a result of chemotherapy].

Children at Love Canal experienced the same teasing.[16] So did victims of the Times Beach dioxin contamination. When a resident eating in a restaurant was identified as having appeared on television, many customers left. Victims found that laundries would not do their wash.[17] Three Mile Island residents, too, experienced these reactions: when a Pennsylvania family visiting Disneyworld was identified as coming from Middletown, the hotel bellhop refused to take the luggage. Another family fled at the time of the accident to a sister's house, where the brother-in-law refused to allow them inside.[18]

Such stigmatization is common in toxic waste disaster areas. Sometimes it results from anger and fear about property values and the city's reputation, but it is also a psychological defense against the fear of being contaminated oneself. At Love Canal, residents were "feared as the contaminated carriers of mysterious diseases."[19] Michael Edelstein found that residents in the Legler section of Jackson Township, New Jersey, were labeled as having poisoned water; their homes were considered to be marked and thus unsalable. By extension—a "courtesy stigma"— the whole community can become stigmatized.[20] Health concerns also leave their mark, often tangible, sometimes anticipatory: "Once contaminated, many exposure victims view themselves differently, in part because they fear dreaded health impacts, such as cancers, threats to un-born children, and cross-generational genetic defects. Victims also discover that others see them differently as well. Their homes and neighborhoods are downgraded by observers who exhibit 'anticipatory fears.' "[21]

Like whistle-blowers who expose corruption in cor-porations and government agencies, toxic waste organiz-ers are often seen as oddballs disrupting the normal flow of events. Indeed, being an activist means pitting oneself against the established order and is in itself a form of deviance. Not only do toxic waste activists threaten the established political, economic, and social order, but they are also seen as obsessed with a toxic waste problem. Anne Anderson's initial water hypothesis for the Woburn leu-kemia cluster was treated in exactly this way. At Love Canal, "nonbelievers" who were skeptical of any relation-ship between chemical contamination and health prob-lems stigmatized the "believers" as radicals, liars, cheats, and crazies.[22] By focusing on an alleged obsession, critics of the activists psychologize the situation, making the ac-tivists appear emotionally disturbed and thus not to be taken seriously.

Although Woburn residents faced considerable oppo-sition and stigmatization, some also reported supportive comments and attitudes. The father of a surviving child remembered:

As time went on and you would get comments from people like, "This is a great thing you are doing and we wish you luck and everything," you started to gain more confidence and feel even more justified in what you were doing.

Neighbors who feared that their property was declining in value were not always hostile:

Our neighbors have all been supportive. They all want to know the answer too. A few have said we dropped the property values but they haven't said it directly to me.

A New Frame of Reference

Woburn residents faced a more subtle and difficult challenge than simply overcoming obstacles and withstanding abuse: they had to remake their basic picture of the world. Generalizing from his study of Love Canal and Legler, Michael Edelstein emphasizes the difficulty of reframing one's outlook on the world in which one lives. People have a "lifescape," or a frame for understanding their surroundings, of which they are generally unaware until their normal set of behaviors (their "life-style") is disrupted or their assumptions are contradicted in some other way. This disruption may not by itself trigger adequate realization and action; it must be accepted or recognized as a challenge. Victims often react to toxic waste exposure by denying the problem or its severity. They may also accommodate themselves to the problem rather than challenge it, or they may panic.[23]

Residents may become habituated to contamination. A survey of inhabitants of Love Canal found that persons who had been aware of contamination at an earlier time

were less likely to perceive the contamination as dangerous, especially in the absence of noticeable health problems. The researchers concluded, "Perhaps the longer one
lives with potential dangers, the more likely one will become reconciled to the condition, if the effects are not
acute in nature."[24]

Both psychologically and experientially, people are
simply not prepared to notice the signs of toxic waste exposure. During the period of incubation, when people are
unaware of the developing crisis, there may be clues of
an impending disaster that are not understood as such.
In Legler, New Jersey, there had been random problems
with water quality, but these were taken as matters of individual concern. People recalled the bad taste and odor
of water and remembered viewing the dumping of chemical barrels and colored sludge, but they did not understand and therefore accommodated themselves to the unusual situation.[25] Even when public attention is drawn to
a disease cluster, many people cannot reorganize their
perceptions. Some Love Canal residents who themselves
suffered unusual health problems argued against a linkage to chemical swales. When pressed, they admitted that
they would prefer not to know about a linkage if one was
proved, because it would be too scary.[26] Nonbelievers often
based their opinions on the lack of personally experienced effects. In Woburn, victims reported that many
people argued:

> I drank the water for twenty years, I never had a
> problem. . . . I've had no problems with it; why
> should I worry about it? It is happening to somebody
> else, not to me.

For a person who takes this view, the problem simply
cannot be seen and therefore does not exist. Invisibility
surrounds nearly all environmental and occupational haz-

ards. A Massachusetts public health study summed it up: "Estimates of the proportion of cancer deaths attributable to exposures to carcinogens in the workplace range from a low of 2 percent to a high of 38 percent. Even if we take the lowest of those figures, the number of cancer deaths in Massachusetts contracted in the workplace is on the order of one per day. If the 30 workers a month who die of occupational cancer were killed by a scaffold collapse, it would make national headlines. Yet its equivalent in terms of human life lost is tolerated month after month, year after year."[27]

One might expect doctors to more readily see health patterns that are invisible to others. Their work, after all, consists in making intelligible the diverse signs and symptoms that patients present yet may not understand. Doctors might ideally serve as key sources of knowledge in toxic contamination situations, but they do not. They rarely look for environmental causes of diseases and thus fail to legitimize environmental health concerns.[28] When Woburn victims complained of cardiological and gastroenterological problems, their physicians often thought they were hypochondriacs or suffering psychosomatic disturbances. Most of the people we interviewed found neither their own nor other Woburn doctors particularly helpful in viewing their epidemic in any larger context.

Similarly, at Love Canal, the county medical society turned down community activists' request for assistance.[29] Love Canal residents, like people in other toxic waste sites, reported such symptoms as shaking, headaches, skin rashes, respiratory disorders, vomiting, stomach pains, and bloating; these are symptoms that often elude medical diagnosis, particularly if they do not match a known constellation of effects. Love Canal families reported that most doctors could not or would not make the connection between illness and chemicals. It was the families who made sense of the data, Fowlkes and Miller suggest. "Viewed from the perspective of traditional medicine, the health problems of the families were a collection of incoherent anomalies. Viewed with reference to the chemicals, their problems began to make sense. The chemicals provided a framework for understanding their health experiences that accorded them a legitimacy that professional medicine was unable or unwilling to give them."[30]

Why is it so hard for toxic waste contamination victims to recruit medical support? First, medical education provides little if any study of environmental and occupational health. Nor is specialization in those fields well developed or respected. Second, toxic waste victims suffer from what Henry Vyner calls "medical invisibility," which stems from "latency invisibility"—the long, unknown period between contamination and disease. It also derives from "etiological invisibility"—the difficulty of determining the causal pathway of disease. Causality is invisible because there are rarely any observable lesions, the disease may have other causes, and people may be unaware that the responsible contaminant exists or that a causal relationship exists between contaminant and disease. Moreover, the symptoms do not fit a typical pattern. As a result, toxic waste health effects are particularly difficult to diagnose—they present "diagnostic ambiguity."[31]

Nevertheless, when a specific disease is finally detected, people face what Vyner calls an "adaptational dilemma"—"a situation in which a person finds that an empirically informed and thus satisfactory adaptation to an invisible exposure is not possible." In particular, "it is virtually impossible to assess and protect oneself from the dangers of exposure to an invisible contaminant." In practical terms, victims are faced with potentially life-and-death choices along with a lack of information. Whether residents of the area surrounding the contaminated Three

Mile Island nuclear plant should or should not evacuate is an example.[32]

Victims experience a wide range of uncertainties—about their previous exposure, their present exposure, whether to evacuate, the boundaries of contamination, how much of the contaminant they received, the significance of that dose, the latency period of the disease, the etiology of the disease, its diagnosis, its prognosis, its treatment, how to cope with the situation, and how to deal with the financial elements.[33] These ambiguities and uncertainties are highly stressful and prevent victims from coping well with the threat to their health.

People damaged by toxic waste exposure find that the logical sources of information and support are not very forthcoming. Without information, it is hard for them to break with the routine assumptions of everyday life, although their situation challenges those assumptions to the limit.

> Toxic waste directly assails several fundamental social beliefs: that humans have dominion over nature; that personal control over one's destiny is possible; that technology and science are forces of progress only; that risks necessary for the good life are acceptable; that people get what they deserve; that experts know best; that the market place is self-regulating; that one's home is one's castle; that people have the right to do what they wish on their own property; and that government exists to help.[34]

It is surprising, in view of his approach, that Vyner emphasizes that people can develop "nonempirical belief systems," which are "deductions based on data that are qualitatively or quantitatively inadequate from a scientific standpoint." To some extent these belief systems stem from the contradictory yet authoritative messages from government officials. Such systems are also attempts to achieve certainty in a general context of extreme uncertainty.[35]

It is not surprising, under psychological pressures of this severity, that some victims of invisible environmental contaminants may develop apparently irrational outlooks, although this response does not seem to be typical of community groups. In fact, most individuals and groups successfully develop accurate belief systems based on concrete investigations. That is clearly what happened in Woburn with the FACE/Harvard School of Public Health health survey and in many other contaminated communities. Most important, community efforts at forming logical hypotheses and undertaking appropriate research have often surpassed the efforts of government and professionals.

One of the Woburn mothers listed what she considered the main obstacles to understanding and action:

> I think we all think, somehow we are all very comfortable thinking that industry just wouldn't do this to us, government wouldn't allow industry to do this to us even if industry wanted to, and it is a very difficult thing to grasp in the first place. Second place you really don't want to know because it is not a comfortable thought. Because what can you really do about it . . . how much can you really do? How much can you fight industry? How much can you fight a government? So it is almost like a lost hopeless cause. People just don't want to grasp it because after you finally understand it, then what? Then all you are going to do is feel frustrated and frightened by it. There are so many areas of pollution, and every day, the more you learn about it the more difficult it becomes. So who wants to learn any more about it? Who wants to learn about it? It is not comfortable.

Resigned Acceptance

As these words imply, many people face high risks with resigned acceptance, which is a common response to knowledge of toxic hazards. We consider resignation a passive response to a powerful set of social forces and therefore detrimental, because it does not lead to remediation. People are willing to live with risks, even life-threatening risks, for a variety of reasons that often point to forces beyond individual control, such as job security and government policy. Sometimes the reasons are internalized attitudes about the "normal" way of living in the world, such as unwillingness to show fear.

Resigned acceptance is similar to denial, in that it ignores the existence of a problem. Yet denial may be a more active approach in which people find supportive coping mechanisms. With resigned acceptance, people merely accept the inevitable, passively allowing themselves to be victimized. In their position as victims, they are even more powerless. For that reason, attaining personal and group power and efficacy is a central issue in toxic waste organizing.

Much of what we know about the phenomenon of resigned acceptance comes from studies of workplace hazards. Coal miners, for instance, accept phenomenally high risks that are well known. Similarly, shipyard workers in Bath, Maine, have spoken openly of being unable to leave their work even when they know of the serious asbestos danger. Dorothy Nelkin and Michael Brown's interviews with seventy-five workers uncovered a variety of rationales for accepting risk. Some workers accept risk as part of what they get paid for, some because of a related need for efficiency: "We'd never get anything done if we had to wait around to find out if things are safe."[36]

Nelkin and Brown found that when workers felt unable to control conditions of their work life, they accepted with resignation situations they recognized as grave: "Everyone's going to die sooner or later"; "If this doesn't get you, something else will." These respondents felt that it was useless to work for improved conditions in the workplace. This conviction was not tied to a particular job; people believed they would face the same or other risks in other jobs, assuming they kept the same kind of work. Some preferred known risks to new unknown ones. Some felt that their trade was by definition a risky one and that risk was part of the tradition. Some feared demotion or firing if they complained. Others felt they had few alternatives because their education and training were limited. Some interviewees liked the "rush" of danger or the high wages that came with the risky job. Other parts of the job might be good; people took the good and bad together. Still other workers created individual solutions, such as changing their diets and developing positive attitudes. Several had fantasies of personal invulnerability. Some feared the anger and frustration of co-workers or accusations of cowardice.[37]

The fears, concerns, and attitudes of workers in the risky jobs are similar to what community residents feel when exposed to toxic waste contamination. Although many communities with toxic waste contamination do unite, most do not—the social structural forces and the psychological obstacles are just too powerful. Economic forces, such as environmental blackmail by corporations who would prefer to leave the area than clean up, have also kept many contaminated communities in check.

People living at toxic waste sites must overcome a blind faith in scientific experts and the rationality of technology, the dominant paradigm of our society. Of course, most people do not act with perfect rationality in the sense of operating on the basis of statistical probability, knowing all risks, and balancing those risks. Rather they select from salient information and make choices for personal ends. The fact that they do not employ a strict rational choice model does not mean their fears are groundless.[38] As the Woburn residents and their counterparts across the country have shown us, personal fears are often more rational than corporate-scientific views. In Woburn and elsewhere it is the ordinary people who detected toxic waste hazards and who protect the environment.

Increasingly, however, government agencies, corporate officers, and many scientists follow a rational model of decision making based on risk assessment. Risk assessment utilizes economic approaches to analyze cost-benefit ratios, and psychological methods to study risk acceptance by individuals. Typically, a bureaucratic scientist might use risk assessment to determine whether to allow a corporation to continue production or emission of toxic substances or to allow a government unit to site a toxic dump, nuclear weapons lab, or other hazardous facility. There are several problems with this approach. First, risk assessment compares "natural" risks such as hurricanes with human-created ones and implies that victims of the latter should view their own suffering in the light of other more serious risks. It also depreciates complaints about toxic hazards when there are higher local risks to health, some of which stem from personal habits such as smoking. Second, risk assessment is often based on unclear or unsubstantiated risk levels for toxic chemicals and on poorly conceived studies of the health effects of toxic exposure. In Woburn, this approach would have told residents that the statistical probability of disease was so low as to be practically nonexistent. Third, as many toxic waste victims and a growing number of scholars now realize, risk assessment often involves valuing corporate profit and government stability more than human safety. Fourth, risk assessment offers a technological approach to a human problem. It ignores people's perceptions and feelings in favor of alleged absolute measurements.

But an individual's perceptions of a problem are important. With doctor-patient relationships, for example, medical sociologists have shown that trust, exchange of opinions, and informed consent are not only humanitarian but also critical to a good patient-provider relationship and better health. Further, even when community perceptions and fears of toxic hazards seem exaggerated to officials and experts, they have a rational basis in the many disasters of recent years and the poor official response to them.

The American people have witnessed widespread contamination and frequent closing of municipal water supplies. A decade after the near meltdown at Three Mile Island, they see that the nuclear power industry has not yet fully implemented the government recommendations stemming from the accident. They hear of leakages and mismanagement in the federal government's nuclear weapons production plants. They have experienced the continuing contamination of food supplies by pesticides. At the same time, Americans have watched their government allow the export of dangerous products, such as the contraceptive Depo-Provera, which are ruled illegal for use domestically. In short, we have seen uncontrolled toxic pollution, accompanied by scientific and government inaction. It is inappropriate for experts and officials to brand public perceptions as inaccurate. Further, even when community residents do have apparently inaccurate perceptions of a particular situation, their concerns ought not be discounted. The very fact that a large number of people and communities share a type of perception indicates that a significant social phenomenon is involved.

In fact, distrust of traditional wisdom and information

sources usually comes only after a long-standing unwillingness to consider alternative explanations. Woburn families spent a long time in proper channels before they began to doubt the reliability of official responses. So too did Love Canal citizens. But public health officials give contradictory messages about leaching paths, toxicity levels, degree of risk, boundaries of contamination, and measurement of health effects. Residents begin to distrust traditional scientific authorities when those authorities contradict the experiential knowledge the community has collectively gathered and developed.[39]

Residents further learn that the response of government is not concerned primarily with the scientific components of toxic waste crisis, but rather is intensely political and concerned to protect the government and corporate status quo. They learn that democratic inputs for citizens are sharply restricted, and that the public good is not central to public policy. When they realize that they actively distrust government, they then begin to act on their own.

Communities afflicted by toxic waste contamination are hard to organize because victims have lost control of their lives on several levels. Victims must face the reality of living in an environment poisoned by forces beyond their reach. They exist under actual or potential threats about which little is known. Many decisions about their health and lives are made far away and without their input.[40] Faith in the political and economic system falters and sometimes crumbles in the wake of toxic waste crises, because corporations have usually caused the problem and government has typically prolonged it. Understandably, Woburn residents displayed much distrust of government and corporations, as did inhabitants of other toxic waste sites. In the wake of the near meltdown at Three Mile Island, area residents showed exceptional distrust of fed-

eral and state officials and utility companies. Their scores
on general attitude scales for mistrust were also higher
than in national samples conducted at the same period;
women were more distrustful than men of authorities.[41]

Distrust can lead victims in two contrary directions. On
the one hand, it can lead to mobilization, because people
feel a need for power after being abandoned by traditional social and political institutions. On the other hand,
distrust can lead to helplessness, because most people find
it too difficult to challenge the entrenched institutions of
society. Further, even if distrust leads people to organize
politically, they may still suffer emotionally from the failure of their ordinary ties and norms.

Thus distrust of the government and corporations may
not be enough to mobilize individual victims. They must
still bridge several gaps between private and social life.
Social support can buffer severe stresses and help people
maintain their health. But normal social networks often
break down in toxic waste crises. Because the community
or municipality as a whole is an important link in the social network, as victims challenge the established order
they loosen the bonds of social collectivity. They find that
they must organize and help themselves.

Victims of toxic waste must, moreover, transcend the
impression that their problems are merely personal. They
must understand and make others understand that their
personal troubles are indeed social problems.[42] The shift
from a personal to a social viewpoint can benefit people
who participate in community organizing efforts. At Love
Canal, although people reported losing friends as a result
of the crisis, many more reported making new friends.[43]

Researchers have found a strong relationship between
victims' neighborhood ties and their understanding of a
toxic waste crisis. In a sample of sixty-three Love Canal
residents, one-third were "minimalists"—they believed that

contamination from the landfill was limited in scope and had few if any serious health effects. Two-thirds were "maximalists"—they felt that the contamination was pervasive, that it extended beyond the official boundaries, and that it had probably caused serious health risks. Minimalists were older, had no children at home, often had a history of working for a chemical company, and had few neighborhood ties. Maximalists were younger, typically had children at home, and had stronger local ties.[44]

Other social factors may make it harder for victims to come to terms with their situation and act. A community may be frightened by the strategy of environmental blackmail, in which polluting corporations threaten to run away or government agencies warn that corporations may flee if they are charged. Even without environmental blackmail, people may simply accept corporations as valuable local resources. Hooker Chemical escaped much blame at Love Canal because the company was central to the local economy. The Love Canal minimalists, questioned after the local contamination became generally known, remained unconvinced that there was any relationship between people's illnesses and the chemicals. They further claimed that if there were any risk, it was part of a fair trade for the benefits of modern chemical technology.[45]

Likewise, Dow Chemical's reputation as a good citizen protected it in the Midland, Michigan, dioxin case. As the major employer there, Dow succeeded in its public relations campaign to stifle the notion that it caused dioxin contamination. The director of the county board of health agreed with Dow executives that the corporation's safe practices and concerns for the environment actually made Midland a safe place in which to live. He broadly asserted, "We are alive and well in Midland, Michigan, and we welcome others to come and enjoy life with us." The city council joined the clamor of support for Dow, passing a resolution that dioxin posed no threat to public health. Even those with deep suspicions held their tongues, at least in public. A sixty-four-year-old woman, her husband recently retired from Dow, spoke to a reporter only when he was out of earshot, and she began her account with a qualification:

> Dow has been good to us, but I can't help thinking of my friends. It's all around us, cancer. Another neighbor across the corner just discovered she has cancer; a neighbor next door had brain surgery, and the second neighbor on the other side had cancer. The neighbor who just moved out of the house next door had breast cancer. The person we bought our house from had breast cancer. I know a family with two sons-in-law with testicular cancer, at the same time. If I'd known then what I know now, I would have raised my children elsewhere.[46]

Resigned acceptance sometimes takes a belligerent form as an aggressive acceptance of the status quo we call "boosterism." This reaction was evident in the large demonstration held in Institute, West Virginia, in support of Union Carbide, following a leak at its local plant that occurred soon after the tragedy at Bhopal. Boosterism involves a transformation of knowledge and belief that causes people to act against their own interest. Texas Eastern Gas Pipeline Company, for example, announced in 1987 that for the last 35 years it had been burying wastes containing PCBs. Despite the concerns of some residents who live near the burial pits, residents have come to the support of the company in the belief that it would not do anything unsafe. The mayor told a *New York Times* reporter, "If it is a problem, I feel sure Texas Eastern will take care of it." The town librarian added, "I have no quarrel with it. I don't see anything wrong with it because we know they're going to clean it up. They keep the place looking nice. They have a ball park they let people use. Scout troops have picnics there."[47]

The Pollyanna tone of these remarks is symptomatic of a condition in which people believe they are exercising their power and making informed decisions when in fact they have handed their power over to corporate and governmental authorities who they trust will do what is proper. One tragedy of toxic waste contamination is the intense powerlessness felt by the victims: the tragedy is compounded when people do not even realize that they are victims and have given up their power.

Contrary to the sentiments of the boosters, government officials and agencies too often obstruct communities' efforts to remedy contamination. The entire history of citizens' attempts to get government help is replete with resistance by public servants. Each level of government has its own reasons for not meeting victims' needs. Generally, government seeks to preserve the status quo, whether it is an economic base consisting of one or more large local employers, the defense of a state public health monitoring system, or an ideological perspective in which toxic waste activists are seen as anticapitalist and un-American. Government officials have conflicting roles as public servants, bureaucrats, scientists, technocrats, promoters of private enterprise, and regulators of compliance with the laws. These roles make it hard for officials and agencies to focus their efforts on the best environmental strategy. Bureaucratic overlaps and poor coordination between layers of government make the situation worse.[48]

Victims of toxic waste must confront not only officials and bureaucrats in local, state, and federal government but also scientific experts in government units and other institutions. Because of disparities of knowledge and power, victims feel at a disadvantage when dealing with experts. They often emerge from contact with experts feeling incompetent and powerless. Yet frequently—as in Woburn—ordinary people are capable of putting together scientific data gathered from many experts and seeing gaps or patterns in those data that the experts are blind to.

People living in contaminated areas may also be inhibited by the economic stakes in their houses. At Love Canal, few renters considered their homes to be unsafe. Most of these renters lived in a housing project widely considered to be the nicest in Niagara Falls and would have to move to lower-quality or more expensive housing if they left. Although homeowners were far more likely to perceive the threat, they too felt considerable anguish about perhaps losing years of work and equity that might represent the largest part of their savings.[49] Because a home represents much more than the value of the property, toxic victims experience what Edelstein terms the "inversion of the home," the loss of the psychological comfort of haven and refuge.[50]

Besides the difference in income, another feature of the owner-renter split at Love Canal was that 65 percent of the renters were black. Although there was no clear evidence of overt racism, a number of the Homeowners' Association members made the renters feel less important, since it was felt that they could easily move out of the Love Canal area to other rental apartments.[51]

Toxic waste sites that have come to national attention have been in primarily white neighborhoods, although a disproportionate number of toxic waste sites are in minority communities. Part of the problem is that organized environmental and toxic waste groups have had largely white memberships and have not done enough to reach out to minorities. At the same time, the very significant organizing efforts in minority communities has not received much press. In 1982, for instance, residents of Warren County, North Carolina, mostly black and led by civil rights organizations, marched to block the dumping of PCBs. Fifty-five were arrested, although arrests rarely occur in toxic waste activism.[52] Freudenberg describes a number of toxic waste struggles involving Native Americans and Hispanics and suggests that these groups find it easier to distrust the status quo: "Middle-class Americans are often reluctant to believe that corporations or their government could deliberately engage in activities that might sicken or kill people, but the historical experience of nonwhites has led them to believe otherwise."[53] Nevertheless, racism remains an obstacle to toxic waste organizing, as it is to all other forms of social change.

Most of the difficulties in toxic waste organizing present themselves even before residents learn the full extent and cause of their problems and seek remedies. Before the FACE/Harvard health survey, for instance, the Woburn families already believed that their personal troubles added up to a clear social problem, that the corporations and government were standing in their way, and that a unified organization was necessary for action. The next steps in the process—the health survey, the pursuit of the trial, and the continuing struggles with government agencies—were very wearing. The Woburn activists needed an enormous amount of fortitude to carry on with the task. Toxic waste litigation typically lasts eight to ten years, and cleanup may take even longer. Of course, the contamination itself may have extended over a still longer period. In Woburn, Anne Anderson began what has been termed her "shoe-leather epidemiology" in 1972; in 1990 the two Superfund sites in Woburn were still not cleaned up and the trial was still in the appeals stage. Consider also the pollution by Velsicol in Hardeman County, Tennessee: a state regulatory agency brought it to attention in 1964; in 1966 the United States Geological Survey got involved; in 1972 Velsicol was ordered to close the dump; in 1977 affected residents organized; and in 1988 the appeal of their case was heard.

To pursue a project such as the Woburn case, residents need not only skills, contacts, allies, media attention, and internal unity but also patience. We and many others have observed a remarkable degree of patience on the part of the Woburn residents. Notwithstanding their intense anger and desire for justice, the families have displayed enormous self-discipline and restraint in the face of provocation. Similarly, FACE has continued to communicate and work with the Massachusetts DPH, the EPA, and other government agencies, despite many rebuffs and criticisms.

All these barriers to the formation of a community active against toxic wastes are more than an assortment of individual factors; to overcome them calls for a reframing of traditional perspectives on the social order. With a new frame of reference, and effective leadership and organization, victims can unite to alleviate the toxic waste problem. In the process they can empower themselves to manage their personal suffering, overcome stigmatization, and trust in their own abilities to understand and deal with problems.[54]

The Roles of Community Organizations

Once a community group such as FACE coalesces, it plays other roles besides galvanizing community support, dealing with government, working with professionals, and engaging in health studies. A community group becomes the primary source of information for people living in a contaminated area, and often the most—or the only—accurate source. The Love Canal Homeowners' Association (LCHA) was a constant source of reliable knowledge about health studies, evacuation plans, and negotiations with the government. For instance, when the state health department gave residents lists of chemical readings from tests of air in their homes but failed to explain what those readings meant, residents came to LCHA for interpretations of the data and guidance about what to do.[55]

Because of its reputation and capabilities, the LCHA could provide significant social and emotional support. Lois Gibbs, the leader of the Love Canal effort, explained:

> Our organization served many times as a mental health crisis center. Residents who were confused, frightened, and at times panicked called or visited the office for support and hope. Many residents felt that no one could understand their problem like another canaler. . . . It was not unusual for me or other LCHA core workers to receive a call in the middle of the night from residents who couldn't sleep, couldn't take anymore, and wanted to end it all.[56]

For LCHA members, as for so many others around the country, participating in the effort was a positive experience. People reported a new awareness of the importance of controlling one's life and of taking part in government and community. They learned a great deal about chemicals, political life, and community organizing.[57]

Such community organizations satisfy three essential needs: social support, information, and power. The organization makes up for a loss of regular social supports, discussed earlier in this chapter. The group's meetings offer the most useful, reliable information. Power derives from the fact that "the group serves as a collective means to achieve commonly shared individual goals. And it helps to reverse some of the psychological damage that occurs from the inherent powerlessness of the situation."[58] In addition to this kind of local self-help group, residents of Legler, New Jersey, reported that their best overall information, assistance, and emotional comfort came from other toxic waste groups in other localities.[59]

Without a community organization there will rarely, if ever, be sufficient government and scientific attention to the environmental health risk in a contaminated community. Although individuals often play key roles, they are limited in their personal energy and their social efficacy. When efforts become solidified in organized groupings, the potential for success grows. How difficult such mobilization is comes into full focus only when we see the extensive physical and emotional problems confronted by the Woburn families.

3

The Sickness Caused by "Corporate America"

Effects of the Woburn Cluster

No Safe Place

Woburn is a highly toxic environment. Corporate contamination of the public water supply, compounded by government inaction, has harmed the entire community as well as the known leukemia victims. The litigant families suffered from illness and death due to leukemia, from other diseases, and from intense psychological turmoil accompanying the illnesses. They are quite aware of their problems, although the community as a whole is less prepared to understand that exposure to contaminated water has harmed the health of the entire town.

When we asked interviewees why they did not consider moving, in view of the troubles they faced from Woburn water, most answered along the same lines as the bereaved mother who said,

> There's no safe place anywhere, and every day it gets worse.[1]

The concept "no safe place" refers not only to Woburn families' limited geographical mobility; it alludes also to the persistence of the toxic substance in the body and to the general environmental crisis plaguing human beings, wildlife, and plant life everywhere.

The toxic waste victims and their families felt that in Woburn they at least knew what they were dealing with, since wells G and H had been shut down and the areas previously served by the tainted wells started to receive tested water from a Metropolitan District Commission (MDC) reservoir. The families feared that if they moved elsewhere they would subject themselves to risks of unknown contaminants. Some people combined this with a desire to fight the polluters:

> Well, why leave? Stay and fight it instead of walking away from it. You would just be walking into the next town that has it. And I don't think there is any clean water in the whole country anyhow.

Residents of the Legler section of Jackson Township, New Jersey, had similar reactions:

> Why should we move somewhere else, all towns are alike?

> We didn't consider moving. If we were looking for a place, we would not know where to go. The problem is everywhere. If it's not smog, then it's the water. No matter where you move, how do you know you're not moving into the same nightmare elsewhere?[2]

One Woburn mother still thinks about moving, but,

> Where do you move to? How do you know it's safe? I worry about where my kids will live and work.

The widespread contamination of water was especially relevant to one Woburn family:

> Before we moved here we were actually going to move down to Pembroke, and while we were going through

this suit we found out that the exact area we were
going to move into they found toxic waste in that
area. So we would have been sitting right on top of it
as well. If I moved to New Hampshire—beautiful
country, nice rolling hills—until they find out what the
hell is underneath it. So where do you really know
where to go?

Another family member explicitly tied the fear that no
place is safe to the W. R. Grace company, which has many
facilities in New England, some under investigation for
chemical leakages and others for suspected toxic disease:

Where are you going to move to? W. R. Grace would
have the landfills. It is probably all polluted. They are
all over the region.

He mentioned a new development in Billerica (about fifteen miles from Woburn) where "everybody on the street
has a brain tumor."
A teenaged survivor of leukemia had yet to make the
choice about moving. In response to the question where
he would like to live when he is older, he told us,

I might live in Woburn. I don't know. I haven't
thought about it.

When asked if he would feel safe anywhere the boy said:

I don't know. Not really. I would probably get a
[water] filter right away.

Nor do people trust that technology will be able to help
them select a safe place:

If you can say to yourself, "OK, I know this 300,000
square miles of this backwoods—nothing I can see under the earth," then you might say, "Put me right in
the middle." But there ain't no such thing. I don't
think technology will ever get that good.

In his study of Three Mile Island residents, Robert Jay Lifton tells of a woman in her sixties who tried to escape the contamination site, along with her husband, in a mobile home, to find a safe place for themselves and their adult children:

> We started going here and there, I can't even tell you where we were. We were all over the country and when we'd go we'd find a new group and ask them, "What's in this area?" It turned out that there was either a nuclear plant or a waste dump or weapons storage or missile silos or something, a Love Canal or Nevel Island—you know they had them all over the country. So we don't know yet where we're gonna be able to go. And each place where the danger is bad . . . the people say . . . "Well, I'll just stay here where I'm familiar with this area and I'll die here." And that's what we may have to do too before we're done. I don't know. I still hope we can find a place that's safer.[3]

Our Woburn families were very preoccupied with future health problems. This preoccupation is a form of the feeling that there is no safe place. When the contaminant is already inside the body, clean water or air in another part of the country will not help the victim. Lifton found this fear among Three Mile Island victims: "If I'm going to die from [this] atomic business, I'm going to die no matter where I'm at."[4]

Health Effects

Exactly how ill were people in Woburn? The full extent of health problems throughout the community was revealed only by the Harvard/FACE study of reproductive and childhood health problems. The survey included 4,396 pregnancies that terminated between 1960 and 1982. Controlling for important risk factors in pregnancy (such as smoking, maternal age, and history of pregnancies), researchers found access to contaminated water to be associated with sixteen perinatal deaths since 1970, eighteen eye-ear anomalies, and twenty-seven central nervous system/chromosomal/oral cleft anomalies. The central nervous system (CNS) anomalies were mainly cerebral palsy, mental retardation, and spina bifida; seven of the nine chromosomal disorders were Down's syndrome. They found that exposure was not associated with spontaneous abortions (511), low birth weight (201), perinatal deaths (stillbirth or deaths within seven days of birth) before 1970 (49), or with musculoskeletal (55), cardiovascular (43), or "other" (45) birth anomalies.

For analysis of childhood disorders, data were available for 4,978 children. Exposure to contaminated water was associated with kidney/urinary tract (43) and lung/respiratory (192) disorders. There was no association with allergies (476), anemia (77), diabetes (19), heart/blood pressure (21), learning disability (218), neurologic/sensory (113), or "other" disorders (77).[5] If only the in utero cases are examined, the positive associations are even stronger.[6]

Although we are, of course, concerned with the effects of environmental pollution on the whole town, our emphasis is the leukemia cluster and the affected families' personal experience of illness. By official count, twenty childhood leukemia cases were logged between 1964 and 1983; by the activists' count there were twenty-seven. This cluster was the source of people's recognition of the tragedy, and it remains the most salient phenomenon.

Physical Health Effects

The eight families that confronted often fatal leukemia experienced a multitude of other health problems as well.

Medical literature shows clear associations between TCE exposure and cardiac arhythmias, rashes, and immunological problems. This is borne out by assessments during 1984 and 1985 of the immunological, cardiological, and general medical status of twenty-five surviving members of the eight litigant families. In comparison with controls, the eight families showed a significantly greater occurrence of lymphocytosis (as measured by elevated T-cells) and clinically abnormal ratios of helper to suppressor cells (T4/T8) that were unstable over time. They also had an increased number of autoantibodies. Accompanying these signs of immune system problems was a higher incidence of infections and dermatological problems than would normally be expected. Twenty-two of twenty-five case subjects (88 percent) had frequent or chronic sinusitis or rhinitis without a seasonal component. Thirteen (52 percent) had gastrointestinal complaints including chronic nausea and irritable bowel syndrome (episodic diarrhea and constipation). Thirteen (52 percent) had recurrent rashes beginning after exposure to wells G and H water; in all but four persons, these rashes disappeared after exposure ended. Three had anal pruritis that began and ended with their exposure to TCE. Fourteen persons (56 percent) had cardiological symptoms, including unexplained rapid heart rate at rest and palpitations or near syncope. Of eleven of these persons who were subject to more detailed study, including echocardiograms, eight showed serious ventricular arrhythmias and seven had premature ventricular contractions. Six persons required cardiac medication.[7]

The families also experienced neurological damage, as measured by their blink reflexes. The blink reflex correlates with the functioning of the fifth and seventh cranial nerves, which are known to be injured by TCE exposure. The differences between the case and control populations were highly significant.[8] Taking all these findings into account, scientists who studied the Woburn victims concluded: "Since neurological, cardiological, and dermatological abnormalities have been previously seen in humans exposed to TCE, the Woburn population, which has all of these abnormalities, probably represents a true syndrome of toxic exposure."[9]

Depression and Other Mental Health Effects

Physical abnormalities, however, were only the beginning of the damage the families experienced. Most strikingly, depression pervaded virtually every aspect of their lives. A psychiatrist examining the families on behalf of the companies' defense attorneys found so much despair that the defense attorneys chose not to call him as an expert witness, and only an order from the judge enabled the plaintiffs to obtain copies of the notes containing his findings.

At the time of the initial interviews in the spring and summer of 1985, three families had maintained their children's rooms and possessions exactly as when they were alive, even though years had passed.[10] One family had picked the day of the family interview to put down new carpeting in the child's room and bring it back into use. Pictures of the deceased child were prominent in each house. One family, the members of whom were all quite depressed, always kept the lights turned down low: they were literally and figuratively living in darkness. Judging from their accomplishments and life histories, the families of the leukemia victim were probably not clinically depressed before the diagnosis of leukemia. Only one family member had been previously treated for depression and had responded well to antidepressant medication.

We were struck by not only the severity of the depression but also its chronic, unremitting nature. The two families whose child was in remission were somewhat less depressed than the others. The depth of depression also appeared to be correlated with the length of time the child had been ill before death, which was also the time families had been under stress and in which they had developed a special bond with the ill child that deepened as the illness progressed. Many of the parents eloquently described how special this bond was and how different it was from anything else they had ever experienced.

In order to understand better what these families were experiencing, we spoke with child psychiatrists experienced in working with families that had lost children to leukemia and other forms of cancer. They confirmed that although depression is expectable in families who lose a child, their reactions usually progress in stages that culminate in some form of resolution. The loss of a child is never forgotten but is usually resolved in a way that allows families to proceed in a functional manner.

This pattern simply did not hold for the Woburn families. None of them showed signs of recovering even though in some instances a number of years had elapsed since the death of the child. Persistent depression appeared to stem from several different factors. First, the sheer length of the illnesses had depleted the families, and especially the parents, of their psychological reserves. Although their own mortality was not threatened, from day to day they did not know whether or for how long their child would survive. Every cough or headache provoked anxiety and concern. As mentioned above, this anxiety helped create a deep bond between the parent and child, about which one mother said, "It was like we were one." Certain aspects of this bond resemble the pleasurable symbiotic fusion most mothers experience with young infants. But with the child's death, the expected and yet traumatic termination of this fused relationship creates a void in the parent's life that simply cannot be filled.

As one would expect, parents whose children survived reacted differently. They were certainly less outwardly depressed, although one mother did become manifestly depressed when the child was determined to be in remission and no longer in need of chemotherapy. She came to understand that she had appropriately drawn a causal connection between the child's improvement and the chemotherapy. When the chemotherapy pills were discontinued she panicked, fearing that the child would become ill again. She said:

> I felt secure when he was on the medication. I think that not having the medication going into him left us wide open.

She had herself become dependent on her child's pills.

She also alluded to the cumulative effects of years of stress. Thus an appropriate perception of a causal relationship between the medication and her child's improvement had evolved into a more concrete connection. The dissolution of this connection triggered extreme anxiety, which then precipitated a major depressive episode in a woman who had experienced depression previously and thus was presumably vulnerable to it. She felt better after taking antidepressants and was later able to gain a great deal of psychological insight into what had happened.

The mother in another family whose child survived, although she had no prior history of such symptoms, developed a strong obsessive-compulsive syndrome. She scrubbed and rescrubbed floors until her hands became raw. She became very concerned with germs and cleanliness. Both she and her husband reduced their interactions with one another and the outside world, trying to make their home into a sterile fortress against infection.

The mother considered her growing preoccupation with cleanliness pivotal in her child's recovery, in that she had been able to protect the child from secondary infection. Now that the child was in remission, this preoccupation did not go away and in fact seemed to increase steadily. She felt that only by creating as sterile an environment as possible could she ensure that her child would not relapse.

This hypervigilance is common in toxic waste sites, as residents become preoccupied with searching for causes of and responsibility for contamination and with protecting their future health.[11] A woman at Three Mile Island kept her police scanner on day and night for four years, hoping to find out the reason for the frequent sirens heard in the Three Mile Island complex.[12] Hypervigilance may allow for the quickest possible response to a dangerous situation, but at a considerable psychological cost.[13]

In the family described above, the father responded to his child's disease with an existential depression, in which he felt everyday events to be part of a meaningless existence. The shock of the illness had jolted him out of his usual worldview, and he now saw ordinary human interactions as trivial and inconsequential. This pattern persisted and even intensified after his child went into remission. He complained, "My life has changed in a way that I can't describe," and added:

> It upsets me to hear people get upset about a baseball strike or about hockey games. How can you get upset about that sort of thing? . . . I can't make small talk any more. It seems trivial.

Parents whose leukemic children survived remain unable to feel safe, since they live in perpetual anxiety about their children's remission. A number of fathers made points such as "If they're OK then why can't you buy life insurance?" One father reported:

> I have a terrible fear inside that my child will relapse. I can't loosen up. It really bothers me that they poison the water like this. I think it is all a big cover-up.

The circumstances surrounding their children's leukemia were further cause for depression. Instead of being comforted in their agony, parents had to fight to gain public recognition of the pollution. Parents whose children died slowly came to recognize that their loss was unnecessary, a direct result of human carelessness in the handling of substances known to be toxic and potentially lethal. This recognition provided a focus for parental anger, but it also intensified the loss—"It didn't have to happen"—and made the death of the child all the more heartrending.

The litigation itself contributed to ongoing depression by forcing the parents to relive the horrors of the child's illness through the seemingly endless process of depositions, testimony, and consultations with independent experts for both defendants and litigants. We heard of one father who watched excavations at the W. R. Grace site in Woburn that clearly indicated that Grace had misrepresented its disposal method for large quantities of toxic materials (a great deal had simply been buried around the plant site, allowing it to seep into the groundwater). Even though these revelations, which were videotaped and witnessed by EPA officials, greatly enhanced the litigants' case, this father experienced not victory but anger, followed by extreme depression. The excavations had dredged up his feelings and the revelations drove home the fact that a tragedy need not have happened.

The last example points to one of the most disturbing

aspects of community action on toxics: remedies and justice are available only at the cost of reliving and displaying publicly the suffering and losses already experienced. People are robbed of privacy in which to experience their sorrow; they are forced to grieve in public, even to accommodate journalists who want constant replays. One mother complained that a television crew, filming her child's return from hospital treatment, asked if he could return to the car and limp to the house once more. After more than a decade of public display, the families lose their perspective about what are private feelings and what is the public record. They feel that they must justify their suffering by legal proof or it will be diminished and discredited. Perhaps that is why it is so difficult to mobilize contaminated communities in general, and why it was so hard to recruit all the Woburn leukemia victims to the lawsuit. This contradiction is another source of anguish.

At Love Canal depression was common. Many residents threatened suicide and several carried out their intention. Anxiety and stress were rampant. Residents threw books at officials and threatened them with bodily harm. As in all toxic waste sites, women suffered the most, particularly mothers of young children.[14] Three Mile Island residents also experienced high levels of depression. During the year after the accident, the mothers experienced new episodes of affective disorder at a rate three times higher than a nonexposed control group; this finding is considered striking since the baseline rates of affective disorder in both areas were identical before the Three Mile Island leak.[15]

Although we did not see post traumatic stress disorder (PTSD) in Woburn, it was the primary mental health problem in Hardeman County, and has been reported in other toxic waste sites. PTSD involves preoccupation with the traumatic event; various anxiety symptoms related to that event, including fears, hyperalertness, exaggerated startle reaction, insomnia, and recurrent nightmares; sudden feelings of the traumatic event reoccurring, usually because of association with environmental or ideational stimulus; different kinds of bodily complaints; feelings of detachment or loss of interest and of diminished feeling or "psychic numbing"; guilt in relationship to behavior during the traumatic event or to people who have died; memory impairment and trouble concentrating; and avoidance of activities that arouse recollection of the traumatic event.[16]

The syndrome can be catalyzed by public policy as well: "The Department of Defense and the Veterans Administration, by electing not to help the atomic veterans cope, in a systematic fashion, with the health effects of the tests in which they participated, created conditions that encouraged those men to become preoccupied with their health."[17]

Why did we find depression rather than post traumatic stress syndrome in Woburn? One explanation might be that depression can be the outcome of unresolved post traumatic stress.[18] Lack of resolution may be due to the persistence of the legal appeal. Another explanation may be that despite widespread knowledge of the Woburn cluster there was no massive disruption by flood, spill, evacuation, or relocation. Also, unlike disasters that visibly affect an entire geographical area, Woburn's crisis primarily affected a small number of people, albeit very seriously. The families largely suffered on their own, without the community sense of shared catastrophe that often yields PTSD. Instead, emotions were internalized as depression.

General Psychological Effects

The Woburn leukemia families do, however, share most characteristics of what Lifton calls the "general constellation of the survivor," found in disasters such as floods or atomic bomb blasts. First, they retain a "death imprint" of images and memories of the disaster and feel a strong "death anxiety." Woburn residents were hyperaware of the details of their own, their children's, and their spouses' diseases and deaths, and they continued to be worried about future health. Second, most of the family members experienced "death guilt" based on feeling that they could have done something to prevent the loved one's death. Third, many suffered "psychic numbing," a diminished capacity for feeling, particularly apathy, withdrawal, depression, and overall constriction in living. The Woburn families likewise suffered "impaired human relationships," sometimes manifested as an inability to comfort one another, even when family members knew they needed mutual support. Finally, they attempted "to give their death encounter significant inner form." That is, they attempted "to find sufficient explanation for [their] experience so as to be able to resolve the inner conflicts described under the other four categories." For people like the Woburn victims, that explanation is usually not forthcoming, since they know their disaster was not natural or ordained by God but of human origin. Thus survivors are faced with "disruption of the moral universe."[19]

The generalized distress experienced by those who live near toxic waste sites can be understood as "demoralization," a feeling of being considerably upset and out of control. Demoralization is widely used in psychiatric epidemiology to measure the emotional state of the non-mentally-ill general population. Bruce Dohrenwend and his colleagues, who studied the Three Mile Island locale, compared the demoralization of residents with the clientele of a community mental health center. With a higher score indicating more disorder, the overall mean scores were 28.3 for mental health center clients, 30 for the women of Three Mile Island, and 25 for the men of Three Mile Island. Twenty-six percent of those interviewed directly after the accident showed severe demoralization. Although the percentage declined over the next four months, the researchers calculated that 10 percent of the area's population suffered extreme demoralization directly attributable to the accident.[20]

Researchers who gave a self-rated psychological distress scale to seventh, ninth, and eleventh grade students at Three Mile Island found a substantial degree of distress. The students were similar to mothers at Three Mile Island and elsewhere in that they experienced considerably more distress if they had a preschool sibling. Those with higher psychological distress scores also reported more somatic complaints.[21]

The mental health effects of disasters last a very long time. In one study, researchers followed over time a group of people who experienced a human-made catastrophe, victims of the 1972 Buffalo Creek, Kentucky, flood. A coal company's poorly constructed, inappropriately used slag dam, rather than nature, was widely blamed for the flood. Two years afterward, victims demonstrated more anxiety, depression, social isolation, somatic concerns, and disruption of daily activities than did a control group. Even after four years victims suffered higher degrees of disturbance. At the site of the Three Mile Island nuclear plant, both at the time of the leak and two years afterward residents had more symptoms, poorer task performance, higher risk for psychiatric problems, and higher levels of catecholamines (a reliable biochemical marker of stress) in their blood than did controls who lived near an undamaged nuclear facility.[22]

Toxic waste sites can produce stress even in the absence of known leakages or health problems. A study compared samples of residents living within one mile of a New Castle County, Delaware, dump the EPA ranks the second most hazardous in the nation with residents in a nearby neighborhood at least five miles from any known hazardous waste site. The researchers, who had studied the health effects at Three Mile Island, employed the same measures of psychological and physical health self-report, behavioral tasks, and biochemical markers of physiological arousal. Mean scores in the waste site neighborhood for all measures were significantly more abnormal, and in most cases more than double the scores of those of the control area.[23] Even the planned siting of a toxic hazard can cause distress, as found in a survey of a rural community near Phoenix, Arizona, where a hazardous waste facility was to be built. Using the mean demoralization data from Three Mile Island, investigators found that 36 percent of their sample scored higher on demoralization than the mean score of community mental health center clients.[24]

We are now also beginning to see prospective studies of mental health effects of hazardous sites. Knowing that the Three Mile Island reactor was going to be restarted, a research team looked at a sample of mothers of young children, a group known to be at high risk for environmental psychological problems. A panel of 385 women who had been interviewed during 1981–1982, after the incident, provided baseline information. Of these, 52 percent returned questionnaires that were mailed to them one month after the restart. A composite measure of subclinical symptoms of depression, anxiety, and hostility was used, and the researchers found that symptomatology did in fact increase after the restart. Symptoms were higher in those women who had had a serious clinical episode before or during the eighteen months immediately following the 1979 accident.[25]

Despite our growing knowledge of mental health effects of human-made disasters, there is a backlash against this knowledge. When evidence of psychological effects of exposure is discussed, opponents of community activists often turn that against the victims. Opponents claim that not only are the psychological problems imaginary, but that the physical problems also are somaticized symptoms of prior emotional instability. The trauma victims are thus blamed for their illness, a tactic that may cause the victims to abandon a key weapon. "As a result, the exposed individuals often come to be suspicious of any mention of the psychological trauma associated with an involve exposure. They regard such discussion as an attempt to discredit their claims that their illnesses are organized diseases caused by the contamination to which they have been exposed."[26]

Victims are encouraged to deny and be ashamed of the trauma they have suffered.[27] In the pretrial actions in the Woburn litigation, for example, corporate attorneys pointed to prior psychiatric problems that were not attributable to toxic waste contamination and intimated that contamination could not possibly cause depression.

Life Experience in Toxic Woburn

In Woburn, as elsewhere, reactions to toxic contamination did not always fall clearly into the categories of illness. A parent's anger at Grace Chemicals and Beatrice Foods may be at the same time a gnawing psychological pain and a public, political expression. A parent's feelings of hopelessness may be simultaneously a component of depression and a reflection of the crisis of toxic waste contamination in America.

Living with Childhood Leukemia

Living with the reality of childhood leukemia, family members experienced a depression that was tied up with their hopes and expectations for remission as well as with their guilt about the disease. They reacted both similarly to and differently from the families in a sociological study of childhood leukemia in 60 children admitted to a hospital in England in 1976 and 1977. In the earlier study, researchers found that delay in the initial diagnosis prompted anxiety and guilt feelings in the parents, who felt they had failed to recognize early, vague symptoms common to numerous ailments or failed to prevent a putative cause (such as prenatal X-rays, working with chemicals, bottle-feeding rather than breast-feeding).[28]

The Woburn families continually brought up such guilt feelings. One mother remonstrated with herself for having given extra water to her children in the belief that it was healthy to drink lots of water. Such guilt also appeared in relation to breast-feeding. A mother who lost her son says she no longer blames herself, but

> I used to blame myself because I am the one that
> drank the water, and if I didn't breast-feed him . . .

For some Woburn parents there was guilt of an even vaguer sort:

> I think that when a child is diagnosed with having a
> disease that is life-threatening, I think the first thing
> that you do is turn inward and ask, "What did I pass
> on to this child? What have we done? What weakness
> in us have we given him?" And that I am sure every
> parent reflects on and it comes back to them.

These feelings were heightened by the dramatic improvements in diagnosis and treatment of childhood leukemia in the last two decades, producing remissions of five or more years in about one-half of victims. Parents thus had higher expectations for success in treatment. They felt a constant hope for remission. Yet even when children were doing well, parents continually feared that the next illness or routine medical test would reverse their child's successful course. These fears and expectations were clearly noticeable among Woburn parents. The parents of a girl who survived spoke of their ongoing anxiety:

> You listen to other doctors talk about immune systems
> and chances of relapse, and you just feel as though
> there is never a time when you are out of the woods.
> There is always some little part that is affected by it
> forever.

Our interviews did not confirm results from the study of English leukemia victims, in which the parents' search for an explanation for the illness was inconclusive and continuous, often asserting itself strongly after a relapse or death. The uncertainty about causation prompted families of victims to move from "proximate" (biomedical) explanations, to "encompassing" (cosmological) or even metaphysical explanations (such as divine retribution). The Woburn families fared differently in this matter—their constantly growing understanding of environmental causation led them to remain clearly within the framework of proximate biomedical explanations. Indeed, they were lucky to be able to trace the biomedical process to a toxic pathway, which allowed for both a private and public struggle for justice and a possible remedy. We have pointed out that it is painful continually to relive and testify about one's suffering, yet it is also a way of achieving empowerment. Even though most parents in the English study discussed nagging concerns about hidden carcinogens in the environment, they had neither the scientific evidence nor community support necessary to pursue that evidence. The Woburn families were able to document such a relationship and to attain a degree of certainty for themselves.

Fear of Future Disease

Although the stricken families were quite certain about the causal pathway of their children's leukemia, they were absolutely uncertain about their future health. Everyone worried about becoming sick as a result of toxic exposure. Many people did have cardiological and immunological problems, as mentioned earlier. One mother with a heart condition told us,

> I woke up one day and [my husband] is looking at my
> arm because I have these little bruises all over my
> arm, and he was concerned. I mean, it is like every
> day, if something little comes across your body . . .

In one family whose son had died, the mother had skin cancer and the father contracted both skin and jaw cancer after the son's diagnosis, from which he later died. They were particularly aware of the many cancer cases, miscarriages, and stillbirths in their neighborhood and could reel off details with remarkable familiarity. Other families were also extremely aware of other people's maladies, and this awareness added to their fear of future disease. Parents with surviving children worry about the side effects of radiation treatment on those children. The parents of one girl who has experienced some coordination problems fear future learning disabilities, which they know have affected other children in radiotherapy.

All parents told us that they worried about their children, even in very routine illnesses. Fairly typical is this

response from a woman whose husband died of leukemia:

> Every time they go to the doctor and they have blood
> work done, it is like sitting here and waiting with
> bated breath. Every time they have a symptom. [My
> son] had a bloody nose just before we went to Florida
> and I had a hard time stopping the bloody nose. And
> that is how [my husband] started—with a pinprick on
> his leg. And you have to kind of get beyond that and
> say "It is only a bloody nose." You have to stop it;
> don't become hysterical. But I think the tendency is
> always there to become panicky.

In Woburn, as in Love Canal and Legler, many people
were afraid to have more children. Love Canal residents
were specifically warned of such risks to pregnant women
as miscarriages. Toxic waste victims in many locations have
themselves observed the frequency of miscarriages, birth
defects, and childhood disorders. One Legler couple put
it this way: "We argued over having another kid. I refused unless we first had genetic counseling. If it weren't
for the water, we would have conceived another child."
The mother in a Legler family concurred: "We are afraid
to have children because of the possibility of chromosome
damage. The baby we just had wasn't planned. We worried during the pregnancy. The doctor did tests. When
the doctor came out to announce the birth, my husband
asked if it had all its fingers and toes."[29] Toxic crises attack what is to many people the most sacred, important,
and rewarding goal in life—having children who will live
and be healthy.

Although all people living in the midst of a toxic waste
crisis fear future disease, the Woburn families experienced an added dimension of fear because they already
knew of a leukemia case and had suffered various other

ills. We are not talking merely about elevated risks, but about actual disease. It is not surprising to find the Woburn families preoccupied with their current and future health. In fact, they harbor a feeling that they have not really survived, but have only been given a reprieve, with a threat of disease—even a death sentence—over themselves and their loved ones.

Marital Impact

All but two of the couples reported that stress on their marital relationships increased after they discovered their child's leukemia. Two of the couples divorced while their child was sick. It appeared that one of the two failed marriages had significant fundamental problems, but the other one might well have remained intact had the child remained healthy. One expert on toxic waste health effects who has examined many sites finds that divorce is a common result.[30] In Legler, eleven divorces and twelve near divorces occurred during that toxic waste crisis. Marital stress takes diverse forms: attempts to blame a partner for moving to Legler, resentment over lifestyle changes, tension over dealing with the toxic waste problem, disrupted sex lives, and anger at a spouse's deep involvement in the community organization.[31]

The two Woburn marriages that seemed to weather the crisis well are also of interest. One couple seemed simply to have a very sound relationship and a supportive extended family. This family was also very good at delegating roles. The other couple who did not appear to be overly stressed by the crisis was extremely religious. This couple's ability to "turn everything over to God" relieved them of guilt. They also felt sure that they would see their son again in the afterlife. Their religion brought with it a strong supportive group of friends from the church. The night their son died, a large number of people from the church gathered in their home to pray for his soul.

In the marriages that were stressed but did not break up the patterns of distress varied, but with some common themes. As might be expected, the most common was blame. One husband who had wanted to move out of the area some years before blamed his wife for wanting to remain close to her family of origin. In another family, in which the immediate cause of death was an infection, the mother blamed the father for not being more careful about washing his hands. The mother of one family that lost a child had earlier had a tubal ligation at her husband's urging. This created a great deal of tension, because their surviving child wanted a brother or sister, and the bereaved parents wanted another child. In one family, the stress of the illness brought back to the surface a marital conflict that had been resolved years before.

At the follow-up interviews in 1987 the marriages were doing better. Two years earlier, the litigation had reawakened all the stresses and horror of the child's illness, causing married couples to revert to some of the defensive strategies they had used during the course of the illness. The marriages that seemed to be strengthened by the ordeal were probably more able to tolerate the stress and make it through the difficult period. Having made it through a difficult ordeal together strengthened them, as did the increased understanding the process brought about. Marriages that were dissolved were simply not strong enough in the first place to stand the strain of the illness.

Effects on Children with Leukemia

We do not have much direct testimony from the affected children. Those who died did so before we met their families. We could speak only with the surviving children, and they could not recollect much from their young years. Even as teenagers, the surviving children spoke very little, allowing their parents to dominate in the interviews. The same was true of the siblings of leukemia victims. We thus rely largely on parents' impressions of the effects.

The children were robbed of childhood by the severity of leukemia. Parents reported how difficult it was for sick children to play with friends, to make weekend plans, and to attempt vacations. One parent described the effect of treatment on the life of a boy now cured:

> He went through three years of intensive chemotherapy, and then four more years of pills, and it kind of got to be a way of life.

A girl in remission is constantly preoccupied with her health, according to her mother:

> The poor kid, when she comes home tonight she is crying because she has a cold. And I said, "Honey, it is just a cold." Well, what am I going to do? Everything is catastrophic to her.

This surviving child is upset because her coordination problems affect her dancing. She also worries that her treatment has hurt her intellectual capacities.

Parents recalled their sick children's abilities to transcend their own suffering. One boy who died expressed concern in his last years for his parents, who had previously lost a child in an auto accident. The boy told his nurse he hoped his expected high chances for remission would be borne out "because my parents already lost one boy." The parents remembered this story and their son's comments on returning from treatment one day:

> Out of the blue he said, "Ma, I think you better have another baby." It scared me. I was praying that every-

thing would be all right. He was in remission. Unbeknown to us he was starting to relapse. He must have known something. I didn't know what to say. We just kidded with him and then four months after he died we found I was pregnant.

Impact on Siblings of Leukemia Victims

Young siblings found it hard to watch a brother or sister endure the infections and weakness of leukemia and to see them go through the nausea and other effects of chemotherapy. Persons they loved were suffering and dying: that was simply not what childhood should be like. The siblings lost out on much parental attention because the mothers and fathers had to spend so much time and emotional energy with the sick child. Thus the siblings of leukemia victims were also robbed of their childhood.

Brothers and sisters adjusted to their stressful situations in various ways. One was for the eldest daughter to assume the role of surrogate mother. The mother devoted all her energy to caring for the sick child, while the daughter ran the household and looked after the younger children. In two extreme cases, the role change lasted several years and turned the girls into "parentified" children. Both girls expressed many somatic complaints. One had become expert at reading her mother's facial expressions for clues about how things were going with her sick brother. As a result these two girls were hyperalert to the signs and symptoms of those around them and had a correspondingly overdeveloped sense of responsibility.

Another common pattern was that of the protective older brother. In one instance, this protectiveness began with sticking up for a younger brother who was teased because he lost his hair after chemotherapy and evolved into a serious problem, in which the older brother picked fights long after his brother died. His anger and aggression most likely served as a defense against depression over the sibling's death.

Among younger children, the most common reaction to a sibling's illness was jealousy. These children did not understand how ill their sibling was or how painful the treatments were. Instead, they focused on the attention the ill child received. Even when they were older and could understand the severity of their sibling's illness, they still acknowledged lingering feelings of having in some way been cheated. They could also feel guilt, as one girl did:

> I really did not understand what was going on. I resented it; I was jealous and then later I felt very guilty about it.

Her mother noted, "She has apologized [for her jealousy] about a dozen times over the years."

Parents noted the burdens on the brothers and sisters of leukemia victims. One mother believes that the tension caused her son to do so poorly in high school that he could not go to college. In another family, a brother developed a noticeable behavior problem at home and school as a result of his brother's illness. At several points he mentioned wanting to kill himself. One child developed a nervous tic, another incontinence.

All the children showed more concern about their own bodies, which was understandable in the light of the intense general focus on health, the critical illness of a family member, and the illnesses in many other families. The children expressed fear of future health problems. The sister of a leukemia victim worried that her skin moles might be melanoma, as her father's had been. The girls were also worried about whether they would be able to have children and what the consequences of toxic exposure on future children might be. One daughter said, "I may have kids with birth defects or I may have cancer."

With one notable exception, the children were not as overtly depressed as their parents. The one child who was overtly depressed was actively able to express how much he missed his deceased brother. This boy had also lost his father through divorce, which compounded the loss and abandonment. Another brother became preoccupied with death and feared that his parents might die when they were away from him.

The Woburn children resembled children affected by toxic waste elsewhere. Many Love Canal children feared their own early death or the death of their parents. In the preface to this book we recounted the dread of a Legler child who thought he might die after inadvertently brushing his teeth with tainted water. Lois Gibbs summarizes similar fears on the part of Love Canal youngsters:

> Picture yourself five years old watching the 6 o'clock news report. Your mother is being interviewed, saying, "There is dioxin in there . . . dioxin kills . . . I don't want my babies to die." What is that child supposed to think? Another example is that during the construction to clean up the Love Canal there were standby buses, school buses, throughout the neighborhood. The buses were placed there in case there was an accident and the residents had to quickly be evacuated. The small child getting on a school bus can't help but wonder: Will that bus take Mommy away while I'm in school? Will the canal blow up and Mommy with it while I'm gone? Or, will Mommy die in the basement from the dioxin?[32]

Coping Mechanisms

How did the families who had to bear so much suffering cope? A number believed that the loss of their loved one was "God's will" and that they would be reunited in heaven. Families who expressed this sentiment seemed to believe it deeply; it allowed them to handle the loss and the perceived injustice. One mother with this religious faith actually became more cheerful when she talked about her dead son. A father went as far as to say that God was warning people about pollution:

> We think that when God takes children he takes them for a reason. And I think he is giving us a warning right now. I think he is giving the people in this world a warning. He is taking a lot of kids.

One woman told us, "If I didn't have my faith I would be in a mental institution."

Some families coped by shutting out external input and focusing on their sick child and on other family members. To some degree, the physical and temporal demands of the sickness made this strategy necessary, but some parents used it to cope with their suffering. One family turned their living room into an activity center with a mattress to sleep on, drew the curtains, and barricaded their sick daughter from the external infection that can be so dangerous to a leukemic child. As discussed earlier, this coping style seemed more disturbed and in fact contributed to the mother's obsessive-compulsive problems and the father's depression. One might expect any family to try to protect a leukemic child from opportunistic infections, but this family had transformed a normal alertness into a frozen defensiveness.

There was much denial. Some parents pushed away their conscious awareness of the sick person's suffering. In some families, members refrained from sharing with each other their feelings about the crisis. Some fathers acted as if they were optimistic when they were not. In one case, a father who maintained an optimistic facade for his family expressed his pessimism only in an individual interview outside of the home, where he confessed that he had gone to pick out a burial plot and a gravestone. In another case, a family painted a positive picture of how well they were coping, when in fact the mother had had two psychiatric hospitalizations and the daughter had been in therapy. Keeping the child's room untouched, as noted earlier, is a form of denial as well. A father went even further, prohibiting anyone from saying his dead son's name.

For some family members, helping other families in crisis provided relief. A mother who lost her son reported:

> I find it rewarding in a whole lot of ways working in a hospital, even with dying patients. Just knowing that somebody is there to care about them and comfort them. It sort of gives me some peace and it is not like I don't feel I did that with [my son] because I really think I did. But I know how some people are in the hospital, how some nurses are. They don't give a whole lot of care to dying people. And I think that a lot of them haven't experienced maybe real close personal deaths or tragedies in families and they don't know how to deal with them. So in a lot of ways it is rewarding in that respect.

Another father whose son succumbed to leukemia helps out in a Ronald MacDonald House, which provides temporary housing for out-of-town parents of hospitalized children. One brother participates in athletic fund-raising activities for leukemia victims, about which he says, "It makes me feel better to do something to help."

The suit against Grace and Beatrice helped most people to cope with their troubles. For one mother who lost a son, the litigation crystallized familial social support:

> I came to understand a little more of what others in the family were going through, that we had never

really talked about much ourselves before because we just more or less wanted to protect and insulate each other from what we were feeling ourselves.

For a family whose son recovered, the suit brought support from a larger network, despite the hurt:

By getting involved in the case and meeting these other families and sharing everything with them, it did bring back memories, some of the memories of [our son] being sick and in the hospital and different things like that there. But the camaraderie among the group, though, I thought that was very rewarding—to us anyway. So I was very pleased with that. In fact I kind of missed part of it when the original settlement with Grace was made and the judge threw the Beatrice case out. It was kind of a sense of something that you were involved with, a just cause, and it took a lot of your time, and the fact that it was over, it left you with kind of mixed emotions really—with me it did anyway. The fact that it has gone to appeal now, we are kind of getting back together again, it seems like the cause has been resurrected or something and I am kind of pleased about that. But it did bring back memories though.

Another mother responded, to our questions about the beneficial aspects of the litigation,

Yes [it helped] a lot of times, a lot of times through the depositions, going through medical records and having to remember different situations and times that [our son] was sick, trying to remember dates. It made me do a whole lot of thinking that I hadn't done, and it still goes on, too.

To some extent, the litigation bound up and displaced a great deal of the suffering. But for that very reason the end of the frenetic litigation brought problems. The woman whose husband died of leukemia said,

> Now that things are settling down I get more depressed. I get anxious about crazy things. I have a hard time getting myself going. My theory is just to keep busy and everything will fall into place.

Positive and Negative Aspects of the Health Survey and Litigation

Although the lawsuit helped many families to cope with their suffering, it also brought up painful memories for all the people involved. In the discovery phase of the suit, there was pain from the companies' repeated attempts at obfuscation, as exemplified by the scores of documents obtained that arrived with most of the relevant sections blacked out. During discovery, as more and more information was uncovered that actually benefited the suit, many litigants found themselves becoming more depressed because the material indicated that their loved ones had died or suffered needlessly. For some, the Harvard/FACE health survey was similarly depressing. One person told us:

> You pray to God that they don't find anybody [with disease], but, you know, you don't know which way you really want to go. You hope it doesn't work out, but you know damn right well it is going to.

Family members who volunteered to make phone calls for the survey found doing so particularly hard, since they had to maintain objectivity:

> I know that I was a very, very careful interviewer. We were cautioned over and over again not to jeopardize the study. It was too important, and you didn't add anything to anybody's answers. You only asked what you were told to ask, and even when people spoke

about the tragedy of "those parents, those with [sick]
children," I never commented on it.

It was very difficult for me because it wasn't long after
I lost [my son] and there were days and days that
would go by and I just couldn't pick up that phone. I
just couldn't do it; it would cost me too much.

During the next phase, deposition, families suffered not
only from endless retellings of their troubles but also from
the defense attorneys' attempts to discredit them. In one
example, a woman litigant had previously undergone a
tubal ligation. Because her insurance paid for ligations
only after a third live birth, she had to sign a paper saying that she could not cope emotionally with more children. The defense attorneys located that paper in her
medical records and tried to use it to discredit her.
Throughout the discovery and deposition phases and into
the trial litigants also faced endless media attention and
public exposure.

As could be expected, the suit was a tremendously
painful experience. A bereaved mother told us that

it was really an agony. It was very difficult. It was a
constant living with and re-experiencing all the negative things that had happened because of [my son's]
illness.

Yet people were able to maintain a larger notion of the
suit as a positive form of personal and social action. A
mother whose child had died wanted

to get something more out of it than just seeing my
son suffer and die. Help others, help my older son
. . . and if there is anything I can do to prevent him
from getting anything like that or clean up the water
that we all drink or that his kids might drink one day,
then I am going to be out there fighting for it. And it

is not just my own relations, it is a lot of people and their families.

After the settlement with Grace, families and their attorneys stated publicly that they had won a victory, if only an out-of-court settlement. But underlying this sense of a public victory—definitely an honest sentiment—was anger and hurt. A mother whose child died expressed dissatisfaction with the outcome of the suit:

> No, [I'm not satisfied] only because I guess I will just never forgive them and I don't feel like it has ever ended or it ever will end, on my side with W. R. Grace, my own personal fight, it is an internal thing. But it is never going to make me feel at peace with them just because of the settlement, and I know I am going to feel the same way about Beatrice or any other company that is ever found for contaminating.

Another mother felt the same:

> I thought more positive things were going to come of it. In retrospect I guess that Grace really didn't have anything to lose, or hasn't lost much at all, even monetarily, or in any way, I guess. But when we settled, that wasn't necessarily the case, but as I get further away from it, I don't think that they really suffered much at all.

All families were angry that there was no corporate admission of guilt. They would have preferred to have no monetary settlement or award if they could get an admission of Grace's responsibility. As one parent put it,

> If it [the monetary settlement] was nothing and they had said yes we did it, and we will fix the problem, we will never dump any more. If they had just said that I would feel a whole lot more at peace with everything.

All the people we spoke with echoed the same sentiments about the money:

> When we did get the money and it was in our hands and our bank accounts, it was very very hard to even think about using it. I just had a real hard time dealing with that. I have told my family that and I have told Jan that, and the other families, and everybody says, "You know I can't understand the way you are thinking, they owed it to you." But I still feel like it is a payoff. As long as I feel like that, I can't stand the thought of using it . . . I feel like it was in exchange for my son, and money for his life. . . . There is no price for my son. And I feel like they are saying to me, well he was only worth $8 million or $1 million. Who are they to say that to me, to put a price on my boy's head? I hate it. I really hate it and that makes me even more mad and makes me want to fight and make more money.

Woburn litigants often confronted accusations that they were primarily after money. After the out-of-court settlement with Grace, several reported that people thought they must be rich. One mother remembered asking a visiting child not to jump on a couch, and the child responded, "You're rich; you can buy another one." Compare this with Edelstein's report of a townsperson who accused a Legler, New Jersey, victim, "There's nothing wrong with your water; you're only out for the money."[33] Love Canal victims were accused of trying to "make a bundle" from the government.[34] Whereas some other citizens see the money as central, the litigants themselves consider it to be "marked" and "tainted." As we saw previously, everything in the toxic contamination setting takes on the same stigma.

But the families remain hopeful because of the belief, expressed by their lawyers and shared by most of them, that Woburn offered an important public lesson about corporate responsibility. A man who was otherwise quite pessimistic said,

> I got a feeling that corporate America really sat back and took notice. I really believe they took notice this time.

Another father believes:

> What we did was a start, I think. That is square one. It did show the people out there that if you are wronged by a corporation that arbitrarily pollutes your water or your yard or your air or something like that, that, yes, there is an avenue that you can pursue to bring about a just [solution]—to cease it.

He thinks that "a lot of groundwork was laid for future cases that will impact on corporate America."

Social and Political Aspects of Illness Experience

Like this father, the litigant families often placed their efforts in the context of overcoming government inaction and struggling against "corporate America." Without any prior involvement in social movements, they had developed a new distrust of those two pillars of the social structure. Living in toxic Woburn formed the basis of a new and vastly different life experience.

Because their new life experience included both social and political components, we may speak of social and political forms of illness experience. In the language of social scientists, "illness experience" encompasses the ways in which people experience their illness, as distinct from the narrowly medical "disease." Illness experience, far more variable and complex than a clinical disease, includes a broad range of factors such as perception of self and of work and family roles. Sociological studies show that people ordinarily organize a good deal of their lives around their perceptions of and ways of dealing with health and illness. In toxic contaminations, victims' entire lives are taken over by the situation and the experience of illness has many nonmedical features.

Affixing Blame: Natural versus Human-Made Disasters

When social and behavioral scientists began to study chemical spills, toxic waste disasters, and similar phenomena, they likened them first to natural disasters. Fires, floods, and earthquakes were well studied from the 1950s through the 1970s, particularly in terms of their psychological impact, and such a linkage seemed to make sense. But more recently researchers have discovered key distinctions between natural and human-created disasters.

In particular, human-made disasters seem to provoke longer-lasting and often more serious effects. In one study comparing Times Beach residents who experienced dioxin contamination, floods, or both, victims of flood alone were twice as likely to report full recovery from symptoms as those who suffered exposure to dioxin with or without flooding.[35] It appears that the more clearly victims perceive a human cause, the greater is their emotional distress.[36]

Human-caused disasters lead to attributions of responsibility. Earlier we emphasized that all the Woburn families blamed W. R. Grace and Beatrice and the government agencies that belittled the problem or hedged on the investigations of the contamination. Many of the victim families volunteered that it would be easier if the leukemia cluster had been God's will or a result of natural causes. In those cases, they would be able to accept that there was no alternative. But in the case of human failure or intentional harm, resentment lingers. Robert J. Lifton, in his study of Three Mile Island, wrote that "when there is a sense of gross negligence or callousness, the victims can come to feel that their lives have been profoundly devalued, that they have not been respected as human beings." At Three Mile Island, however, knowing that Metropolitan Edison was at fault did not help. That knowledge allowed people to be angry at the perpetrator, but they received no satisfaction from blaming the company. The utility always claimed it was in control, when in fact it was out of control, "thereby profaning people's suffering and denying that they had anything to fear rather than attending to what they feared."[37]

Because there was human responsibility in a disaster such as Woburn, the parents of the sick children felt that they too might be responsible. Our respondents told us that they felt guilty for feeding polluted water and water-based products to their families. After all, if they had only known in time, then they could have diminished the extent of toxic ingestion. As we have discussed, the severe psychological impact of toxic waste sites includes feelings of personal responsibility and guilt for the actual and potential health problems of their children. At Three Mile Island, parents who evacuated and those who did not experienced guilt about children later born with birth abnormalities. Parents' fears of future defects appeared as "images of grotesque deformities in subsequent generations."[38]

What are the long-term effects of a continual search for blame? The search is an ongoing moral dilemma, since people may not be completely sure who bears the blame and how much. Even when the victims are certain where the blame lies, they must continually try to win over those who disagree. If they fail to convert the nonbelievers, they may feel further guilt for not doing enough, and this sense of failure can erode their self-esteem.

Human-made disasters are not as easy to trace as natural disasters, which usually follow an observable pattern, appearing and disappearing by a single route.[39] By contrast, the human-made disaster is almost "occult": cause and effect are difficult to find.[40] It is not easy to identify all the immediate victims of technological disasters, nor is it possible to identify all future victims. These disasters lack clear limits in time and space. As a result, people's future health and lives presumably remain at risk. Since people confront unknown, frightening potential dangers, the psychological components of human-made disasters become especially significant.

Exacerbating the impact of human-made disasters is the slowness or absence of response and assistance. We have previously spoken of residents' difficulties in getting government officials and scientists to accept that a disaster was occurring and to provide aid. In addition, victims do not know what to expect. In a natural disaster, there are precedents for relief efforts—medical care, insurance benefits, legal proceedings, relocation, private and government relief services—that do not exist in human-made disasters. Solutions such as clean-up, storage of waste, and permanent or temporary relocation are often unavailable or experimental and subject to change on short notice.[41] But victims need an immediate care-giving response. To recognize this need sends a message to the victims that their suffering is acknowledged and validated.[42]

Human-made disasters strike at the heart of rationality and our expectations about life in a modern technological society. We expect our technology to work; the failure of technology indicates general loss of control over something once perceived as controllable. By contrast, natural disasters involve a breakdown where such control never existed and was thus never capable of being lost.[43] Rationality cannot adequately explain technological disasters for another reason: these events are not merely human-made, in contrast to natural or God-given; they in fact seem unnatural or supernatural to many victims. Environmental contaminants are invisible, even occult. They exist in a demonic netherworld, neither natural nor human.

Even in the class of human-made disasters, toxic waste crises are distinctive. Fowlkes and Miller view toxic waste contaminations as "unnatural disasters," "simultaneously predictable, inevitable, and avoidable, and in those respects, non-accidental." The conventional human-caused disaster resembles an accident in which "something goes wrong, breaks down, blows up, collapses." The unnatural disaster, by contrast, unfolds in two stages. "The first stage . . . entails the actual or potential exposure of the population to invisible risk; the second awaits the passage of time and the emergence of debilitating health or environmental effects in consequence of that exposure." Along the way there are signs of a problem that often go unheeded. It is not the sudden appearance of disease clusters that makes for the unnatural disaster, so much as "the convergence of a set of conditions that gives rise to a new definition of an existing situation." Rather than a slowly developing event, the unnatural disaster is a "slowly unfolding consensus" of the affected population.[44]

Environmental disasters sometimes affect a specific number of persons in a geographic area, but they can devastate an entire community. In Love Canal, in Legler, in Buffalo Creek, and in Hardeman County, whole neighborhoods or towns were ravaged, with permanent disruption of the land, inhabitants, and social institutions. A number of toxic waste incidents have required temporary evacuation or permanent relocation. In such cases, a community is tangibly destroyed. Lifton puts it well: "Families everywhere are anchored by their home, which is both a physical structure and a profound symbol of

family integrity and viability. Therefore, a major source
of trauma at TMI was its threat to family homes in terms
of both those meanings. Indeed, some of the most excru-
ciating emotions encountered at TMI have to do with the
undermining of individuals' relationships to their area in
general and to their homes in particular."[45]

Perhaps this devastation is what it truly means to speak
of "environmental disasters." In such a context, community organization requires more than well-motivated individuals; it requires community cohesion to repair the
community rupture. In Buffalo Creek, Lifton and Olson
observed that victims lost the larger religious or moral
universe. This loss, too, must be considered when we speak
of the destruction of community.

In view of the totality of the disaster, we have all the
more reason to define toxic waste contamination as a political rather than solely a medical phenomenon. The main
political element is the community that creates the bud-
ding consensus. In Woburn, an important aspect of victims' illness experience was a change in their attitudes
toward political institutions and political action.

Distrust of Corporations

Woburn residents grew up like many other citizens with
a basic trust in corporations and government. As one
woman told us,

> I thought that factories, industries, all those compa-
> nies that were producing things for people really had
> a conscience and were doing things in a way that
> wouldn't harm people. And on top of that I thought
> that the government was watching to make sure that
> they were proceeding in a way that wouldn't hurt peo-
> ple.

She learned otherwise:

It [the entire Woburn crisis] has taught me a lot about
responsibility. We get comfortable in assuming that
they were protecting us. . . . You have to do it yourself, you have to always be on guard and you have to
do your own homework and do your own everything
in order to see that what you want done is done.

This woman sees that corporations have found a way to
continue polluting, despite government attention:

The fines don't mean anything to industry because
they don't hurt. It just isn't cost-effective. It is easier
to dispose of it [toxic waste] in an illegal way rather
than having it trucked to a proper disposal place.

Another family member agrees that large corporations
can afford the fines and it will be the smaller firms that
will implement new environmental policies:

I would like to think it is because they want to protect
the public, but I just believe it is because the public is
being a watchdog now and they are being watched.

The families' anger is, of course, focused on Grace and
Beatrice. In one interview, a leukemia victim's brother burst
out,

They knew they were dumping stuff and they
shouldn't have been putting it in the ground.

Almost all the family members felt that corporations' pollution stemmed from the profit motive. A sister con-
tended that "The company made millions while poisoning people." A father whose daughter succumbed to
leukemia cried:

I would like to blow W. R. Grace up. It is a billion
dollar company and nothing is going to affect them.

Some residents find it hard to focus their anger beyond the somewhat amorphous corporate entity. A bereaved father was angry because

> Grace Company had a library that had these publications for at least thirty years on the different chemicals and what they do; they knew what these chemicals did. They said they didn't know about it but the publications sitting in their library said they did.

Nevertheless, he found it difficult to focus his anger:

> You can't put your finger on an individual and get mad. I resent what they may be doing to others. . . . There is no one person you can point to. If a person tries to shoot you you can identify him and get angry. Maybe that is where our frustration comes from—a lack of being able to do something direct.

We found this ambiguity to be a dominant theme among the victim families: they needed to pinpoint the responsible individuals. The corporation is intangible and nonpersonal; its identity transcends individuals. Indeed, that is the classic benefit to capitalism of the corporation—personal responsibility is replaced by the fictitious person of an organization that controls capital and serves its interest. The Woburn families knew that real people signed memos and gave orders that polluted and covered up. They knew that real people were working—at huge salaries—to disclaim responsibility and to deny the families' problems. But nowhere did the families have the opportunity to address the victimizers. Even in court, they could not confront the corporation's executives, only its lawyers. Everything was always a step removed from any hope of assigning responsibility.

The impersonal interaction with corporate officials in turn makes the suffering of the families more intangible.

Victims of human-made disasters always find it harder to win assistance and credibility than do victims of natural disasters. The invisibility of the environmental contaminant is in large part the cause of this difficulty. In addition, the invisibility of the people of the corporations contributes to the lack of accountability and thus to the lack of public and personal legitimation of the victims' suffering. Most glaringly, corporate personnel are allowed to escape punishment for actions taken inside the corporation that would be punishable outside. Only in the last few years have individuals faced felony charges for their deeds as corporate actors, and it is not clear whether that trend will grow.

The Woburn families have a larger understanding of corporate malfeasance, as exemplified by one woman's statement: "I know it is not just W. R. Grace. I know it is many, many corporations." Their pervasive distrust includes a general mistrust of the environment, which they may even come to view as a malevolent force.[46] Most litigant families now have water filters, even though their water supply undergoes frequent inspection. A victim's mother predicted: "Where VCRs are in now, well, water filters are going to be the in thing." Another family moved to Florida and reported:

> When we traveled to get to Florida, it took us ten
> days. We went through a lot of big cities that smelled.
> And I am [saying], like "OK. Everybody roll up your
> windows, turn the air conditioner on, and make sure
> none of these chemicals get inside the car."

Environmental mistrust can also lead to vigilance and self-care. The six-year-old brother of a deceased child puts out his parents' cigarettes to stop them from smoking, and he tells people in stores not to buy foods made by Beatrice. The father of another dead child has changed his job, which had put him near solvents, and has pushed his company to be careful about disposal of toxics. Another father says: "You don't buy anything unless you read the whole back of it to find out what is in it." A woman reports:

> I think I am much more careful about what is going on. I won't let anyone spray my lawn with fertilizer. I won't use fertilizer that kills any type of weed. I look at cans to make sure there is nothing like benzene in them. You just become more label-conscious. You try to use as few chemicals as you have to.

Distrust of Governmental Authority

Woburn residents involved in the lawsuit have developed a deep distrust in government, which, like their counterparts in other toxic sites, they believe has failed them. They attribute some of this failure to incompetence, but most they see as resulting from self-protection, self-interest, and collusion with corporate America.

Families said they had gone time after time to town authorities to complain about the water and were told that they were deviant or disturbed. A mother said:

> I don't trust anybody any more. For a long time we were being lied to. I am sure the city knew what was going on.

A woman whose husband died voiced the same sentiments:

> I have no faith in them [city government]. If it weren't for our case they would turn on the wells tomorrow.

According to one father:

> Government regulations go as far as the dollars in front of them. It is who can pay the government. I

don't care how honest they think they are, they are
also very, very slow.

The Woburn families made a number of connections
between government and corporations. In particular, they
believed that J. Peter Grace, head of W. R. Grace, had
considerable pull with the federal government, which made
the EPA reluctant to side with the families. In fact, in
1985 J. Peter Grace headed the President's Private Sector
Survey and Cost Control Commission (Grace Commission), a body charged with offering plans to streamline or
privatize various governmental functions. When reporters and public interest groups examined Grace's corporate activities at the time of the Grace Commission report,
they found that more than thirty Grace (and subsidiary)
sites were being investigated for health hazards or had
violated environmental or workplace requirements over
the past ten years.[47]
Our respondents also made connections between the
corporation ethic and the governmental process in other
public health arenas. One father brought up the anti-
smoking campaign of U.S. surgeon general C. Everett
Koop, charging that the tobacco industry was too eco-
nomically powerful to allow the government to take strong
measures. In another family, someone used the tobacco
industry as an example of how "the establishment" was
trying to block litigation,

> because they don't want to bankrupt the whole coun-
> try, the whole corporate America, because it seems
> that that is what it would boil down to sooner or later.

He was also concerned about nuclear waste and what he
considered to be phony unemployment statistics; he sum-
marized a long discourse by saying that "I have just lost
my faith in the government."

The distrust experienced by the Woburn families has both positive and negative elements. On the positive side, distrust of corporations and the government allows people to overcome serious obstacles in the way of justice and remediation. In this sense, distrust contributes to empowerment. On the negative side, mistrust can leave marks on the personality; one may become inappropriately distrustful in personal relationships. Distrust may thus lead to cynicism and a diminished capacity to enjoy life and to look forward to the future. In this sense, distrust leads to disempowerment. Toxic waste victims must live with both sides of this experience—not the only contradiction they experience.

The Efficacy of Political Action

Pervasive distrust was just one unanticipated result of the lengthy, all-consuming Woburn lawsuit. All litigant families told us that they had no idea what they were getting into when it started. In the words of one plaintiff:

> It was just like one step at a time. As with everything, you take one step at a time and that step leads to the next one, to the next one, to the next one, and you just kind of watch and see what happens with it. All we knew was that we wanted to file suit so that something would happen, and it was a kind of wait and see.

They are now very familiar with the difficulties of community organizing, ranging from internal conflicts in their plaintiffs' group and in FACE to the external conflicts with their town.

All feel a sense of mission and purpose. One family member who is very active in FACE feels that

> the organization accomplished an awful lot, and it has given credibility to this kind of problem. And it has

given people courage to stand up and make noise about something that they think is wrong in their community, and get attention.

For another activist, the suit was the appropriate vehicle to obtain justice and attention:

> It was the only way to go, the only way to make anybody listen. If we left it up to the city or EPA or any of the governmental agencies, nothing would have ever been accomplished because they are just all—you know, they appoint one commission after another, or a committee to take care of the problem so that it never gets done. So filing the suit was the only thing that I could see that would bring something about really quick and take care of the children.

The suit was clearly not an attempt to secure mere economic retribution. It began with a sense of mission in its fight against corporate toxic waste dumping and government inaction, and the sense of mission grew. The widow of a leukemia victim told us:

> In the beginning I felt really self-conscious. I am not one to sue anybody but the longer the case goes on the more I realize it is important because nobody is going to watch out for the public. The governmental agencies aren't going to watch out for us; obviously the city isn't going to watch out for us. . . . Unless people band together and try to do what they feel is right and try to stop the illegal dumping to make these companies become accountable for their actions, nothing is going to get done, because nobody can protect us except ourselves.

But many people retained doubts about the effects of their long struggle:

> It hasn't changed pollution. It hasn't changed standards. It hasn't changed laws. It hasn't made it any

easier to fight corporate America. It hasn't changed, probably, their dumping techniques.

Nevertheless, pessimism did not keep this man or others from continuing to do what was necessary to pursue the case. He continued:

When Jan [the families' lawyer] calls me I am willing to do just about anything. . . . Oh, I won't give up. . . . I would feel guilty if I did nothing.

For these ordinary, previously nonpolitical Woburn citizens to lose faith in government, to see it as a protector of the abuses of "corporate America," and to mobilize themselves is quite significant. Their mainstream conceptions of the social order have been destroyed. One study of twenty-five toxic-contaminated communities found that the residents consistently lost basic trust in government. To challenge the ideology that sustains and legitimizes dominant institutions, residents must adopt an "injustice frame," a belief that "the unimpeded operation of the authority system, on this occasion, would result in an injustice."[48] Residents then move further to "break the bonds of authority": "Political socialization that encourages obedience to authority and supporting cultural belief systems may make the bonds of authority a major challenge to unauthorized collective action. To succeed, challengers must loosen the bonds by delegitimizing the authority that is the target of their challenge."[49] In addition, community residents must create or maintain an organization among participants. This train of events is by no means easy for the average citizen, and the very fact that we see it in Woburn is testimony to the strength and vitality of the local movement.

The progression of distrust and the genesis of political action is illustrated by the community response to toxic

waste in South Brunswick, New Jersey. Local activists began with a single-issue pragmatic response to immediate
dangers but expanded to "a window on a world of power
hidden from them."[50] The leader of the South Brunswick struggle, Frank Kahler, had previously seen himself
as a patriot with a deep faith in governmental abilities to
protect people. In the process of uncovering toxic dumping and the local and state governments' unwillingness to
deal with it, Kahler first realized that government was not
immediately responsive to citizens. Kahler then came to
think that government was basically protecting industry,
although he still believed that the judicial system would
resolve the problem. But Kahler then discovered that legal proceedings were cumbersome and imbalanced in favor of wealthy and powerful parties. He also decided that
the judge was partial to the defendant corporations. Kahler finally no longer believed in the abstract concept or
"esoteric phantom" of "my country," but grasped the hidden structure of political power.[51]

The typical Woburn litigant does not express herself
or himself in such a politicized fashion as Frank Kahler.
But the family members do have a developed understanding of what has happened to them and how they
have affected the world around them. As one might expect, the degree of knowledge and analysis varies among
the families. Some are particularly knowledgeable about
scientific and legal issues; they would often bring up other
current toxic waste cases, about which they kept abreast,
and other examples of corporate malfeasance, such as the
case in which Beech-Nut was found guilty of selling arti-
ficial baby juice as pure apple juice. Other family members are less aware of corporate deviance in other areas
but have a firm grasp of the specific issues in the Woburn
case. The families have been closely enmeshed for some
time, and together they have amassed a collective body of

knowledge and made a collective political and scientific effort.

The Woburn families have coped with their suffering largely through their sense of mission. They have focused anger at the polluters and at the government forces who have neither blamed the polluters nor cleaned up the waste site. The families' anger and search for justice has also been channeled into the lawsuit and its implications for toxic waste problems throughout the nation. All the litigants expressed a deep desire that the Woburn case serve as a warning and an example to other communities.

4

Taking Control
Popular Epidemiology

The public's knowledge of the Woburn problem stems solely from the residents' actions in discovering the leukemia cluster and pursuing the subsequent investigations. In researching this book, we read countless articles in newspapers, popular magazines, scientific journals, and health publications and followed television and radio coverage of the Woburn events. Uniformly, reporters and commentators view the Woburn citizens as the most powerful instance to date of a lay epidemiological approach to toxic wastes and disease. Although one of us (Phil Brown) some time ago coined the term "popular epidemiology" to describe Love Canal residents' organizing efforts, Woburn actually furnishes the first example of popular epidemiology strong enough to allow for the detailed formulation of the concept.

Traditional epidemiology studies the distribution of a disease or a physiological condition and the factors that influence this distribution. Those data are used to explain the causation of the condition and to point toward preventive public health and clinical practices.[1] In contrast, popular epidemiology is the process by which laypersons gather scientific data and other information and direct and marshal the knowledge and resources of experts to

125

understand the epidemiology of disease. In some respects, popular epidemiology parallels scientific epidemiology, although they may proceed in different forms and tempos. In some cases, such as the discovery of Lyme Disease in the early 1980s, laypersons solved an epidemiological mystery before trained scientists. Despite similarities to traditional epidemiology, however, popular epidemiology is more than a matter of public participation in traditional epidemiology. Popular epidemiology goes further in emphasizing social structural factors as part of the causative chain of disease, in involving social movements, in utilizing political and judicial remedies, and in challenging basic assumptions of traditional epidemiology, risk assessment, and public health regulation. Still, the starting point for popular epidemiology is the search for rates and causes of disease.

We shall restrict the label of adherent or practitioner of popular epidemiology to residents who develop and apply the work of popular epidemiology in their communities. Sympathetic scientists may become supporters of popular epidemiology, but lay involvement in the discovery and pursuit of disease in such cases as Woburn is so significant that we shall apply the term only to laypersons. Adherents believe strongly that science, like government, must serve the needs of the people. Just as they question the political apparatus that typically discourages lay investigations into toxic hazards, so do they question the detached attitude of many in the scientific community who champion supposedly value-neutral scientific methods.

Popular epidemiology is a pursuit of truth and justice on behalf of the public that involves both laypersons and professionals. Popular epidemiology is not merely a system of folk beliefs, although they certainly deserve attention from professionals. Most centrally, popular epidemiology unites lay and scientific perspectives in an effort to link science and politics.[2]

Although our discussion of popular epidemiology focuses on toxic waste contamination, the approach is valid for many other phenomena such as nuclear plants, pesticide spraying, and occupational disease. Popular epidemiology is an extremely significant advance for both public health and popular democratic participation.

Defining the Problem

The Quality of Lay Observation

Popular epidemiology is important for medicine and society because people often have access to data about themselves and their environment that are inaccessible to scientists. In fact, public knowledge of community toxic hazards in the last two decades has largely stemmed from the observations of ordinary people. Similarly, most cancer clusters in the workplace are detected by employees.[3]

Even before observable health problems crop up, lay observations may bring to light a wealth of important data. Pittsfield, Massachusetts, residents knew before any authorities did about polychlorinated biphenyls (PCBs) that leaked from storage tanks at a General Electric power transformer plant and polluted the Housatonic River and the local groundwater.[4] Yellow Creek, Kentucky, residents were the first to notice fish kills, disappearances of small animals, and corrosion of screens and other materials. As one resident put it, in discussing a successful struggle to clean up a PCB site in Marlboro, New Jersey: "You didn't have to be a scientist. Trees were down, grass wasn't growing. You'd think you were on the moon or something."[5] Helene Brathwaite, leader of a struggle to remove asbestos from schools in Harlem, made a similar claim: "Nobody knew any more about this than I did. If you assume you're going to get experts to help you, you're in trouble. Most of the time on environmental issues there are no experts, and if there were we wouldn't have these problems."[6]

This "street-wise or creek-side environmental monitoring"[7] occurred in Woburn, where residents noticed water stains on dishwashers and a bad odor long before they knew of adverse health effects. Love Canal residents remembered persistent bad odors, rocks that exploded when dropped or thrown, leakage of sludge into basements, chemical residues on the ground after rainfall, and irritations on children's feet from playing in fields where wastes were dumped.[8] Residents of South Brunswick, New Jersey, noticed foul-tasting water and saw barrels labeled "toxic chemicals" dumped, bulldozed, and ruptured.[9]

Judith Broderick, from Reading (next to Woburn), noticed previously that she became ill for three months after exposure to chlorine leaks from a nearby factory. Later, she smelled the rotten-egg odor of hydrogen sulfide from decaying animal hides at a former glue factory. She remembers that "People felt nauseated. We had headaches, our eyes would burn, we had difficulty breathing, sleeping, eating."[10] Broderick knew that among the eight women of childbearing age on her block, there were six miscarriages and three stillbirths. At a nearby school, three of five pregnant teachers miscarried. When she looked out of her window she saw three special education buses coming to pick up children with various learning disabilities and handicaps. She thought, "Too many lost babies, too many damaged children."[11]

Out of such observations, people develop "common sense epidemiology,"[12] whereby they hypothesize that a higher than expected incidence of disease is due to pollution. In some cases, laypersons carry out their own study or initiate a study for experts to carry out. For example, in Pittsfield, a retired engineer was concerned about elevated cancer rates and known PCB contamination. He initiated a study which showed a high correlation between working for General Electric and having PCBs in the blood. Other residents then linked those blood levels with their knowledge of elevated cancer rates.[13] In Yellow Creek, Kentucky, a woman who helped organize a health survey remembered: "Every family told of kidney troubles, vomiting, diarrhea, rashes. One family showed us big welts right after they showered. And there were huge numbers of miscarriages. I cried every night. We gave our data to Vanderbilt University and they found high rates of these diseases. The Centers for Disease Control found some leukemia but said it wasn't statistically significant. Statistics don't tell you. People do. I've walked this creek and I've seen the sick people."[14]

In 1973 a Michigan farmer, Rick Halbert, noticed that his cattle were becoming hunchbacked, bald, sterile, and crippled by overgrown hoofs before dying. He conjectured that those symptoms were caused by the cattle feed and carried out an experiment to test the idea. He fed twelve calves on that feed alone. Five died within six weeks, and most of the rest died during the next two months. Halbert reported these data to the Michigan Department of Agriculture, but they were not willing to repeat the experiment with cows. They gave the suspect feed to mice, all of whom died, but the supply company argued that the animals died from eating cattle feed instead of mice food. Halbert then hired scientists who, employing a mass spectrograph, found bromine in the feed. Eight months after Halbert's first observations, investigators learned that Michigan Chemical Corporation had accidentally supplied the Michigan Farm Bureau with sacks of fire-proof-ing chemical PBB, which is known to cause cancer, genetic mutation, and birth defects. During the crucial eight-month period between the farmer's first observations and the discovery of the accident, a great deal of contamination had already occurred. Human breast milk was found to contain PBB; many farm animals were poisoned too. Tens of thousands of livestock and millions of chickens were slaughtered as a result.[15]

Another example of lay detection is offered by the dioxin contamination in Moscow Mills, Missouri, one of several Missouri dioxin sites besides the well-known Times Beach. In 1971, horse rancher Judy Piatt noticed a strong smell after a waste hauler sprayed road oil to keep dust down in the stable area. The next day she saw dying sparrows; in the following weeks cats and dogs lost hair, grew thin, and died. Forty-three of eighty-five horses in the exposed area died within one year, and of forty-one newborn horses, only one survived. Three months later Judy Piatt's daughter was hospitalized with internal bleeding. Based on her supposition that the waste oil was responsible, Piatt followed the route of the salvage oil dealer for over a year, noting sites where waste oil and chemicals were dumped. She sent her information to state and federal officials, but no action resulted. It was three more years until the CDC found dioxin in the oil, at 30,000 parts per billion; anything over one part per billion is considered dangerous.[16]

Patricia Nonnon of the Bronx provides an additional illustration of creative case finding. When her nine-year-old daughter contracted leukemia, she remembered hearing of other cases; in fact, there were four in the three-block area bordering on the Pelham Bay dump. Prior complaints to the state environmental agency had brought no results, so Nonnon tried a different approach. She set up a telephone hot line in 1988 and received more than

300 calls reporting many diseases: twenty-five cases of childhood leukemia, sixty-one cases of multiple sclerosis, ten lupus, nine Hodgkin's disease, and six rare blood diseases. All respondents lived less than a mile from the dump. Residents knew the landfill was hazardous, because a few years before several firms had been convicted of illegally dumping hundreds of thousands of gallons of toxic waste over a decade at five landfills, including Pelham Bay.[17]

In addition to collecting information, laypersons employ logical tests of the relationship between location and health. One Love Canal resident reported: "As far as the relationship of this to the chemicals, let me put it this way, when we go away from here, we feel fine. We just spent a month out west, no eye problems, no nerve problems, felt good. I slept like a log. We're back home, we have the same problems again. Headaches, eyes, nerves, not sleeping."[18] A number of other Love Canal residents reported changes in their family's health after their official relocation.[19]

In Woburn, residents were the first to notice the leukemia cluster, through both formal and informal methods of identification. Then they framed a hypothesis linking pollution to disease and pressed local, state, and federal agencies to investigate the cluster. They particularly asked authorities to test the water that they suspected of being a cause. After state environmental officials found high concentrations of TCE and PCE in wells G and H, residents argued that those known carcinogens were the cause of the cluster. To bolster their hypothesis, Woburn residents joined with biostatisticians from the Harvard SPH to carry out the community health survey.

Without community involvement, this study would not have been possible because of the lack of money and personnel. The very fact of lay involvement led professionals and government to charge bias. Nevertheless, extensive analyses by the researchers demonstrated that the data were not biased, especially with regard to the use of community volunteers as interviewers. Resistance to the idea of lay participation is harmful, since professional and governmental distrust of the public can delay amelioration and cause additional disease and death.

The Myth of Value-Neutrality

Popular epidemiology opposes the widely held belief that epidemiology is a value-neutral scientific enterprise that can be conducted in a sociopolitical vacuum. It also challenges the belief that epidemiological work is properly conducted only by experts. Critics of the Harvard/FACE Woburn health study—among them the CDC, the American Cancer Society, the EPA, and even the SPH's Department of Epidemiology—argued that the study was biased by the use of volunteer interviewers and by prior political goals. The possibility of volunteer bias is a real concern, but on a deeper level the criticisms assumed a value-free science of epidemiology in which knowledge, theories, techniques, and actual and potential applications are themselves devoid of self-interest or bias.

As was the case in Woburn, popular epidemiology can include methodological and statistical controls for bias. Indeed, without skewing any evidence it can overcome some fundamental limitations of scientific endeavors. In practice science is limited by such factors as finances and personnel. Without popular participation it would be impossible to carry out much of the research needed to document health hazards. Science is also limited in its conceptualization of what problems are legitimate and how they should be addressed. As we have pointed out, physicians are largely untrained in environmental and occupational health matters, and even when they observe environmentally caused disease, they are unlikely to blame the disease on the environment. Similarly, epidemiologists and public health researchers are not sufficiently attuned to problems of toxic waste contamination. Funding agencies are reluctant to support the kinds of investigations needed at toxic waste sites. And, most fundamental, scientific approaches to toxic waste contamination are directed by an old paradigm that no longer fits reality.

Environmental health activists are by definition acting to correct problems not adequately addressed by the corporate, political, and scientific establishments. Popular involvement is usually necessary for professionals to target the appropriate questions, as is clear from the history of the women's health movement,[20] the occupational health and safety movement,[21] and the environmental health movement.[22] These movements have significantly advanced public health and safety by pointing out otherwise unidentified problems and showing how to approach them, by organizing to abolish the conditions that give rise to them, and by educating citizens, public agencies, health care providers, officials, and institutions. Popular participation brought to the national spotlight such phenomena as DES, Agent Orange, asbestos, pesticides, unnecessary hysterectomies, abuse of sterilization, black lung disease, and brown lung disease.

Issues of Scientific Method

Standards of Proof

Despite the successes of popular epidemiology, we must take a closer look at critics' concerns about breaches of scientific method. Does popular epidemiology adhere to the appropriate standards of proof? Authorities in fact disagree on the level of statistical significance required for intervention in environmental hazard settings. Many communities that believe they have uncovered environmental health risks find themselves challenged because they lack enough cases to achieve statistical significance. Some professionals who work with community organizations stick closely to accepted standards of statistical significance,[23] while others argue that such levels are as inappropriate to environmental risk as they are to other issues of public health and safety, such as bomb threats and possible epidemics.[24]

We believe it is imperative to follow Ozonoff and Boden, who distinguish between *statistical significance* and *public health significance*. An increased rate of disease may be of great public health significance even if statistical probabilities are not reached. Further, clinical medicine tends to err on the safe side of false positives (claiming a relationship when there is none), and epidemiology should mirror clinical medicine rather than laboratory science.[25] Some researchers have noted that recent epidemiological research has a tendency to accept an increasingly lower level of false positives.[26]

Traditional epidemiologists prefer false negatives (type II error) to false positives (type I error); that is, they would prefer falsely to deny an association between variables when there is one than to claim an association when there is none.[27] To achieve scientific statements of probability requires more evidence than is necessary to state that something should be done to eliminate or minimize a health threat. In the view of one observer,

> The degree of risk to human health does not need to be at statistically significant levels to require political action. The degree of risk does have to be such that a reasonable person would avoid it. Consequently, the important political test is not the findings of epidemiologists on the probability of nonrandomness of an incidence of illness but the likelihood that a reasonable

person, including members of the community of cal-
culation [epidemiologists], would take up residence
with the community at risk and drink from and bathe
in water from the Yellow Creek area or buy a house
along Love Canal.[28]

Indeed, those are the kinds of questions presented to public
health officials, researchers, and government members in
every setting where there is dispute between the perceptions of citizens and officials.

For residents near toxic waste sites, proved toxicity is
not required for alarm and action. Someone in Love Canal
put it well:

I think the most important question that people ask,
they always ask, "Well, how do the chemicals affect
your family?" That really has nothing to do with it,
because having two children, and living in that neighborhood, you had no choice. You had to get out of
there whether the chemicals affected us or not. You
cannot live a good, happy life always wondering.[29]

In a further excursion into the politics of epidemiology, Beverly Paigen, a scientist with the New York State
Department of Health who was instrumental in aiding the
Love Canal residents, discusses a conversation with an ep-
idemiologist from her office:

We both agreed that we should take the conservative
approach only to find out that in every case we disagreed on what the conservative approach was. To him,
"conservative" meant that we must be very cautious
about concluding that Love Canal was an *unsafe* place
to live. The evidence had to be compelling because
substantial financial resources were needed to correct
the problem. To me, "conservative" meant that we
must be very cautious about concluding that Love
Canal was a *safe* place to live. The evidence had to be

compelling because the public health consequences of
an error were considerable.[30]

Paigen offers valuable insight into the scientist's choice
between type I error (being more likely to accept false
positives) and type II error (being more likely to reject
false positives).

> The degree to which one is willing to make one or the
> other kind of error is a value judgment and depends
> on what one perceives to be the consequences of mak-
> ing the error. To conclude that something is real
> when it is not means that a scientist has followed a
> false lead or published a paper that later turns out to
> be incorrect. This may be embarrassing and harmful
> to a scientist's reputation. In contrast, to ignore the
> existence of something real means that a scientist fails
> to make a discovery. This may be disappointing but it
> does not harm the scientist's reputation, so the scien-
> tist is more willing to make type II errors. However
> those charged with protecting public health and safety
> should be much more concerned about the second
> type of error, for a hypothesis that is not recognized
> drops out of sight.[31]

Of her own scientific experience, she writes:

> Before Love Canal, I also needed a 95 percent cer-
> tainty before I was convinced of a result. But seeing
> this rigorously applied in a situation where the conse-
> quences of an error meant that pregnancies were re-
> sulting in miscarriages, stillbirths, and children with
> medical problems, I realized I was making a value
> judgment.[32]

Paigen argues that the value judgment involves deciding
"whether to make errors on the side of protecting human
health or on the side of conserving state resources." The
same logic applies to the choices between protecting pub-

lic health and accepting "environmental blackmail" and the primacy of corporate development and profit.[33]

Thus the competing paradigms of risk are not merely clinical and epidemiological, but also intensely political. On the one hand we have what David Dickson terms the "technocratic paradigm," in which the desire to protect the business community shapes regulation. In contrast, the "democratic paradigm" starts from the victims' perspective, values safety over profit, requires less than conclusive proof in order to take action, and provides those likely to be affected with an active voice in determining risk and making decisions.[34]

How Good Are Official Data?

Even when citizens accept standard significance levels, they may suspect that the collection and analysis of official toxic hazard data are erroneous. Massive public complaints about Massachusetts' response to excess cancer rates in twenty communities (including Woburn) led to evaluations by the state senate and the University of Massachusetts Medical School, which found that the Massachusetts DPH studies of those excess rates were poorly conceived and methodologically weak.[35] The DPH studies were often unclear about what problem concerned the community or the DPH. Most studies had no adequate hypothesis, failed to mention potential exposure routes, and as a result rarely defined the geographic or temporal limits of the population at risk. Methods were presented inconsistently, statistical terminology was confused, case definitions were weak, and environmental data were rarely presented. Further, statistical tests were inappropriately used to explain away problems. In the case of elevated cancer in towns of Upper Cape Cod, initial analysis found no towns with excess rates. When a later analysis combined two adjacent towns, the data were compelling for the elevation of several cancer types, yet the DPH claimed that excess lung, colon, and rectal cancers had life-style rather than environmental causation.[36] Activists and sympathetic scientists find such arguments unacceptable; they view them as blaming the victims while denying possible external causes.

The Massachusetts commissioner of public health appointed a Study Commission on Environmental Health Issues in 1983 to report on problems such as these. The Study Commission's complaints mirrored those of the citizens:

> Despite its public mandate, DPH is seen by such members of the community as an obstacle and an adversary, not as an agency that is helpful and sensitive to their needs. The Environmental Health Services Bureau routinely responds to a citizen concerned with local chemical contamination by minimizing the problem, stating, in effect, "We can't bother to investigate every unsubstantiated claim or concern," or, "When you can provide some hard scientific or statistical evidence, please call us again."[37]

The commission found that despite its mandate to err on the conservative side of health protection, the DPH imagined the political risks to be too great and took the opposite tack to avoid antagonizing industry.[38]

Massachusetts is a particularly interesting example because the damaging effects of the poor studies and nonresponsiveness to the community included the resignation of the public health commissioner. Elsewhere researchers often used exposed groups diluted by unexposed individuals and comparison groups that were inappropriate because they were likely to be exposed to the same health threats as exposed groups.[39] In the Michigan case of PBB-contaminated cattle feed, the state health department carried out a study so poorly designed that

70 percent of the control animals showed the presence of PBB. But the state would not admit the flaws in its work.[40]

Lay individuals and groups trying to uncover and remedy environmental hazards have far fewer scientific and financial resources than do government units and are therefore at a scientific disadvantage.[41] Most communities that consider themselves at risk or as victims of environmental disasters have no stable source of scientific data. If they are lucky, they can mobilize local scientific support. But university-based scientists frequently consider applied community research to be outside the regular academic structure of challenge and reward. Often they see the work of uncovering environmental problems as fairly routine compared with work on frontiers of science such as molecular biology.[42] Furthermore universities have become increasingly dependent on corporations and government for support, and scientists have lost both autonomy and the urge to challenge established authority.[43]

Scientists who ally themselves with citizen efforts are sometimes punished. When Beverly Paigen aided Love Canal residents in their health studies, she was harassed by her superiors. After Paigen spoke out publicly, the New York Department of Health withdrew a grant application she had written without telling her. They refused to process papers on another grant already funded, thus denying her the funds. She was told that because of the "sensitive nature" of her work, all grants and research ideas had to go through a special review process. Her professional mail was opened and taped shut, and her office files were searched after working hours. Paigen's state tax return was audited, and she saw in her file a clipping about her Love Canal work. Later, the state tax commissioner wrote her and apologized. Paigen was not the only scientist harassed for siding with Love Canal residents. William Friedman, regional director of the Department of

Environmental Conservation, and Donald McKenna, senior sanitary engineer in the regional office, were demoted and transferred, respectively, for raising questions about the state's investigation of Love Canal.[44]

Similar cases of retaliation have been documented elsewhere. Melvin Reuben, director of the Experimental Pathology Laboratory at the Frederick Cancer Research Facility, Frederick, Maryland, was forced to resign for warning that malathion was carcinogenic; Irwin Billick, head of the Division of Environmental Research at the U.S. Department of Housing and Urban Development was fired for "unnecessary" work on lead poisoning.[45] In 1981, Peter Infante, a staff scientist for the Occupational Safety and Health Administration (OSHA), was threatened with dismissal for too energetically reporting the carcinogenicity of formaldehyde.[46]

A cardinal assumption of scientific research is that the truth and validity of science are affirmed through open access to data, yet lay inquiry into environmental health risks is often obstructed by secret scientific data and analysis. Officials sometimes withhold information on the basis that it will alarm the public, that the public does not understand risks, or that it will harm the business climate.[47] The above-mentioned University of Massachusetts evaluation of DPH studies of excess cancer rates grew out of public pressure on the legislature. Citizens were angry that the health department did not seek the input of citizens, communicate data to affected towns, or share information when asked. Local health officials reported that they typically heard of elevated cancer rates through the media rather than from the DPH. Perhaps a good deal of the governmental and professional resistance to popular epidemiology derives from the fact that lay efforts very often point to the flaws and biases in official data that we have noted.

Lay investigations of environmental contaminants require full information. Although the right to know is usually associated with workers' right to know of toxic hazards in the workplace, the notion of a community right to know has developed recently. Community groups want all existing data to be available to them whether or not there are identifiable health effects. Although the agencies safeguarding the data defend secrecy on the ground that people will become alarmed, the people who request data from state health departments and cancer registries are clearly already alarmed. Another official excuse is that the media may make a story out of nothing. "Media hype" occurs throughout society, however, and is simply the price of democratic access to information.[48]

Federal secrecy in investigations of the Woburn cluster violated residents' right to know. As mentioned previously, the EPA conducted a secret investigation of Woburn and thereby denied the public access to important scientific data. Past EPA administrator William Ruckelshaus formed the study group in 1984, but its existence was not discovered until May 1988.[49] That episode is reminiscent of the New York State Department of Health's response to Love Canal. Following a long train of events, in which the state did not release data to independent scientists, Governor Carey appointed a special commission chaired by biologist Lewis Thomas. Activists who invoked the New York Freedom of Information Act learned that the commission violated the law by not announcing meetings and not holding them publicly.[50] Indeed, knowledge makes a difference. One large population survey determined that the level of concern for environmental toxics rose with the number of information sources.[51] Another study found a positive correlation between information about the Diablo Canyon nuclear plant and the opposition to licensing it.[52]

In addition, the federal government has dramatically affected the contours of environmental issues by loosening the acceptable levels of toxic hazards and regulatory agency enforcement.[53] The Reagan administration reduced controls on air and water pollution, stalled the recognition and prevention of acid rain, and reduced the regulatory power of EPA and OSHA. In December 1987 the Supreme Court limited the scope of the Clean Water Act when it ruled that citizens and environmental groups cannot sue companies for past violations.[54] Since people have long been denied access to necessary information, this decision is particularly unfair.

Government Resistance

In looking at official resistance to acknowledging toxic waste contamination, we cannot really separate government and scientists, although they are not always the same. What we actually have are combined government and professional units, such as DPH, EPA, and CDC. None are solely governmental or solely professional, although the government uses professional models in its deliberations. Toxic waste activists realize that their main target is often government agencies, since it is they that have the power to act. Further, government agencies are essentially in control of scientific inquiry at toxic waste sites and in this role play a prime role in blocking knowledge and participation. Indeed, government agencies often make political decisions couched in scientific terms. In some cases government bodies obstruct citizens by being uninformed users of scientific knowledge. In either case, government officials and agencies constitute a major obstacle to community investigations of toxic waste.

Unfortunately, the "conspiracy theory" holds true too frequently. In one sample of 110 community action groups, 45 percent claimed that government agencies blocked their access to data.[55] In another study of twenty-five contaminated communities, sixteen discovered the problem themselves and petitioned authorities for aid. In all but one case, the victims judged the official response to be inadequate.[56]

A representative example of government obstacles is found in Friendly Hills, a suburb of Denver. Candace Logue, a founder of the Friendly Hills Action Group, reported that at Tupperware parties in the early 1980s mothers compared notes and wondered why large numbers of children were sick or dying. When the state health department and the EPA both declined to study the problem, people canvased door to door. They found that from 1976 to 1984, fifteen children had died: eight from cancer, five from birth defects, and two from immunological disease. A seven-month fetus also died. Thirty-four other children were suffering from those and other serious diseases.[57]

State officials claimed that all illnesses were within expected limits; though there were more childhood cancer cases than expected, they might be due to chance. Residents suspected toxic waste discharges from a nearby Martin Marietta Corporation facility. One week after officials pronounced the discharges safe, the Air Force, which runs a test facility on the Martin Marietta site, admitted that the groundwater was contaminated by toxic chemicals. Thereupon, the water board shut down the water treatment facility, for reasons it claimed were related only to its age. Residents found that Martin Marietta had a record of toxic spills. Water board officials then responded that the nearby water treatment facility, which would have been contaminated by such spills, did not supply water to Friendly Hills. The Friendly Hills Action Group found water board maps that showed this to be untrue. Furthermore, Martin Marietta was in fact fined by the state health department for many violations of water discharge permits. The Air Force had acknowledged toxic wastes underground. Several months later EPA scientists found serious contamination, including TCE, in a plume, or underground wave, stretching from the Martin Marietta site toward the water plant.[58] The belated discovery of what residents knew long before is eery and infuriating—and, sadly, it is common to many toxic waste sites.

In addition to obstructing citizens' desire for information, government officials often advise people to alter their life-styles to minimize their risks.[59] A Yellow Creek citizen who asked a state official about health effects on future children was told that it was best not to get married. When asked about threats to food gardens, the official advised residents to stop growing their own food.[60] State health officials recommended that Love Canal residents who were pregnant or had young children move, although the state was not yet prepared to fund such relocation.[61] Such responses trivialize realistic worries and treat citizens as annoyances. As Judy Broderick recounts, her calls to local and state officials about pollution in Reading were treated as "just a nuisance."[62]

Initial shock at the existence of toxic substances often gives way to anger at public officials who minimize or cover up the problem. Residents at toxic waste sites feel angry at the corporate polluters, of course, but they initially trust that their government will serve them and remedy problems. When the government fails to do so, citizens confront a breach in their essential concepts of democratic governance. We have dealt with this in an earlier chapter, showing the deep antagonism between Woburn residents and their elected and appointed officials.

A Velsicol victim in Hardeman County, who has since died, told a reporter, "We thought people from EPA would help us. Next thing one of them is working for Velsicol. The government won't watch the industry."[63] Another victim said:

> I knowed they was dumping stuff, but they said it wasn't dangerous. One day I found this snake and threw him in one of the pits and he moved around a bit and then he died. But I never thought it'd get in our water. I'd take a bath and break out, like chicken pox. Take another and there's the pox again. I took a water sample to the health department; they said nothing's wrong with it. I thought they was good people, smarter than I was. But they wasn't.[64]

There are, of course, some well-intentioned government bodies that nevertheless cannot act effectively in toxic waste crises. Public health departments may have problems with their own organizational boundaries, such as in relation to state environmental agencies, and also face tensions between the public and private sectors, in which they attempt to minimize their regulation of private enterprise. Further, state health and environmental agencies commonly exhibit a bureaucratic tendency to minimize and underestimate toxic waste problems.[65] Another component of the bureaucratic mentality is the tendency of state and federal officials to focus on site cleanup rather than on the health of the population. This perspective is not only incomplete but also antagonizes residents who are deeply concerned about their health.[66]

Institutional inertia and boundary disputes are common in all areas of social policy. In environmental policy, we find extreme disorganization and confusion. The EPA enforces eight separate laws and is organized disjunctively, with little integration and cooperation among component parts and little overall mission. In carrying out its work, the EPA deals with ninety different congressional committees.[67] At both state and federal levels, regulation and legislation are too specific to the medium of contamination—air, water, soil. An integrated effort would be more appropriate, but agencies and institutions protect their own areas, fearing to lose power and budget allocations in a unified, cross-media reform. Individual scientists usually protect their narrow specializations and remain focused on a single medium.[68]

As with medical care, mental health care, and other major elements of social policy, environmental laws and regulatory mechanisms are rarely conceived of in terms of long-term planning. Rather, they are approached incrementally through an agglomeration of partial programs tailored for particular interest groups. Lack of planning hampers effective policy for the long run, as well as current efforts at specific toxic waste sites.

Issues of Professionalism

Professionalism and Information Control

Scientific obstruction of popular epidemiology must be seen in a wider context. Widespread professional antagonism to popular participation in scientific endeavors usually has nothing to do with disputes over scientific facts. Instead, scientific professionals object because they need to defend their professionalism, institutions, or political-economic alliances.

A huge gulf separates professional and lay perspectives and behaviors. Scientists, like other professionals, are a tightly knit community of experts who generally accept the belief that science and technology are best left to scientists and engineers.[69] They often display scientific paternalism and "professional hubris," holding that laypersons cannot be involved in scientific decision making.[70]

Health care activists have effectively criticized and discredited this attitude in the health care system.

Professionals generally do not want to let laypersons take on the work they control as professionals. This jealousy is particularly ironic in epidemiology, since the original "shoe-leather" epidemiological work that founded the field was much like popular epidemiology today. The Woburn residents' efforts resemble John Snow's classic study of cholera in London in 1854, but the stakes in epidemiology have changed since John Snow's day. If scientists do not control the research process, they lose scientific status and funding.

Professionals' claims to autonomy in directing scientific inquiry rest in part on the notion that epidemiological science can reach a high degree of certainty. In truth, however, scientific knowledge is full of uncertainty, especially in the field of toxic waste contamination. Uncertainty, combined with the sociopolitical context of toxic waste crises, provokes scientific controversy. As Thomas Kuhn has pointed out, all science is about controversy, particularly when paradigms of "normal science" are challenged by anomalies and "revolutions."[71] The production of scientific facts, Bruno Latour adds, is a collective effort and always involves controversy. "Nature" cannot, he claims, settle controversies, since "nature" itself is determined by the outcome of the controversy. To understand scientific controversies in a specific field, we must "follow scientists in action," observing what parties are involved and how they collaborate in the social construction of scientific facts.[72]

Toxic waste activists have been watching science in action and find much reason to doubt its unqualified veracity. Even about such a well-documented site as Love Canal it is hard to know exactly what happened: "Given the persistence of dissension among officials, community leaders, eminent scientists, government agencies and the residents themselves, it is probable that any 'truth' about Love Canal will always be provisional. As a participant in this study observed, 'That's the whole summary of the canal. Everybody knew what was going on and when you got right down to it, nobody knew what was going on.' "[73] Not only was the community at odds with officials, but the official agencies disagreed with one another. There was no consensus. In the absence of scientific clarity, people's "understandings and explanations had to be constructed substantially in terms of experiences, attitudes, and values."[74] In a setting of such ambiguity and uncertainty, social and interpretive approaches to toxic waste disasters will thrive.

From their comparative study of the communication of risk, Krimsky and Plough point out that there are two models, based on "technical rationality" and "cultural rationality." Cultural rationality appeals to folk wisdom, peer groups, and traditions. It asks questions that are not part of the technical sphere, such as "Why do we need this product?" It looks at direct and personal effects of the environmental risk. Technical rationality, however, has a narrower range of interests and is concerned with transferring information specifically geared to a technical solution. In addition, this information is usually supplied only on demand rather than voluntarily, since public education is not generally among the technical rational aims. Unfortunately, many official agencies consider the cultural view to be an error and thus butt up against it rather than work with it to serve as "translators" between the two models.[75] When two models with different assumptions and goals are in combat, uncertainty grows and spreads.

Uncertainty also infects the "margins" of clinical and epidemiological knowledge, such as transgenerational effects of toxics, chronic low-dose exposure, and disease

clusters. There is much scientific debate about these issues, resulting in a high degree of uncertainty. At the
margins, professionals assert their dominance even more
strongly than usual because of this uncertainty.[76] They
redouble their claims to a spurious certainty. Uncertainty
exacerbates public dissatisfaction as well, because it often
leads to inaction or inappropriate action by scientists. In
this cycle, professionals become even more adamant about
their scientific prerogatives and even more averse to lay
involvement.

Professionalism embodies a high degree of information
control. At its most basic, this control involves the exclu-
sion of laypersons as we have mentioned. In addition,
professionals' need to control information leads to incomplete and unspecific communications about risk. "A scientist speaking in a community about the health effects
of a hazardous waste site is part of a political ritual that
aims to evoke confidence and respect. The technical information in the message is secondary to the real goal of
the communicator: 'Have faith; we are in charge.' "[77]

The directors of the health study of the Missouri dioxin
contamination initially planned to notify residents of specific laboratory results. On reflection, and without consulting the community, those professionals decided that
the information was "too technical." As a result, "low he-
matocrit" followed by a specific percentage was replaced
with "abnormal blood count," and "elevated cholesterol"
followed by a number was replaced with "abnormal blood
chemistry."[78] Residents at Love Canal and other sites
complained about the same vagueness of information.

Such bowdlerization of data demeans the courage and
intelligence of the victims and unfairly deprives them of
information crucial to management of their health. Uncertainty causes an alarmist response. Another risk-com-
munication technique that causes uncertainty and alarm

is the practice of defining sharp cutoff points above which human exposure is considered to be unhealthful. This is always both a scientific and a policy decision, since whenever a situation is declared unhealthful some remediation, such as a company-supplied water filter, is called for. But residents at toxic waste sites are also taught to accept the epidemiological notion of a dose-response curve, in which higher degrees of exposure lead to more health effects.

One commentator makes an analogy to the highway speed limit. It makes no sense to say that it is only unsafe to drive over fifty-five miles per hour. After all, auto speed is directly related to fatalities. The occupant of a car can escape injury at ninety-five miles per hour, though this is less likely; similarly the occupant can be injured at thirty miles per hour. There is no speed at which you can say that risk is absent. Similarly in toxic exposure, a dichotomy with a "trigger point" is inappropriate; it is confusing as well, when people have already been told they should believe in a continual, metric relationship.[79] Many contaminated communities have even been told they were not victims of exposure, precisely because no one had yet verified a dose-response curve. Massachusetts officials, for instance, applied this logic to Woburn.

Our observations of Woburn families and FACE activists, combined with what we know of activists in other sites, tell us that citizen activists can become quite sophisticated about toxic waste issues. Indeed, as we have continually emphasized, community residents are indispensable to the toxic discovery process. To treat them as inferior is not only unfair but also detracts from contributions to scientific knowledge.

Professionalism, Politics, and Economics

When environmental health groups and toxic waste activists challenge the scientific canon of value-neutrality and traditional standards of proof, they attack some core assumptions of professional scientists. By putting forth their own political goals, activists may challenge scientists to acknowledge that they too have political agendas, although covert, unconscious, or unrecognized. Toxic waste controversies often reveal scientists' alignment with corporate interests. For instance, corporate attorneys make much of the charge that citizen activists are untrained and incapable of making valid judgments regarding pollution.[80] This charge fits with the view of many professional scientists. Popular participation threatens not only the division of knowledge and power between laypersons and professionals, but also the corporate system that produces environmental hazards.

Scientists long accepted industry's cost-benefit approach to toxic chemicals. For corporations, the key question was whether it was worth cleaning up the workplace. Public opposition to the toxic waste crisis has made this position less tenable. Thus, more recently, scientists, regulatory agencies, and corporations pursue a "better science," in which there is "endless tinkering with standards." As a result, according to Nicholas Ashford, "we spend $300,000 on animal studies of one chemical, yet never ask if we can substitute something for the chemical. This is just what industry wants us to do."[81]

Similarly, scientists in regulatory agencies often accept corporations' research on toxicity without critical evaluation. They may even let corporations test their own toxic contamination sites and implement their own remediation procedures. For instance, in the case of Temik aldicarb pesticide contamination on Long Island, both the EPA and the producer, Union Carbide, ignored warnings that Temik could persist in soil and thus penetrate aquifers. They were relying, at least in part, on data that were not designed to address that particular question. Some scientific studies were concerned only with the relationship be-

tween the pesticide and the soil, some with reaction ki-
netics. Company chemists felt that they had demonstrated
that there were no surface water problems and therefore
it was pointless to look further. The fact remains, some
EPA and state agricultural extension service scientists had
warned of dire effects, and officials refused to act on those
warnings. Agricultural staffers who requested further data
were rebuffed by both Union Carbide and the EPA. After
EPA, the public, and the media recognized a crisis, the
EPA accepted Union Carbide's request to delay making
the results public. Union Carbide was even given responsibility for conducting water sample tests, notifying residents, and providing water filters.[82]

Most persons who criticize lay-scientific method believe
that science cannot be value-free and that the positivistic
methodology of epidemiology serves the interest of those
in power.[83] Toxic waste activists are also dissatisfied with
the new field of risk assessment, which fails to take into
account deeper social and cultural forces. The positivist
cost-benefit analysis and psychometric studies of risk assessment cannot provide adequate information on health
risks, because both the risks and perceptions of the risks
are shaped by economic, ideological, and political concerns.[84] Indeed, the very language of risk is highly sub-
jective and controversial, laden with underlying political
theories of society.[85]

For instance, in debates over occupational health, industry advocates approach health risks from the assumption that the economic system is reasonable, efficient, and
nonexploitative and that illegal practices are the ill-ad-
vised acts of the few. Those advocates see conflicts over
workplace safety as prompted by uninformed, unscien-
tific, or irrational fears about chemicals. Labor advocates,
on the other hand, assume a conflict approach in which
industry trades lives for profits.[86]

Even when risk-perception research—often conducted

by psychologists—does not expressly serve the economic system, it supports existing notions of scientific rationality, in opposition to cultural rationality. Rather than build a culture-based theory of risk perception, psychometricians usually just enter more variables into a single equation, such as voluntary/involuntary, familiar/unfamiliar, human-made/natural. This approach rationalizes "cultural noise" and maintains the dichotomy between expert and lay risk perception.[87]

The alleged value-neutrality of risk assessment is further challenged by the fact that corporate and governmental risk-assessment guidelines are for the most part political rather than scientific. Reagan-era deregulation has led to arbitrary reductions in toxic hazards control, accompanied by increases in allowable pollution levels.[88] Thus citizens groups have no stable foundation on which to base their expectations of intervention and redress of grievances.

Scientific and governmental attitudes and practices have not, however, been monolithic. Partly in response to citizen organizing, and partly as a result of scientific and scholarly developments, a growing number of scientific and environmental professionals seek to increase public knowledge and participation. As toxic waste activism is also a social movement, a burgeoning corps of scholars in the social sciences and humanities are refocusing social attitudes toward risk assessment and communication, joined by a small number of epidemiologists and other scientists.[89] Some of these scholars work in tandem with community groups, while others address a more general public.

Lay-Professional Alliances

When scientific, medical, and public health experts become involved in popular epidemiology, it is always in alliance with citizen activists. Indeed, the community activists tend to be the leaders, in contrast to the more formalistic input they offer most state and federal advisory bodies. Although laypersons can learn to utilize expert knowledge and acquire some expert skills themselves, we are concerned that excessively high levels of epidemiological research will become the accepted standard. This would be unfortunate, since most organizations might not be able to marshal the level of research undertaken in Woburn.

In medicine, some practitioners criticize patient involvement in treatment as "antimedical," much as nuclear power proponents hold that antinuclear activists are "antiscientific." Such charges stem from preconceptions rather than a worked-out judgment on the merits of the case. Opponents may similarly accuse popular epidemiology of being antiscientific because it expresses a different concept of what science is, whom it should serve, and who should control it. Environmental health activists want to work with professionals. They have shown their mettle in some very significant cases where their efforts in organizing resources and carrying out research have been invaluable. One survey found that 89 percent of community groups interacted regularly with scientists, and that scientific experts were the main source of information for groups.[90] In Woburn, sympathetic scientists Steven Lagakos and Marvin Zelen were valuable allies, as was Beverly Paigen at Love Canal. Irving Selikoff, well known for his work on asbestos-induced disease, played a large role in the Michigan PBB contamination of cattle feed.[91] Such scientists have cooperated well with lay activists and are either unhampered by the organizational constraints government investigators face or willing to take the risks of being whistle-blowers.

By allying with epidemiologists and other professionals, activists provide valuable inputs. FACE members and

SPH scholars constructed the questionnaire in a consensual fashion. Barbara Wessen, who managed the Harvard/FACE study, writes: "The sessions were an educational give and take, at once mini-seminars in statistical and epidemiological methods for the community members and learning sessions for the 'experts.'" In this process, she continues, "FACE people provided creative input in such key areas as the lay phrasing of questions, defining vernacular units of measurement, such as using pounds rather than grams to define low birthweight or defining 'miscarriage' as pregnancy loss before 6 months, and determining endpoints."[92]

Community residents can also point experts to additional issues for study, such as community integration and political organization. As in the health care system, lay citizens can receive certain practical training so that they are not completely dependent on professionals. Marvin Legator and his colleagues have written a manual to enable lay groups to do just this—*The Health Detectives' Handbook: A Guide to the Investigation of Environmental Health Hazards by Nonprofessionals.*[93] The Environmental Action Foundation has also prepared a handbook, *Making Polluters Pay: A Citizens' Guide to Legal Action and Organizing,* dealing with both legal and health matters.[94] Barry Commoner, one of the earliest scientist activists in environmental affairs, argues that scientists have a special responsibility to inform and educate citizens and to work with them. He cites many successful collaborations, often on public initiative, on such issues as nuclear plants, pesticide controls, air pollution standards, and the mercury pollution of Lake Erie. This partnership, he holds, is "the clue to the remarkable upsurge of public actions on environmental issues."[95]

The Activist Nature of Popular Epidemiology

Popular epidemiology is by nature activist, because it involves the lay public in work that should be done by corporations, scientists, and officials. Popular epidemiology activists attack the corporate and governmental status quo. Popular epidemiology includes citizen-propelled investigation of naturally occurring diseases for which no firm is responsible. For instance, Lyme disease (first discovered in Lyme, Connecticut), was spread by deer ticks, but citizen activists became active around the issue because they considered health officials to be dragging their heels in the matter. Nevertheless, popular epidemiology is particularly powerful when the issue is environmental pollution, occupational disease, nuclear power, or drug side effects. In those cases the public sees persons, agencies, and corporations acting against the public health, often with clear knowledge of the dangers. Popular epidemiological investigation is furthermore essentially activist because its findings are immediately employed to alleviate suffering and causes of suffering. Popular epidemiology thus extends beyond the immediate effects of the local pollution. The Woburn plaintiffs' efforts went beyond their personal health problems from toxic waste: by uncovering evidence of Grace's dumping of TCE and other toxics, they aided an EPA investigation that led to a federal grand jury indictment and conviction against Grace for lying to the EPA about that dumping.[96]

By definition, environmental health activists act to correct problems that are not resolved by the established corporate, political, and scientific communities. The first logical step in protecting people from the hazards of toxic chemicals is corporate responsibility for the judicious use and safe disposal of toxic chemicals. It is well known that manufacturers are often lax in this sphere and frequently violate established laws and safe practices. For this reason, and because corporations purchase land and factories without knowing what toxic chemicals have been used there in the past, public agencies present the next line of defense. These include state and local boards of health, local water boards, state environmental agencies, and the federal EPA. Laypersons often begin at the agency level rather than the corporate level. But as the case studies of Woburn, Yellow Creek, Legler, South Brunswick, Love Canal, and many other sites indicate, public officials are often skeptical about, even hostile to, the advice and requests of citizens.

Even when public agencies agree to carry out studies, they often demand a different level of proof from what community residents want. Furthermore, agencies tend to undertake "pure" epidemiological research without reference to practical solutions to the problem. Even if they want to, many public bodies have no legal or effective power to compel cleanups, and they rarely can provide restitution to victims. Popular epidemiology emphasizes the practical side of environmental health issues, and activists often become impatient with the cautious approach of public agencies. As in so many other areas of public policy, the fragmentation of agencies and authority contributes to the problem. Community activists cannot understand why more immediate action is not taken, particularly because they are more apt than officials to define the situation as a crisis.

Popular Epidemiology and Social Movements

Because popular epidemiologists consider injurious products or actions a result of corporate and governmental action and inaction, they seek to place blame and responsibility on the appropriate parties and to obtain political, social, and economic redress. In many cases local activism is linked to similar cases around the country and to a specifically focused political movement.

Popular epidemiological projects lead many practitioners to a broader social understanding and political activism in other toxic waste issues on a national level. More than half the groups in Freudenberg's study cited accomplishments that extended beyond their own communities.[97] Activists often start out as citizens who notice that something is wrong; the obstacles imposed by corporations, political leaders, and public health officials force them to become activists. Frank Kahler from South Brunswick, Anne Anderson from Woburn, and Lois Gibbs from Love Canal provide examples.

Not all participants necessarily become full-fledged activists, but a noticeably critical attitude enters into the thinking even of those who do not expand their actions on a larger scale. Our Woburn interviewees, for instance, showed a great deal of antagonism to large corporations and unresponsive officials. Residents who joined the litigation against W. R. Grace and Beatrice Foods hoped that their suit would place blame on the corporations and focus attention on their actions in order to prevent future environmental health crises. Public health officials do not share this desire to blame companies; indeed, they shy away from doing so.

All social involvement can lead people to greater politicization. Environmental issues, along with other health issues, have become very salient, in part because of breakdowns in the environment and the social system and in part because of a new awareness. Environmental politics, which originated in natural resource protection, now emphasizes human health and safety. This change merges environmental politics with the tremendously significant health politics of recent years to create a major new social force in American society.

Like social movements in health care, the toxic waste movement stresses the public's right of access to specialized knowledge. Although residents in Woburn and other toxic waste sites struggle on many fronts, their efforts in the arena of scientific knowledge are especially significant. In their challenge to traditional science, they resemble antinuclear activists, the occupational health and safety movement, and the women's health movement, which resulted from and contributed to a public skepticism about the omniscience and beneficence of science and technology.

Popular epidemiology strongly criticizes the traditional view of scientific knowledge. Adherents know that they have made the difference in pinpointing toxic-waste-induced disease. When people realize their own scientific abilities, they develop strong self-esteem and self-efficacy, develop new frames of reference, and feel empowered to challenge political, economic, cultural, and scientific leaders and institutions.

In social composition, toxic waste activism differs from many other social movements, including the older environmentalist movement. Rather than largely middle class and upper middle class, members of toxic waste groups are typically middle or lower middle class. They are less educated and their leaders and members are most often women.[98] Indeed, large population surveys of environmental attitudes demonstrate that unlike other progressive ideologies, environmentalism is weakly related to social class. Summary measures of class do not show clear relationships to environmentalism because the components of those measures (education, income, and occupation) do not correlate in the same direction. Education is only slightly positively related to environmentalism and in some cases inversely related. Persons highest and lowest in income are slightly less pro-environment than those in the middle. Occupation relates to environmentalism by category of occupation, with service sector workers more environmentally oriented than those in the production sector.[99]

Also in contrast with other social movements, including the larger environmental movement, toxic waste activism proceeds through local groups. Organizations such as the Citizen's Clearinghouse for Hazardous Wastes offer important publicity and assistance to local groups, but no national membership organization exists. Nevertheless, in the absence of centralized organizations, popular epidemiology activists have managed to draw extensive public attention, because along with local efforts, society has come to see toxic waste as a major social problem. The public has a finite "carrying capacity" for social problems. Activists must compete for public attention, since only a few social problems can attain "celebrity status."[100]

The movement has certainly been fortunate in that public attention to toxic waste contamination has grown dramatically in recent years. Not only have toxic waste activists managed to grab attention by their own efforts, but many social institutions agree that environmental degradation is a fundamental concern of our time. The carrying capacities of certain public institutions (for instance, media, government, schools, civil organizations) have grown to absorb the demands for attention to this social problem. Further, the deep-seated significance of toxic wastes involves so many facets of society that through "problem-amplifying feedback," "activities in each arena propagate throughout the others."[101] For example, the public sees toxic waste contamination problems as firmly linked to such important issues as global warming, revisions in economic planning, product recycling and sustainable development, energy and water conservation, and international ozone protection. Thus although the toxic waste movement is distinct from the environmental movement, it has benefited from the larger environmental consciousness of our times.

This larger awareness is tied to public loss of confidence in scientific and governmental authority. Traditional sources of knowledge and authority have failed to prevent these environmental problems. With declining confidence in the scientific community and scientific solutions, there is a public antagonism to the emergence of an "intellectual technocracy" many feel has become an independent power.[102] People affected by toxic waste have already discovered the flaws in traditional science and government; their experiences have rubbed off on the general public as well.

In short, many people no longer accept on faith statements of scientific fact nor see science as an objective and compelling basis for policy-making, especially in the absence of lay involvement. Controversy, such as we see in toxic waste cases, demystifies expertise, exposes technical and political assumptions, and transfers problems from the technical to the political arena.[103] The questioning of science and technology has provided a nourishing medium in which popular epidemiology could develop.

Influencing Future Public Health Practices

Popular epidemiology can become a major influence on public agencies that initially fail to do their work. The Woburn cluster was the major impetus for a new state cancer registry. The Woburn case also played a significant role in the passage of a Massachusetts law to monitor toxic wastes in water supplies. Many other Massachusetts communities have been spurred by the Woburn activism to demand fuller investigation and disclosure of environmental risks. Woburn activists have made public statements about a number of other community sites, and official and media references to the Woburn precedent are commonplace. In 1986, local groups were able to obtain a state legislative order directing the DPH to release the names of nine sites then being studied for excess cancer; before the rise of local activism, the DPH had kept this information secret.[104]

Woburn activism has also contributed to research on Woburn itself: as we noted earlier, this research includes a prospective and retrospective study of reproductive outcomes by the Massachusetts DPH and the CDC, a new case-control leukemia study by the DPH, a new water distribution model for wells G and H to be used in conjunction with the reproductive outcomes study and a reanalysis of the Harvard/FACE study, and an MIT study of health effects, including genetic changes resulting from toxic wastes. Environmental activism has led to shifts in EPA practices as well, even though the EPA remains weak and often resists popular initiatives. Woburn residents' testimony was crucial for the $9 billion reauthorization of the Superfund in October 1986 and contributed to the national attention paid to the Woburn tragedy. Unfortunately, the Reagan era has instigated deregulation in all spheres, and environmental protection is a particular target for cutbacks.

Environmental health hazards have historically been identified and controlled by scientific research and government regulation. But the environmental activism of the past decade has made community groups a potent third force in environmental hazard action. Freudenberg found that community groups believed that they had been successful in meeting their goals: 37 percent said they had been very successful, 46 percent that they had been somewhat successful. Almost half reported that they had eliminated or reduced their targeted hazard.[105]

Even when government units have felt attacked by

community groups, they have sometimes accepted the fact that lay pressure sped up their response to a toxic waste crisis. This was evident, for instance, at the Stringfellow dump site near Santa Ana, California, where the Parents of Jurupa prompted increased monitoring of the well, collection of air and water samples, and the closing of the site. In Legler, New Jersey, the local government, perhaps one of the most contentious, ultimately recognized the activists' actions.[106] Clearly, popular epidemiology and other forms of community involvement have emerged as significant social forces.

5

Making It Safe

Securing Future Health

As we have seen, residents of Woburn and other toxic waste sites have become practitioners of popular epidemiology, working hard and sometimes obtaining toxic waste remedies and justice. But the burden of fighting against toxic waste should not be borne by the affected communities alone. We must mount a national and international effort to combat existing contamination and to prevent future environmental degradation. Since the environmental politics of toxic waste contamination concerns the whole society, all sectors of society must take responsibility for it. How can we make the environment as safe as possible?

Public Awareness of Toxic Waste Problems

First we must step up public pressure on responsible parties. Such pressure is possible only with public awareness of toxic waste problems. We do have evidence that people are growing more aware of environmental problems. Quality of Employment surveys in 1969, 1972, and 1977 by the University of Michigan Institute for Social Research show growing environmental awareness over time among workers. Between 1969 and 1977, those who said

164

they were exposed to workplace hazards increased from 38 percent to 78 percent.[1]

Another recent survey of 429 citizens found most were concerned about every area of technological risk (contaminated drinking water, nuclear war, accidents at nuclear power plants, cancer-causing chemicals, to name a few). Women were more concerned than men about six out of ten risks. People with higher education were less concerned about six out of ten risk areas, and people with higher income were less concerned about three out of ten areas.[2] These findings contradict sociologists' preconceptions about the relationship of income and education to environmental concern.[3] As mentioned in the previous chapter, the toxic waste movement has a largely working-class and lower-middle-class composition.

When asked what organizations or groups they trusted, 97.6 percent of the respondents considered university scientists to be completely or somewhat trustworthy. Next in trustworthiness were state agency officials (88.4 percent) and public interest groups such as Sierra Club and Common Cause (81.3 percent), although most respondents placed these two groups in the "somewhat" rather than "completely" trustworthy category. Federal agencies were trusted by 74.2 percent, although most of those surveyed considered these only "somewhat trustworthy."[4] This result is surprising, since government officials often cover up or suppress necessary information on toxic hazards while public interest groups are making it public. Perhaps people still have a hard time giving up on the normal institutions of the social order.

When asked who had the greatest influence on decision making about health and safety risks of technology, respondents pointed to politicians but also said politicians ought to have the least influence. Similarly, the respondents preferred university experts to have the most influence, but perceived their influence to be fairly low. The respondents preferred residents in affected areas to have the second most influence, but felt that they ranked last in actuality.[5]

In studies of public trust at local toxic waste sites we find mixed data. In Williamstown, Vermont, where a large dry cleaning establishment contaminated the major municipal well and one elementary school with TCE, the public trusted the local citizens group much more than the town government. The citizens group lobbied for extensive testing, organized demonstrations, led a boycott that urged the schools be closed until proved safe, and founded a statewide group to combat toxic waste throughout Vermont. In Acton, Massachusetts, where two contaminated wells were found, local officials were supportive of activists, stringent about water quality, and quick to act on water purification. As a result, the public was very trusting of both local groups and government.[6]

Evidence for increased public awareness and activism can be seen in the sheer number of toxic waste crises and community mobilizations, a number of which we have discussed in this book. The burgeoning grass-roots movement makes it likely that many people not personally affected by toxic wastes know of the problem. Toxic activism is so much a local effort involving previously uninvolved citizens that the extent of the movement indicates a change in public perception of risk; because many people now view the world around them as full of hazards, they are more willing to organize. Environmental and toxic waste activists have succeeded in winning various federal and state legislation, even if the implementation of that legislation often falls far short of what is needed. This legislation, in turn, encourages greater public awareness.

New Frontiers of Science, Medicine, and Law

Environmental activism has expanded our frontiers of knowledge, which in turn can increase environmental protection. Woburn and other toxic waste cases have helped to create new frontiers in science, medicine, and law. Toxic waste cases have highlighted new definitions of disease, innovative causal linkages and etiological mechanisms, the significance of mental health effects, and the growing understanding of immune system defects. Not surprisingly, these medical and scientific issues are integrally related to new approaches to legal liability, for toxic waste victims and their supporters must go to court for redress and in the process must discover new legal approaches. Indeed, the courtroom is increasingly the forum where scientific knowledge is debated. Several specific legal, medical, and political issues need additional work if progress is to continue.

Insidious and Latent Injuries

To remedy existing and future toxic waste contaminations, we must reconceptualize the causal linkage between substance and disease and rethink the disease process itself. Disease from toxic waste contamination is typically of the type called "insidious injuries": "Injuries are insidious when the links between their causes and manifest symptoms are obscure. This is particularly common where the symptoms are those of a general disease rather than a specific trauma, for example, lung cancer rather than a broken bone."[7] Insidious injuries appear only after a latency period, strike only a portion of the exposed population, affect people widely dispersed through the population, and become manifest by increasing risk rates for diseases that also have other causes.[8] Toxic waste effects can also fall into the category of "latent disorders": "environmentally produced, degenerative diseases in which there is a substantial time lag between exposure and consequence."[9]

In establishing a link between toxic waste and disease, causality is both crucial and problematic. Whereas it is fairly easy to prove that brake failure led to an auto accident, it is much harder to show that kind of connection with toxics. Even with faulty brakes you cannot prove without doubt that every accident would result in the same damage. Juries and judges are generally willing to accept the basic laws of mechanics involved in blaming faulty auto parts or maintenance for accidents. Toxic cases usually seem much less clear-cut:

> Many environmental diseases do not have a unique
> and temporally proximate relationship between cause
> and effect. Long-latent diseases caused by environ-
> mental exposures, such as lung cancer, chronic bron-
> chitis, and leukemia, are also caused by non-environ-
> mental factors. Environmental hazards may also
> increase the severity of diseases caused by other fac-
> tors. While scientific evidence may demonstrate excess
> risk in populations exposed to an environmental haz-
> ard, it is usually impossible to present evidence equiva-
> lent to: "The product exploded, injuring the plain-
> tiff."[10]

Scientific evidence for toxic waste injuries is often indirect because exposure records are rare and exposure is hard to reconstruct. Scientists estimate toxicity by extrapolating from high to low doses and from animal responses to humans, methods difficult to apply to the Woburn leukemia victims.[11] The power differential between corporations and individuals affects the ability to get information and funds to pursue cases involving insidious diseases. It took several decades of legal work for lawyers to amass sufficient evidence to litigate effectively against Johns-Manville. Moreover, individuals have limited life spans, but corporations go on indefinitely.[12] When decades of data are involved, this difference makes the epidemiological task quite difficult. All in all, the murky cause-and-effect connection and long latency period of toxic waste illness are serious problems for activists, lawyers, and the public.[13]

The Problem of Causality

Toxic wastes, perhaps the most common source of insidious injuries, raise thorny questions of corporate versus individual responsibility, the choice of legal doctrines in lawsuits, the power differential of corporations and individuals, and the appropriate role for government. For instance, despite clear evidence that asbestos causes asbestosis, mesothelioma, and lung cancer, the Johns-Manville Corporation argued that "individual susceptibilities" were the problem. Manville wanted to avoid publicity, so it settled claims out of court. It also limited information reaching workers at Manville factories, sponsored research to cast doubt on warnings about asbestos, and withheld from publication any data that showed dangers.[14]

Manville received government support in the form of bills introduced in Congress to create a federal pool of funds to pay claimants. With federal bailout funds, taxpayers would carry what the company considered the burden of changing standards of legitimate business practices.[15]

Despite the problem of determining cause, plaintiffs appear to be winning some toxic tort cases. It is possible that the legal system is accommodating plaintiffs' novel claims of causality: "In general, if a court is given no evidence affirmatively establishing some other cause of the plaintiff's harm and the plaintiff's short-cut causal chain is supported by evidence of observable events, the court will allow a jury to rely on such evidence in rendering its decision."[16] People have commonsense beliefs that exposure could cause certain diseases even without medical proof, and they bring these beliefs to their jury work. Moreover, if an accused polluter has exercised inadequate care and has been willfully negligent, the court is more likely to ease the plaintiff's burden of demonstrating cause. In practice, then, legal determination of cause includes consideration of the degree to which a polluter violated appropriate standards of care.[17]

Some judges have stretched the definition of negligence so that innocent victims could receive compensation. Recently, strict liability standards applied in toxic waste cases have also loosened the legal burden on victims to show direct harm, since many insidious injuries "come from actions that affect the statistical distribution of risk rather than from actions that directly cause such injury or disease."[18] This shift is part of a general trend in the U.S. legal system whereby strict liability has been extended in product liability and even some medical malpractice situations. Still, toxic waste victims have not always fared well in courtrooms. As we mentioned earlier, the appeals court reversed the lower court ruling on the Velsicol case in the matter of immune disregulation.

Immune System Disorder

By their emphasis on immune disorder, participants in toxic waste mobilization have pushed against another medical-legal-political frontier. Immune-related disorders are in the vanguard of modern medical science. Advances in cancer research, the discovery of the mechanism of the AIDS virus, and organ transplant technology all point to the centrality of the immune system in health and disease. Toxic contamination cases add evidence to the immunological puzzle. Researchers and clinicians working with toxic victims have begun demonstrating that immune system defects may follow exposure to toxic chemicals.

The more researchers learn about immune disorder, however, the greater is the disaster portended for our future. Although knowledge may increase our ability to predict disease, it will probably also produce tremendous stress in people who have been or think they may have been exposed. It is interesting, then, to note a potentially strong link between laypersons' immunological knowledge and their emotional suffering. This theme came up repeatedly in our interviews with the Woburn families.

As with many new scientific advances, scientific and legal acceptance of new immunological approaches will take time. With toxic wastes, these two forms of acceptance are tightly linked, and the courtroom is a key platform for acceptance of scientific theories. The increasingly active role of the judiciary in medical and scientific knowledge and practice of the last few decades stems largely from lay challenges to official sources of knowledge. Whenever victims turn to the courts to demand remedial cleanups, medical care, and monetary awards or settlements, they must prove their scientific case, often with innovative theories and models. Toxic waste cases also provide innovative, ground-breaking scientists another forum in addition to scientific journals and conferences. Judicial decisions, as well as media coverage of the litigation, provide publicity that may be more useful to victims than reams of scientific articles.

Science and Society

The new frontiers of scientific knowledge developed not from a value-free forward march of science but from conscious decisions to examine data in a new light and to seek new sources of data. This intersection of science and politics is typical of all areas of science and medicine. Toxic waste tragedies in communities like Woburn contain numerous lessons and suggestions about public participation in science and politics.

Public Participation: Good Science and Good Politics

Some supporters of lay involvement in toxic waste issues view it simply as good politics. In other words, scientists and government ought to provide an appropriate formal mechanism for citizen participation, as in the 1960s and 1970s, when federal agencies agreed to activist requests for public input in environmental impact statements, recombinant DNA advisory panels, health systems agencies, and the National Science Foundation's citizen's panels on a variety of science and technology issues.[19] As it happened, that was not even "good politics," since public inclusion in federal science policy was ultimately undermined by government control of data and by insufficient information, training, and power for lay members of advisory boards.[20]

In some cases, the EPA's attempts to involve laypersons in toxic waste investigations and cleanups have been hampered by unclear definitions and goals. Simply mandating public involvement does not provide guidelines for achieving it. Agencies rarely have specific ideas about the proper extent of popular involvement and remain skeptical that the public can discuss risks and benefits rationally in the emotionally charged contexts of environmental hazard crises. Laypersons often discuss the risks of technology with different assumptions from the EPA and other federal and state agencies, whose highest priority is typically not the needs of affected communities. Bureaucrats may place higher priority on winning local support for EPA's agenda, providing an inexpensive and low-profile risk communication, or increasing the agency's visibility to show that they care for public input.[21] Clearly "public participation" in this context does not necessarily benefit community residents. If residents have experienced direct health effects, agency goals constitute an insult to their real needs.

The popular epidemiological approach to toxic waste contamination in Woburn and other toxic waste sites gives much more credibility and power to the lay public than does the governmental version of public participation. For advocates of popular epidemiology, lay involvement is not merely good politics but also good science, since it changes the nature of scientific inquiry. Community case finding and health surveys have provided data that would otherwise have been unavailable. Nor is popular epidemiology a unique instance of folk wisdom's providing many branches of science with significant data. Ethnobotanists, biochemists, and pharmacologists have learned much from folk medicine; botanists, geneticists, and agricultural planners have gained from the knowledge of farmers.[22] If scientists and government fail to solicit such data they may be lost.

Some state public health officials and agencies have moved toward consciously including input from citizens. In California, public health official Raymond Neutra advocates a general process, developed from a dump-site case that showed officials clearly how important the contribution of community members was. He assumes that residents in affected areas are often the first to notice untoward events, have useful suggestions about exposure routes, and are likely to be aware of transitory instances of high exposure. Apart from residents' rightful role in the process, he argues that local laypersons can be helpful also in the design, conduct, and interpretation of an epi-

demiological study. It is important to remember that, in
view of past experience, residents are often distrustful of
toxic waste studies. Consequently, Neutra argues for an
approach quite the opposite of that seen in Massachusetts: investigators should lay out, rather than hide, uncertainties; they should not avoid distrustful community
members, but seek them out. Officials should ask residents to select an expert to sit on an advisory committee.
Study results should be released directly to the community and distributed as they come out instead of as a finished product.[23]

Already, community efforts at popular epidemiology
have stimulated plans for future research and governmental action. A DPH study of the Woburn cluster led to
the reestablishment of the state cancer registry. The legislature mandated the new registry to collect data about
all tumors in the state.[24] Woburn activism has also contributed to increasing research on Woburn itself: the DPH
and CDC are conducting a major five-year study of reproductive outcomes in the city, utilizing both prospective
and retrospective data, with citizens playing a large role
in the research. The DPH is conducting a case-control
study of leukemia in Woburn. An MIT study will address
the role of genetic mutations caused by TCE in causing
leukemia.[25] Medically, the Woburn case led to the discovery of a TCE syndrome involving three major body systems—immune, cardiovascular, and neurological—which
is increasingly showing up in other TCE sites.[26] This discovery is significant because TCE is a common water contaminant in industrial states.

The Community's Appeal to Scientific Expertise

Despite these successes, popular epidemiology contains
elements of ambivalence, as in many areas of social ac-

tion. In Woburn, community residents developed strong arguments for their case-finding methods and a political basis for epidemiology. At the same time they treated with very special consideration the community health survey community volunteers conducted along with sympathetic researchers from the Harvard School of Public Health. They often spoke solemnly of "The Harvard Study," manifesting a belief (in practice, quite warranted) that the tag "Harvard" provided a special guarantee of validity. Some might argue that this faith in the Harvard study compromised the community activists' independence. To be sure, the Woburn residents were constantly worried about losing control, as they made clear to the Harvard SPH scholars, and settled in advance the degree of involvement. In the end, the Woburn residents' trust in the Harvard scholars was largely due to the mutual respect and involvement that characterized their relationship. The final report of the Woburn health study was authored by the SPH scientists but labeled a joint project with FACE.

The Harvard study was not the only "official" research focus for the Woburn activists. Indeed, they have continually put pressure on state and federal agencies to reorient research goals and methods. FACE and others in the community continue to sit on the Citizens Advisory Council, which participates in all phases of Woburn toxic waste research. These community activists are actively consulted by scientists involved in all the ongoing Woburn research, and FACE members feel they have finally made a mark on the state DPH, which has followed a number of their recommendations for further study.[27]

Although the Woburn activists retain a strong desire for scientific legitimacy, that desire does not jeopardize their independence. It indicates a conscious value-laden judgment in which they frame their political strategy.

They appeal to scientific legitimacy when it serves their needs, which is sound politics: Groups that aspire to a certain goal should marshal the best support they can get.

Their strongly political stance, however, in no way diminishes the underlying attitudes of these activists. They believe that corporations dumped toxic wastes, that these wastes leached into the public water supply, and that the contaminants caused leukemia. They further believe that traditionally cautious epidemiology cannot adequately uncover and analyze the data. They believe that any evidence should be made public and that the public should participate in research to uncover the causes of the problem. In fact, it is largely in the light of governmental and scientific opposition to lay involvement that these groups have developed their own methods of data gathering.

Lay attitudes are instinctive reactions to the problems of toxic waste contamination, not consciously planned programs. Community residents involved in popular epidemiology campaigns rarely have a well-formed conceptualization of their actions, at least in the sense that sociologists might expect. Nevertheless, community residents without backgrounds in the relevant science can develop what is, at least in practical terms, a very sophisticated approach. Popular epidemiology conceptualizations have no strong and explicit theoretical underpinnings. It is only when we look at popular epidemiology from the outside that it makes sense to conceive of it as a coherent approach.

Different Frames for the Social Context of Science

Lacking a set of political principles or a theoretical model to guide their investigations, laypersons who become activists around immediate environmental hazards typically approach their situations empirically, adding facts together in a cumulative manner. Anne Anderson and Bruce

Young, for instance, plotted leukemia cases on a map of Woburn to locate a geographical cluster. Laypersons follow hunches about causal relationships and seek expert help to confirm their beliefs. Anderson's formulation of a linkage between the water supply and leukemia was such a hunch. Because lay investigators believe that corporations or government are responsible both for the problem and the inaction or cover-up, they seek scientific data to buttress their claims. At that point, lay activists become less empirical and more theoretically driven. They recognize not only the causal chain but also the barriers to effective action in corporate and governmental malfeasance and inaction. Although they do not necessarily express themselves in theoretical formulations as a social scientist would, they are nevertheless extremely well informed and can put forth a compelling and logical argument. Many scientists who become involved with lay environmental activists learn to appreciate their knowledge, analysis, and commitment and argue that community activists have pointed scientists toward scientific knowledge previously unavailable.

We might expect that developing a strong new perspective would alter the future beliefs and actions of community activists. As seen in their new perspectives on toxic wastes, on corporate and governmental responsibility, and on the need for lay activism, these people's beliefs clearly have changed. Our interviews with Woburn residents provided ample proof of this. But future action is a different story. Some local environmental activists go on to further activism, but many do not. Woburn residents involved in the litigation have felt too vulnerable or burned out by the lengthy and trying legal struggle. Although they had the tremendous energy needed to deal with their local situation, few wished to expand their efforts. Woburn activists apart from the litigant families have also tended to remain centered in local action. They have not generally become involved in national environmental organizations or other political activism. Their efforts have a national direction, however, in that FACE continually advises community residents across the nation (and sometimes in other countries as well).[28]

Social scientists frame a context differently, referring to a theoretical background that in this case includes the assumption that science is not a value-neutral endeavor. Sociologists' knowledge of the field includes a growing body of literature in the sociology of science and of knowledge, medical sociology, social studies of science, and, more recently, environmental sociology. These studies provide numerous examples of how science is affected by professionalism, political processes, economic power, and institutional inertia. From this theoretical background, sociologists seek out a specific subject matter—in this case, community response to toxic waste problems—and generalize over a number of cases to find similarities and differences.

Scientists, however, do not usually place their efforts in an adequate social context. They believe that scientific knowledge and practice are separate from social factors or that social factors play minimal roles. If scientists do consider the social context of science, their understanding is likely to be an "add-on" to their science. In other words, starting as practicing scientists, they may come to possess a certain social framework. But this framework is unlikely to guide their scientific thinking as much as to temper it.

The new perspective observed in popular epidemiology or similar lay efforts may not be powerful enough to overcome years of professional education and socialization except in a small number of scientists. Those few who transcend the narrowness of their education and socialization may already identify themselves as radicals of one sort or another; they may be found in organized groups, such as Science for the People, and in intellectual/political groupings such as the growing feminist science network. Scientists who have not already launched out in such a departure from traditional science will not necessarily do so as a result of one experience with community responses to toxic hazards.

Lay Hazards and Professional Risks

Scientists may cling to the perspective of risk assessment, for instance, which does not adequately acknowledge the enormous destruction of life and habitat resulting from unfettered economic development. Social scientists, however, have emphasized the value judgments involved in accepting risks. Langdon Winner views the rise of risk assessment in the 1970s as a backlash against environmentalism: "Questions that had previously been talked about in such terms as the 'environmental crisis,' 'dangerous side effects,' 'health hazards,' and the like were gradually redefined as questions of 'risk.' "[29]

The difference between hazards and risks is much more than semantic. "Given adequate evidence, the hazards to health and safety are fairly easily demonstrated. . . . When hazards of this kind are revealed, all reasonable people usually can readily agree on what to do about them." If, however, we are assessing risks, "our task . . . becomes that of studying, weighing, comparing, and judging circumstances about which no simple consensus is available" because knowledge is uncertain:

> As one shifts the conception of an issue from that of hazard/danger/threat to that of "risk," a number of changes tend to occur in the way one treats that issue. What otherwise might be seen as a fairly obvious link between cause and effect, for example, air pollution

and cancer, now becomes something fraught with uncertainty. . . . Cases of actual harm—cancer, birth defects, other illnesses, deaths, damaged environments,
and the like—obviously connected to profit-making industrial practices, [are] yet sometimes treated as if
their reality were merely probabilistic. We may visit
the hospitals and gravesites, if we need to. We may
wander through industrial wastelands and breathe
deeply. But let us not pretend our troubles hinge on
something like a gentlemanly roll of the dice or that
other people's sickness and death can be deemed "acceptable" from some august, supposedly "neutral"
standpoint. That only adds insult to injury.[30]

While scientists and government leaders still defer to a
myth of nearly unblemished scientific success, sociologists
have begun to frame the questions differently. Charles
Perrow has introduced the concept of "normal accidents,"
attributable to the uncontrollable risks inherent in complex technologies. One component can interact (by design
or not) with one or more other components outside of
the normal production sequence, because of "tight cou-
pling," characterized by a lack of "slack" in the system.
Applying a systems sociology to Three Mile Island, ship
accidents, Chernobyl, Bhopal, the Challenger explosion,
and other catastrophes, Perrow shows us how deeply fal-
lible our science and technology are. At the same time,
government and corporate dependence on science and
technology leads to poor regulation and to cover-ups.[31]
Scientists may not wish to acknowledge the uncertainty
and unpredictability of science and technology. Consequently, laypersons without any professional commitment to certainty must be centrally involved in pursuing
information and action in toxic hazard detection, prevention, and treatment.

A Toxic Waste Policy for Securing Future Health

Any society-wide program must first focus on corporate and governmental responsibility. Beneath the numerous examples of corporate and governmental problem making and roadblocks are some general features of the American political economy that create pollution and stand in the way of its solution.

Corporate Malfeasance, Crime, and Cover-Ups

Corporate responsibility for environmental contamination involves legal and illegal actions as well as grey areas in between. The ordinary daily operations of the economy yield enormous, although legal, amounts of toxic wastes. Similarly, through lawful political involvement, corporations exert much influence on regulatory agencies. Because pressures for environmental protection are so recent, corporations used to easy methods of toxic production and disposal are largely unwilling to alter their traditional practices to comply with new laws and regulations.

American industry produces an amazing 250 million tons of toxic substances each year. Pesticides, solvents, plastics, and emissions into the air poison our environment because of wasteful production and the profit motive. Rather than install scrubbers, manufacturers allow their smokestacks to produce acid rain. Instead of disposing of hazardous wastes properly, companies bury them or dispose of them routinely through practices suitable for nontoxic substances. Rather than employ safe organic farming techniques, agricultural corporations overuse dangerous pesticides. Instead of taking the time really to study potential risks, manufacturers rush products to market in order to beat the competition. Instead of engineering durable products, the throwaway economy engages in wasteful production of disposable commodities.

Industrial firms spend millions of dollars annually to lobby against government regulation and to convince the public that corporations handle hazardous materials safely. Manufacturers sponsor corporate-oriented research and use their own partial data to pressure the EPA and other regulatory bodies. Simply by paying higher salaries, private firms can drain the pool of qualified scientists. Petrochemical and agricultural lobbyists put pressure on legislators and regulatory officials. Corporate campaign contributions also play a role; in 1982, twelve members of the House of Representatives who had just voted to weaken the Clean Air Act obtained $197,325 from ninety-three companies that had violated the act's air standards during the year. In addition, many regulatory staffers and officials are recruited from the companies they are pledged to regulate and later return to the private sector. Corporations stall environmental protection by long legal actions as well.[32] For example, in 1977 OSHA lowered the allowable benzene exposure in order to reduce the risk of leukemia. Under the old standards, about ninety-five of every 1,000 workers exposed to benzene on a daily basis were likely to get leukemia. The new limits would lower the expected rate to ten per 1,000. The American Petroleum Institute filed suit, arguing that OSHA failed to conduct a cost-benefit analysis. A federal appeals court set aside the OSHA standards, and the Supreme Court upheld the ruling. OSHA was forced to begin a longer process, and as a result it took a decade to put new regulations into effect.[33]

According to the U.S. Congress's Office of Technology Assessment, there are 600,000 toxic waste contamination sites in the United States. Of these, 888 have been designated or proposed by the EPA for Superfund cleanup, and 19,000 are under review.[34] Many of these sites are no doubt contaminated as a result of ignorance and accident, but many are the direct result of illegal or immoral actions by manufacturers, distributors, transport firms, and waste handlers. Even when companies may have contaminated their locales unintentionally, they have often covered up the outcome to avoid legal and financial liability. In recent years we have seen a growing number of trials and convictions of corporations for bribery, concealment of data, lying to environmental officials, and other illegal practices.

W. R. Grace and Beatrice were aware of the problems caused by the chemicals they employed; they even hid records from the government. Other cases we have cited reveal blatant environmental degradation—Velsicol specifically sought a rural location in which to dump carcinogens, and company officials openly spoke of their knowledge of health risks. Hooker Chemical gave the Love Canal school site to the town while requiring the government to indemnify it from any potential damages. One review of twenty-five toxic waste sites found that most illegal activities were carried out not in ignorance, but with full knowledge of their illegality.[35]

Corporations also utilize illegal dump sites and illicit waste haulers. Waste oil disposal companies sometimes mix toxic chemicals in the oil—the dioxin contamination at Times Beach and Moscow Mills, Missouri, occurred in this way. Many landfill operators ignore or violate legal procedures for storing wastes. Some waste haulers engage in "midnight dumping" or drip wastes out of trucks en route to disposal sites. Some bribe public officials to overlook those actions. Organized crime has made many inroads into hazardous materials handling as well as regular waste disposal.[36] Since many Third World countries have lax environmental protection laws, many American and European chemical companies, tanneries, and manufacturers now dump large quantities of hazardous material in Africa and South America.[37] Companies have also moved production facilities abroad for the same reason.[38]

Corporate corruption reaches even into the profit-making laboratories that test chemicals for toxicity. Investigations by the Department of Justice and the Food and Drug Administration led to a 1981 indictment of officers of Industrial Bio-Test Laboratories, the nation's largest commercial toxicology testing firm. The company falsified data and covered up its crime; its erroneous test data resulted in government approval of 212 pesticides.[39] Similarly, the growing business of cleaning up toxic waste has led to widespread corruption. In 1988, officials of twenty-three companies were arrested and charged with bribing an EPA inspector to overlook violations of asbestos removal policies. The companies represent a majority of all concerns in the New York area that handle asbestos removal.[40]

A particularly vile case of corporate corruption is Norelco's sale of 186,000 water filters between 1982 and 1986 when the company knew that its Clean Water Machine actually contaminated water with methylene chloride, a probable carcinogen. The company in fact still sells replacement cartridges for the filtering machines, although it stopped production of the machines because sales were poor.[41] Norelco's act was especially cruel because people have turned to water filters expressly to protect them from widespread contamination of drinking water.

Abdication of Governmental Responsibility

Corporate responsibility for toxic waste contamination, as we have seen, is integrally linked to the ordinary workings of the economic system. It stands to reason that government involvement will not necessarily erase that link.

Yet to some degree government regulation can be effective.

The early period of federal environmental regulation brought in many committed scientists and lawyers and yielded many positive results. Between 1970 and 1975, air pollution levels fell by 33 percent, largely because of reductions in carbon monoxide emissions. Between 1976 and 1980, children's blood lead levels fell 37 percent, because of reduction of lead in gasoline. The 1976 ban on PCBs led to a large drop in PCB levels in human tissue in the period 1977–1983.[42]

Even in good times, however, regulatory agencies are typically underfunded and short-staffed, unable to perform their tasks effectively. Their statutory powers to fine and otherwise punish violators are weak, and paying fines may be more cost-effective for corporations than reengineering production, distribution, or waste handling. As in most areas of public policy, environmental protection regulation is a mass of complex, often contradictory, statutes, regulations, legal precedents, and agency procedures. In addition, agencies such as the Department of the Interior, the Department of Agriculture, the Nuclear Regulatory Commission, and the Federal Power Commission must account to different congressional committees and associated interest group allies. Protection agencies are divided both vertically (federal, state, local) and horizontally (different agencies at each level), making for further confusion and overlap.[43]

After Ronald Reagan's inauguration in 1981, the government began a severe retrenchment in all areas of occupational and environmental protection. The president appointed antienvironmental officials such as EPA administrator Anne Gorsuch Burford, who had previously sued the EPA to exempt Colorado from some Clean Air Act standards, and interior secretary James Watt.[44] The

EPA's budget was cut dramatically; during its first three years, the Reagan administration eliminated one-quarter of the agency's staff positions.[45] The administration sought to curtail the Clean Air and Clean Water Acts. In November 1986, Reagan vetoed the Clean Water Act amendments that set new restrictions on toxic discharges, regulated municipal storm water discharges, required controls on street surface runoffs, and provided funds for protecting lakes and harbors; Congress overrode the veto in January 1988.[46]

Unfortunately, the EPA has relaxed or proposed relaxations of risk levels and standards for carbon monoxide, lead, and other substances. Beginning in 1982, the EPA's assistant administrator for pesticides and toxic substances, John Todhunter, led a campaign to allow higher carcinogen risks. Without much public attention, the government shifted from tolerating a risk of one extra cancer case per million to one per 10,000. Working with Roy Albert, head of the carcinogen assessment group, Todhunter developed a method by which the EPA would determine the highest dose in animals at which no carcinogenic effect was found, and then divide that by 1,000 to determine a new acceptable level of risk. In the opinion of Umberto Saffioti, chief of experimental toxicology at the National Cancer Institute, this method was "developed in the Stone Age of toxicology" and could be summed up as "Find a no-effect level in animals, divide by 1,000, and pray."[47]

From the very outset of the Reagan administration, EPA enforcement plummeted overall and regional offices were prohibited from undertaking toxic waste site cleanups without prior approval from Washington. This policy expressed a general sympathy with corporate polluters. In 1983 the Chicago regional administrator testified in Congress that he was ordered to allow Dow Chemical to edit an EPA report on Dow's role in dioxin contamination in Midland, Michigan. As a result, the EPA omitted segments of the report that attributed contamination to dioxin releases, that blamed Dow for major pollution of nearby rivers and Lake Huron, and that recommended against eating fish caught locally.[48] Burford preferred voluntary agreements with polluters to using Superfund money for cleanups.[49]

As a result of Reagan-era deregulation, clear reversals in environmental quality have occurred. Improvements in air quality achieved in the 1970s were reversed in the 1980s, partly because the EPA postponed the enforcement date for the Clean Air Act and failed to use sanctions granted by the 1977 amendments to the act. These sanctions include blocking federal highway funds and placing moratoriums on factory construction. EPA officials are concerned that enforcement would lead to economic dislocation.[50] Administration officials declined also to act on acid rain, which has destroyed marine life in so many lakes and coastal areas, for the same reason. In fact, Reagan went so far as to aver that acid rain does not exist. In the 1988 congressional debates on strengthening the Clean Air Act, the administration's indifference strongly contributed to the bill's defeat.[51]

Based on its ideology of unfettered private property rights and its avid opposition to regulation, the Reagan administration has opened fishing grounds to offshore oil drilling and national wilderness areas to mining, oil, and gas development. This policy was formulated by interior secretary James Watt in 1981 as he opened public lands without following legal procedures. The National Wildlife Federation sued the Department of the Interior in 1985, but a judge ruled against them in 1988, allowing over 170 million acres of public land to be exploited for commercial use.[52] Near the end of his second term, Reagan vetoed the designation of a wilderness area of 1.4 million acres.[53]

The Reaganite economic rationale for exploiting the environment led the EPA in December 1987 to refuse to hold oil and gas companies to the same toxic-waste-handling rules as other firms. The EPA was to have produced a study in 1982 on the 1980 legislation that temporarily exempted the oil and gas industry, but it did not begin until sued in 1985.[54] In April 1988 the EPA refused to introduce more stringent standards on sulfur dioxide emissions by power plants, heating plants, and smelters, despite clear medical knowledge of the effects of sulfur dioxide on asthmatic people. The decision was based primarily on the expense to plant operators of installing emission controls.[55]

A January 1988 report by the Center for Responsive Law, a group affiliated with Ralph Nader, asserts that the EPA has been derelict in setting water contamination standards, monitoring water quality, and prescribing treatment methods.[56] Environmentalist litigation was required to speed up the process. As a result of a suit by the Natural Resources Defense Council, a federal court set a deadline for compliance standards, which led to new water pollution rules in October 1988 designed to curb manufacturers' pollution of waterways.[57]

Environmentalists have consistently given poor ratings to the EPA's overall performance. They point out that during the first six years of the Superfund legislation (1980–1986), only six sites were cleaned up sufficiently to be removed from the priority list. A November 1987 report by the U.S. Public Interest Research Group, the National Campaign against Toxic Hazards, and Clean Water Action documented that the EPA had failed to respond well to the 1986 Superfund reauthorization, and was being lax in its cleanup projects.[58] The congressional Office of

Technology Assessment reported in June 1988 that the EPA was not complying with the Superfund amendments and that it suffered from a lack of leadership, a poorly trained work force, and unsafe methods of containing toxic hazards.[59] In September 1988, a report commissioned by the EPA itself found that the agency's research efforts were weak and its detection and prevention of pollution inadequate. The report accused the EPA of having slighted research in order to concentrate on regulatory efforts,[60] which in turn fell far short of what was needed.

EPA regulation of pesticides in food has taken a pro-industry turn. Prior standards under the 1958 Delaney clause of the Food, Drug, and Cosmetics Act prohibited any residues of carcinogens in food. The Food and Drug Administration had previously tried to bypass that clause but was defeated by a federal appellate court. But in 1988 the EPA circumvented that decision by promulgating lower standards, allowing the sale of foods that contain carcinogenic pesticides if the product presents a "negligible risk," defined as one excess cancer case per million.[61]

Outright scandal has rocked the EPA as well. The agency's administrator, Anne Gorsuch Burford, resigned under pressure following public disclosure and congressional investigations of her policy of withholding penalties on polluters. Superfund director Rita Lavelle was fired for allegations of favoritism toward polluters and was convicted of perjury during congressional testimony. Both Burford and Lavelle were accused of selecting or holding off on Superfund cleanups in certain regions in order to further 1982 Republican candidates for Congress.[62]

In the occupational safety and health arena, too, the government has reversed many previous gains and has failed to take adequate action. Reagan's appointee to head OSHA, Thorne Auchter, cooperated with the new labor secretary, Raymond Donovan, to revoke or withdraw many important regulations and policies, lowering acceptable levels of exposure to cotton dust instituted to curb brown lung disease, and abandoning labeling requirements for toxic chemicals in the workplace.[63] Auchter attempted to fire Peter Infante, the scientist responsible for a controversial study of benzene exposure among rubber workers and a vocal advocate of regulation. Infante had also taken a strong stand on formaldehyde levels; subsequent congressional investigation showed that Auchter had been influenced by complaints from the formaldehyde trade association.[64]

In the Reagan administration's first year, OSHA suffered an 18 percent decline in the number of inspectors, a 37 percent drop in the number of serious citations, and a 65 percent reduction in total amount of fines levied.[65] The failure of the Justice Department and OSHA to seek criminal prosecution for occupational health violations is particularly dangerous. A recent study found that states that made a greater effort in such prosecutions had many fewer deaths in the construction industry.[66]

The federal Office of Management and Budget (OMB) also played a role in hindering occupational safety measures. In 1985, OSHA required manufacturers to post hazardous materials warnings on bulletin boards for 1.4 million chemical workers. In 1986, 14 million more workers in 300,000 firms were included and in 1987, 18 million more workers in a variety of other occupations were added. The program was already a compromise, since the Senate defeated a House version that would mandate direct individual warnings annually to about 300,000 workers judged to be most at risk. The American Cancer Society estimated that such warnings, combined with medical monitoring, could prevent 250,000 cancer deaths in one decade. Yet the OMB held up the posted warnings in factories, citing the 1980 Paperwork Reduction Act.[67]

A well-known ideological position of the Reagan White House was that the federal government should continually do less. Despite a federal law authorizing money for the removal of asbestos from schools, the administration rescinded a $50 million appropriation, arguing that asbestos removal was a local responsibility.[68] Similarly, the Reagan-era EPA has maintained that air pollution is largely a local and state concern and that the federal government should not promulgate emission standards. This attitude militates against effective state regulation, since many states prohibit state regulation more stringent than federal regulation.[69]

The government not only argued for state and local responsibility, it even demanded individual responsibility. Federal officials have appealed to those elements of the public who are willing to accept known high risks. In 1983, EPA administrator William Ruckelshaus told Tacoma, Washington, residents that they were "free" to make the choice of health or jobs in regard to arsenic emissions from a copper smelter.[70]

The deregulation of occupational and environmental safety in the 1980s has a number of roots. Conservative, laissez-faire interests were already opposed to active government intervention that would curtail production. The economic crisis beginning in the mid-1970s fed the anti-regulation movement. The same factors underlie OSHA deregulation. Organized labor lost political and economic power as unemployment and falling wages led unions to forgo many safety concerns. At the same time, the economic crisis made the public and legislatures less interested in all forms of social regulation. Continuing economic crisis seemed to point to overregulation as its cause and to deregulation as the economic savior. This common belief persisted even though data show no economic cost to corporations from regulatory statutes. Con-

servative think tanks such as the American Enterprise Institute and legal groups such as the Mountain States Legal
Foundation succeeded in pushing the conservative agenda.
Under Gerald Ford (1974–1976) and Jimmy Carter (1976–
1980), the federal executive branch already was curtailing
activist leaders and staffers in OSHA. Under Ronald Reagan, the deregulatory movement blossomed. As Andrew
Szasz points out: "The social regulatory agencies were of
low priority to the new administration and they were well
hated by the fringe Right. They were ideally suited to be
given to the ultraconservatives as a juicy political prize.
Thus political considerations having little to do with the
environment or regulation per se led the administration
to head up these agencies with persons holding the most
extreme deregulatory views."[71]

The enormity of the problem makes it difficult for even
a well-meaning politician or administration to understand
its extent and to work to alleviate it. The nature of bureaucracy is to diffuse responsibility; it has become almost
an institutionalized way of avoiding issues. Judges may be
afraid to act as well, for fear of being inundated with new
cases.

Litigation and the Alternatives

Because both corporations and government have proved
inimical to environmental protection, persons harmed by
pollution have often turned to the courts. Litigation will
continue to be an important avenue for victims of toxic
exposure. As the Woburn families found, there is often
no other way to obtain the documentation necessary to
explain the disease cluster. In previous chapters, we saw
that the experience of working together on the suit provided the Woburn families with a new and satisfying social network. Their attorney and his colleagues brought

them great comfort and stability. By pursuing the legal action, the families learned a tremendous amount about toxic hazards, achieved prominence in the media, and served as beacons for other contaminated communities.

Sadly, our society lacks safeguards against catastrophes and remedies for traumatic losses, and tort cases have thus become a common way to allocate fault and responsibility. It may be a long time before major social transformations alter this pattern.

Toxic waste litigation is very lengthy, traumatic, and difficult and often fails to clean up the hazards or improve people's health. Alternatively, attorneys and others who have worked on Woburn and other toxic waste sites are trying "brokered" approaches in which communities, corporations, and government are brought together to work out solutions in a nonconfrontational manner. The first known success of this method occurred in 1989 at a toxic waste site in Lowell, Massachusetts. The Woburn families' lawyer, Jan Schlictmann, engineered a $2.75 million settlement between the Colonial Gas Company and eight families forced to move from land contaminated by cyanide and heavy metals. The mediation process took only six months, far shorter than any toxic waste litigation. The state DEQE will use $750,000 for testing and cleanup, and the remainder will provide $250,000 for each family.[72] To be effective, this model will require greater state funding for health studies, as well as health insurance coverage for detailed medical examinations of persons affected by toxic wastes. All parties can benefit from such an approach. Community groups and affected persons can achieve quicker remedies without the pain of litigation. Government bodies can serve the public better and avoid the common problem of disgruntled communities. Corporations can reduce their financial costs and the tarnished images that result from litigation. In addition, they may learn to improve their toxic-waste-handling procedures.[73]

Another alternative to litigation is effective government policy, which would include examining toxic waste sites swiftly and compelling the polluters to take remedial action. Government agencies could have the same statutory power to close down toxic plants and demand cleanup that now exists in public health inspection and supervision of food services. Woburn residents and others might well have been satisfied with a strong government effort on the community's behalf. Federal efforts, however, have so far been limited to cleanup promises (occasionally fulfilled) and sometimes to buyouts of properties from which authorities demand evacuation. No substantial federal or state aid has yet been extended to victims. Clearly, a much more far-reaching strategy is required.

A Program for a Safe Environment

Every community organization and victims group in the country that attacks even the smallest toxic waste problem now plays a role in furthering a progressive toxic waste and environmental policy. The extent of local organizing in the 1970s and 1980s has been astounding and has laid the groundwork for an even larger movement to come. As many activists and researchers note, the difficult task remains of forging a centralized, national movement with coherent leadership, a broad constituency, and a larger political context.

National organizations such as the Citizen's Clearinghouse for Hazardous Wastes, the National Campaign against Toxic Hazards, the Environmental Defense Fund, Environmental Action, and the Natural Resources Defense Council have become significant actors at the national level in this new movement, which is still largely

local and decentralized. The older environmental organizations, usually concerned more with wildlife and nature, have also changed their emphasis to some degree.
The Sierra Club, the Audubon Society, and Friends of
the Earth have taken up more toxic waste issues while
remaining largely conservationist. Newer conservationist
radicals, such as Greenpeace, offer a more militant direct
action approach. There is still no large national organization of toxic waste and environmental activists devoted
to the struggle for a safe environment, nor is there anything approaching the Western European Green parties
that could vie for seats in Congress and effectively raise
environmental issues in national elections.

Nicholas Freudenberg has put forth an outline of a
comprehensive political program for the environmental
movement, covering three major areas: democratic rights,
government responsibilities, and corporate responsibility.
Democratic rights would include community residents' and
workers' recognized rights to know the names, properties, and known health effects of all toxic chemicals in the
area or workplace, to inspect any sites suspected of being
dangerous, and to refuse to participate in any work or
project they find threatening to health and the environment.[74]

Government responsibilities would include strict enforcement of existing laws, more resources for all levels
of regulatory agencies, and a greater emphasis on environmental protection relative to military expenditures. The
government must develop and fund a major research
agenda to prevent or minimize exposure to toxics, to screen
new products for toxicity, and to prevent any exposure
to a substance not proved safe beyond a reasonable doubt.[75]

Corporate responsibility means that corporations would
compensate people and communities for damages and that
when no specific polluter can be located, the government

would tax an entire industry to establish a compensation fund. All toxic materials would be disposed of at the point of production; thus the need for hazardous waste transportation would be eliminated and incentives provided to recycle and to reengineer the production process. The burden of proof would fall on corporations to show, using industry funds and government criteria, that a new material is safe beyond a reasonable doubt. Corporate compliance with safe environmental practices would not include plant closings, layoffs, or runaway shops. Environmental regulations would be applied to U.S. corporations all over the world, thus prohibiting the use of other countries as dumping grounds or as sources for production and distribution of dangerous products.[76]

This detailed program is based on a deep and radical critique of existing social relationships. It offers the vision of a society that centers on human cooperation and a healthy and integrated environment, rather than on the profit motive and the drive to dominate persons and other life forms. The environmental movement addresses the future survival of the earth, now direly threatened by toxic chemical epidemics and poisonings, nuclear power meltdowns, nuclear weapons, climatic disasters such as the greenhouse effect, deforestation, desertification, leakages of recombinant DNA mutant organisms, and eradication of plant and animal species. Because the environmental movement includes all these concerns, it is indeed a most powerful and necessary movement tackling political issues at every level.

Conclusion

In this book we have traveled a long path from the initial discovery of the Woburn leukemia cluster. Although at times we may have seemed to stray from our topic, we are convinced that the individual community-level experience of toxic waste contamination is understandable only in the broader context. Moreover, the growing social awareness of environmental hazards and the impetus to change social and corporate policy result from an accumulation of local perceptions and actions such as the Woburn residents' popular epidemiology. This accumulation is not simply the sum of its parts, but is rather a deeper knowledge base, an activist effort, and a qualitative change in risk perception.

We need to emphasize once more a critical element of the social reality of toxic waste contamination and all other environmental health issues—at bottom, the only reason government and corporations pay attention to environmental and occupational safety issues is that the affected persons have recognized and acted on the problem. As we pointed out in chapter 4, this fact is borne out for many other components of health and illness: social movements have been necessary to bring medical, governmental, and public concern to health problems previously unrecognized or inadequately recognized.

Participants in social health movements do not necessarily grasp the larger framework, at least in the early stages of their endeavor. But fairly soon they experience the interweaving of their and others' efforts. As we have seen from our Woburn families, this experience does not necessarily drive local participants to join national movements, but it does help them to comprehend the national picture. In the future, an increasing number of lay disease detectors will probably choose to be continually active, since more and more people will be affected by toxic wastes. At the same time, more coherent national organizations will be required to catalyze and bind individual activists and groups.

Woburn residents have provided the American public

with an amazing example of what can be done by a determined, creative community that suffers from corporate polluters and government inaction. With no experience in toxic waste issues or in any form of community organizing, the members of affected families and of FACE pursued their cause and brought it to national attention. Along the way, the Woburn families and their allies have had a degree of victory in the out-of-court settlement with W. R. Grace and in Grace's conviction and fine for withholding data from the EPA. They also garnered support from people and groups around the country and encouraged other local toxic waste activists. They look to future victory in the Beatrice appeal for a more complete sense of fulfillment, but at any rate they have already made a significant impact on the country's environmental movement.

It is important to remember that community efforts at lay detection are difficult, painful, and lengthy. We have looked at efforts taking five or ten years or even longer, sapping energy, bringing loss and the pain of publicity, creating tensions in families and communities, and standing a good chance of failure. In the light of these difficulties, we should appreciate deeply the actions of victims and families who choose this route; and we must also be understanding of those who do not so choose. Both groups can be helped by the concerted action of the general populace. Those who take the path of popular epidemiology need individual, community, and national support and require new corporate, regulatory, and judicial policies to make their task easier. Those who have not taken the activist path may be prompted to do so if they have those new sources of support.

We found that crises of toxic waste contamination engender contradictory feelings and responses. People are disempowered and then empowered; they suffer from public attention and litigation yet find strength there as well; they endure stress from working in community organizations, even as those organizations provide needed social support; they lose friends and gain others. They discover that there may be no safe place, but still work to make their own place safe. That is where the struggle starts and ends—the search for a safe place.

Notes

Preface

1. Although the Department of Public Health counts only twelve, the Woburn activists count nineteen cases. We will say more about this later.

2. Joyce Maynard, "The Story of a Town," *New York Times Magazine*, May 11, 1986, p. 20.

3. Michael Edelstein, *Contaminated Communities: The Social and Psychological Impacts of Residential Toxic Exposure* (Boulder, Colo.: Westview, 1988), p. 103.

4. It is instructive that two important recent books on toxic waste exposure open with discussions of plague. Henry Vyner's *Invisible Trauma: The Psychosocial Effects of the Invisible Environmental Contaminants* (Lexington, Mass.: Lexington Books, 1988) begins with a description of the plague that decimated fourteenth-century Europe. Michael Edelstein's *Contaminated Communities* starts with comments on the London plague of 1665. Both authors argue that contamination by toxic chemicals is a plague of our time.

Chapter 1

1. Paula DiPerna, *Cluster Mystery: Epidemic and the Children of Woburn, Mass.* (St. Louis: Mosby, 1985), pp. 106–108.

2. A. V. Carbone, "The Saga of Lake Mishaum," *Woburn Daily Times*, December 2, 1969.

3. "Toxic Waste Problems Aren't New," *Woburn Daily Times,* June 12, 1980.

4. Dan Kennedy, "Riley Reportedly Complained," *Woburn Daily Times,* April 4, 1986.

5. Dan Kennedy, "Witness: Riley Ditch Was Called 'Death Valley,'" *Woburn Daily Times,* April 2, 1986.

6. Evan T. Barr, "Poisoned Well," *New Republic,* March 17, 1986, pp. 18–20.

7. "Pollution on Top of Pollution in River," *Woburn Daily Times,* February 11, 1972.

8. DiPerna, *Cluster Mystery,* pp. 75–82.

9. Ibid., pp. 54–60.

10. Michael Knight, "Pollution Is an Old Neighbor in Massachusetts," *New York Times,* May 16, 1980.

11. DiPerna, *Cluster Mystery,* pp. 111–155.

12. Ibid., pp. 155–161.

13. Ibid., pp. 164–173; Gerald S. Parker and Sharon L. Rosen, "Woburn: Cancer Incidence and Environmental Hazards, 1969–1978" (Boston: Massachusetts Department of Public Health, January 23, 1981).

14. Marvin Zelen, interview, Boston, July 1, 1987.

15. DiPerna, *Cluster Mystery,* p. 175.

16. Zelen, interview.

17. DiPerna, *Cluster Mystery,* pp. 176–199.

18. Kay Longcope, "After the Trial—Woburn," *Boston Globe,* October 17, 1986.

19. DiPerna, *Cluster Mystery,* pp. 200–211.

20. Ibid., pp. 209–215.

21. Diane Wood, "Unifirst Countersues for Toxic Allegations," *Woburn Daily Times,* June 3, 1985.

22. Gary L. Dorion, "One Chemical Contamination Suit Settled," *Woburn Daily Times,* October 25, 1985.

23. Jan Schlictmann, interview, Boston, May 12, 1987.

24. Barr, "Poisoned Well."

25. William K. Burke, "A Double Standard in Toxic-Waste Law," *Boston Globe,* April 5, 1987; Michael R. Edelstein, *Contaminated Communities: The Social and Psychological Impacts of Residen-*

tial Toxic Exposure (Boulder, Colo.: Westview, 1988), pp. 162–163.

26. Edelstein, *Contaminated Communities,* pp. 162–163.

27. "Sixth Circuit Strikes Awards against Velsicol Based on Immune System Injury, Risk of Cancer, *Toxics Law Reporter,* June 8, 1988, pp. 47–49; "Rehearing of Ruling Reducing Award Sought by Plaintiffs in Sixth Circuit Velsicol Case, *Toxics Law Reporter,* June 22, 1988, pp. 111–112; "Remand for Damages Recalculation Clarified by Sixth Circuit Panel in Rehearing Opinion," *Toxics Law Reporter,* September 7, 1988, pp. 448–449.

28. Longcope, "After the Trial"; Schlictmann, interview, Boston, May 12, 1987; Renee Loth, "Woburn, Science, and the Law," *Boston Globe Magazine,* February 9, 1986.

29. Steven W. Lagakos, Barbara J. Wessen, and Marvin Zelen, "An Analysis of Contaminated Well Water and Health Effects in Woburn, Massachusetts," *Journal of the American Statistical Association,* 1986, 81:583–596.

30. Zelen, interview.

31. J. Raloff, "Woburn Survey May Become a Model for Low-Cost Epidemiology," *Science News,* February 18, 1984.

32. Barbara Wessen, interview, Boston, April 3, 1987.

33. Lagakos, Wessen, and Zelen, "Analysis of Contaminated Well Water."

34. Ibid.

35. Ibid.

36. Steven Lagakos, interview, Boston, April 6, 1987.

37. Ibid.

38. DiPerna, *Cluster Mystery,* pp. 168–169.

39. Zelen, interview.

40. DiPerna, *Cluster Mystery,* pp. 251–273.

41. Zelen, interview.

42. Allan Morrison, lecture in the Epidemiology Colloquium series, Brown University, Department of Community Health, February 25, 1987.

43. Zelen, interview.

44. Richard A. Knox, "Professor Criticizes Woburn Study," *Boston Globe,* June 8, 1984.

45. Laurel Lucas, "Civil Liberties Union Wants Court 'Gag Order' Removed," *Woburn Daily Times*, October 17, 1985. Diane E. Lewis, "W. R. Grace Co. Official Denies Responsibility for Pollution of Wells," *Boston Globe*, March 2, 1986.

46. Dan Kennedy, "Pump Tests Tie Riley's Land to City's G Well." *Woburn Daily Times*, March 20, 1986. Dan Kennedy, "Riley Testifies Land Was Never Used as Dump," *Woburn Daily Times*, April 8, 1986.

47. Mark Sullivan, "Charts, Diagrams Show How Chemicals Reached Water Well," *Woburn Daily Times*, May 9, 1988. Dan Kennedy, "A Difficult Week for Plaintiff's Scientist in Toxic Trial," *Woburn Daily Times*, May 19, 1986.

48. William F. Doherty, "Jury: Firm Fouled Wells in Woburn," *Boston Globe*, July 29, 1986. Kennedy, "Witness: Riley Ditch."

49. Dan Kennedy, "Riley Admits He Failed to Comply," *Woburn Daily Times*, April 11, 1986.

50. Dan Kennedy, "Cryovac Worker Tells of Barrel-Dumping," *Woburn Daily Times*, April 14, 1986. Dan Kennedy, "Grace Exec. Tells of Barrel-Dumping," *Woburn Daily Times*, April 16, 1986. Dan Kennedy, "Cryovac Knew of TCE Hazards," *Woburn Daily Times*, April 21, 1986.

51. Dan Kennedy, "Cryovac Manager Requested Barrel Disposal," *Woburn Daily Times*, May 30, 1986.

52. Dan Kennedy, "Chemical Dumping Charges Leveled at Cryovac," *Woburn Daily Times*, August 28, 1985; Dan Kennedy, "W. R. Grace Hits FACE on Tactics," *Woburn Daily Times*, August 29, 1985.

53. Dan Kennedy, "Judge's Ruling Has Something for All Participants," *Woburn Daily Times*, June 5, 1986.

54. Jerry Ackerman and Diego Ribadeneira, "Twelve Families, Grace Settle Woburn Toxic Case," *Boston Globe*, September 23, 1986.

55. Schlictmann, interview, May 12, 1987.

56. Dan Kennedy, "Beatrice Wins Delay in Answering Appeal," *Woburn Daily Times*, July 17, 1987.

57. Jan Schlictmann, interview, Boston, June 3, 1988.

58. "Eight Families Seek New Trial against Beatrice Foods,"

Woburn Daily Times, October 13, 1987. Dan Kennedy, "Families' Lawyer Expects Early Hearing," *Woburn Daily Times,* October 14, 1987.

59. "Beatrice Foods Suit Ruling Is Appealed," *Boston Globe,* February 13, 1988. Anne Anderson et al. v. Beatrice Foods Co., 862 F. 2d 910 (1st Cir. 1988) (brief for the plaintiffs-appellants).

60. Elizabeth Neuffer, "Court Orders New Hearings in Woburn Pollution Case," *Boston Globe,* December 8, 1988.

61. Jerry Ackerman, "Woburn Case Families Press Claim with Aid of Ruling," *Boston Globe,* December 14, 1988.

62. Jan Schlictmann, interview, Boston, December 13, 1988; June 15, 1989; Neuffer, "Court Orders New Hearings"; Nick Tate, "Second Woburn Toxic Waste Hearing Set," *Boston Herald,* December 15, 1988.

63. Elizabeth Neuffer, "Food Giant Accused of Cover-Up," *Boston Globe,* April 7, 1989.

64. Elizabeth Neuffer, "EPA Testimony Sought by Eight Woburn Families," *Boston Globe,* February 2, 1989.

65. U.S. District Court, District of Massachusetts, C. A. No. 82-1672-S, Anne Anderson et al. v. Beatrice Foods Co., Findings Pursuant to Remand on the Nature of the Defendant's Misconduct, July 7, 1989.

66. Jan Schlictmann, interviews, October 23, 1989; January 10, 1990.

67. U.S. Department of Justice, Press release, Boston, U.S. Attorney's Office, January 28, 1987.

68. Ed Quill, "W. R. Grace Admits Lying to EPA," *Boston Globe,* June 1, 1988.

69. Schlictmann, interview, June 3, 1988.

70. Dan Kennedy, "Woburn Leukemia Rate Remains High," *Woburn Daily Times,* December 2, 1987; Richard Clapp, presentation at conference, "Examining Woburn's Health," Trinity Episcopal Church, Woburn, Massachusetts, April 24, 1988.

71. Dan Kennedy, "Markey Blasts EPA Delays in Woburn Cleanup," *Woburn Daily Times,* November 26, 1985.

72. Dan Kennedy, "Markey Using Woburn to Push for Superfund," *Woburn Daily Times,* November 27, 1985.

73. Environmental Protection Agency, "Settlement Reached for Cleanup of Industri-Plex Hazardous Waste Superfund Site," *Environmental News,* January 31, 1989.

74. Gretchen Latowsky, interview, Woburn, Massachusetts, May 26, 1988.

75. Dan Kennedy, "EPA to Say Pollutants Caused Leukemia," *Woburn Daily Times,* May 9, 1988.

76. Environmental Protection Agency, "Status Report of the Ad Hoc 'Woburn Workgroup.'" (Washington, D.C.: Environmental Protection Agency, June 2, 1988).

77. Dan Kennedy, "EPA Report Expected to be Under Fire," *Woburn Daily Times,* June 6, 1988.

78. Longcope, "After the Trial."

79. Richard Clapp, interview, March 13, 1987.

80. Latowsky, interview.

81. Ibid.

82. Dan Kennedy, "Citizens Group Angered by Funding Rejection," *Woburn Daily Times,* January 12, 1988.

83. Nancy Mades, "Commissioner Wants FACE-DPH Pact," *Woburn Daily Times,* April 7, 1988.

84. David Ozonoff, presentation at conference, "Examining Woburn's Health," Trinity Episcopal Church, Woburn, Massachusetts, April 24, 1988.

85. Eliot Marshall, "Woburn Case May Spark Explosion of Lawsuits," *Science,* 1986, 234:418–420.

86. Lois Therrien, Jonathan Tasini, and Richard Hoppe, "Why Business Is Watching This Pollution Case," *Business Week,* March 24, 1986.

87. Anthony Z. Roisman, "Proving Cause in Toxic-Tort Litigation: The Threshold of a New Era," *Trial,* October 1986, pp. 59–61.

88. Ibid.

89. Jane E. Brody, "Immunological Defects Found in People in Michigan Who Ate Food Contaminated by PBB," *New York Times,* August 2, 1977.

90. Ibid.

Chapter 2

1. Gretchen Latowsky, interview, Woburn, Mass., May 26, 1988.

2. Ibid.

3. Ibid.

4. Michael R. Edelstein, *Contaminated Communities: The Social and Psychological Impacts of Residential Toxic Exposure* (Boulder, Colo.: Westview, 1988), p. 141.

5. ICF Incorporated, "Analysis of Community Involvement in Hazardous Waste Site Problems," report to the Office of Emergency and Remedial Response, United States Environmental Protection Agency (Washington, D.C.: ICF, 1981), pp. 28–32.

6. Kurt Finsterbusch, "Citizens' Encounters with Unresponsive Authorities in Obtaining Protection from Hazardous Wastes" (Paper presented at the annual meeting of the Society for the Study of Social Problems, Atlanta, Georgia, August 1988).

7. Latowsky, interview.

8. Edelstein, *Contaminated Communities,* p. 44.

9. Latowsky, interview.

10. Alan Mazur, "Placing Hazards on the Public Agenda" (paper presented at the annual meeting of the American Sociological Association, Atlanta, Georgia, August 1988).

11. Lee Clarke, "Political Ecology of Local Protest Groups" (paper presented at the annual meeting of the American Sociological Association, Atlanta, Georgia, August 1988).

12. Paul Fortin, "The Dump," *Boston Magazine,* April 1981, p. 101.

13. William Sullivan, "Rabbit Irate over Toxic Trial by Media," *Woburn Daily Times,* February 20, 1986.

14. Elizabeth Kolbert, "Upstate Residents' Water Worries Help Move GE to Accord," *New York Times,* May 13, 1986.

15. Philip Shabecoff, "Uncertainties of a Chemical-Filled World Come Home to a Denver Suburb," *New York Times,* April 19, 1987.

16. Adeline Levine, *Love Canal: Science, Politics, and People* (Lexington, Mass.: Heath, 1982), p. 185.

17. Karl Reko, "The Psychological Impact of Environmental Disasters," *Bulletin of Environmental Contamination and Toxicology,* 1984, 33:665–671.

18. Robert J. Lifton, "Psychological Report on Three Mile Island Litigation" (unpublished manuscript).

19. Reko, "Psychological Impact," p. 185.

20. Edelstein, *Contaminated Communities,* pp. 14, 180.

21. Ibid., p. 14.

22. Martha Fowlkes and Patricia Y. Miller, "Love Canal: The Social Construction of Disaster," final report for Federal Emergency Management Agency (Washington, D.C.: Federal Emergency Management Agency, January 1983), p. 98.

23. Edelstein, *Contaminated Communities,* pp. 10–13.

24. Adeline G. Levine and Russell Stone, "Threats to People and What They Value: Residents' Perceptions of the Hazards of Love Canal" (unpublished paper, State University of New York at Buffalo, 1985).

25. Ibid., pp. 27–28.

26. Fowlkes and Miller, "Love Canal."

27. Study Commission on Environmental Health Issues, *Final Report* (Boston: Massachusetts Department of Public Health, February 1984), p. 15.

28. Edelstein, *Contaminated Communities,* pp. 27–28, 50.

29. Lois Marie Gibbs, "Community Response to an Emergency Situation: Psychological Destruction and the Love Canal" (paper presented at the meeting of the American Psychological Association, August 24, 1982).

30. Martha Fowlkes and Patricia Y. Miller, "Chemicals and Community at Love Canal," pp. 55–78 in Brandon B. Johnson and Vincent T. Covello, eds., *The Social and Cultural Construction of Risk* (New York: Reidel, 1987).

31. Henry M. Vyner, *Invisible Trauma: The Psychosocial Effects of the Invisible Environmental Contaminants* (Lexington, Mass.: Lexington Books, 1985), pp. 15–16.

32. Ibid., pp. 18, 30.

33. Ibid., p. 31.

34. Ibid., pp. 11–12.

35. Ibid., pp. 22–25, 90.

36. Dorothy Nelkin and Michael S. Brown, *Workers at Risk: Voices from the Workplace* (Chicago: University of Chicago Press, 1984), p. 86.

37. Ibid., pp. 87–96.

38. Lee Clarke, "Explaining Choices among Technological Risks," *Social Problems,* 1988, 35:22–35.

39. Fowlkes and Miller, "Chemicals and Community."

40. Levine and Stone, "Threats to People."

41. Bruce P. Dohrenwend et al., "Stress in the Community: A Report to the President's Commission on the Accident at Three Mile Island," *Annals of the New York Academy of Sciences,* 1981, 365:159–174.

42. Edelstein, *Contaminated Communities,* p. 81.

43. Levine and Stone, "Threats to People."

44. Fowlkes and Miller, "Chemicals and Community."

45. Ibid.

46. Yvonne Vissing, "The Difficulties in Determining Elite Deviance: Dow Chemical Company and the Dioxin Controversy" (paper presented at the annual meeting of the Society for the Study of Social Problems, San Antonio, Texas, August 1984).

47. Lindsey Gruson, "Town Takes Toxic Wastes in Stride," *New York Times,* March 4, 1987.

48. Edelstein, *Contaminated Communities,* pp. 121–127.

49. Levine and Stone, "Threats to People."

50. Edelstein, *Contaminated Communities,* p. 61.

51. Levine, *Love Canal,* pp. 196–199.

52. Nicholas Freudenberg, *Not in Our Backyards: Community Action for Health and the Environment* (New York: Monthly Review Press, 1984), pp. 182–184.

53. Ibid., p. 212.

54. Ibid., pp. 121–127.

55. Gibbs, "Community Response to an Emergency."

56. Ibid., p. 7.

57. Levine and Stone, "Threats to People."

58. Edelstein, *Contaminated Communities,* p. 144.

59. ICF Incorporated, "Analysis of Community Involvement," pp. 93–96.

Chapter 3

1. In this chapter we draw extensively from our interviews with the Woburn victims and their families. All unreferenced quotes are from those interviews. As we mentioned earlier, we have chosen to keep the victims and family members anonymous.

2. Michael R. Edelstein, *Contaminated Communities: The Social and Psychological Impacts of Residential Toxic Exposure* (Boulder, Colo.: Westview, 1988), p. 66.

3. Robert Jay Lifton, "Psychological Report on Three Mile Island Litigation" (unpublished manuscript), p. 63.

4. Ibid.

5. Steven W. Lagakos, Barbara J. Wessen, and Marvin Zelen, "An Analysis of Contaminated Well Water and Health Effects in Woburn, Massachusetts," *Journal of the American Statistical Association*, 1986, 81:583–596; Steven W. Lagakos, Barbara J. Wessen, and Marvin Zelen, *The Woburn Health Study: An Analysis of Reproductive and Childhood Disorders and Their Relation to Environmental Contamination* (Boston: Harvard School of Public Health, Department of Biostatistics, 1984).

6. Steven Lagakos, interview, Boston, April 6, 1987.

7. V. S. Byers et al., "Association between Clinical Symptoms and Lymphocyte Abnormalities in a Population with Chronic Domestic Exposure to Industrial Solvent–Contaminated Domestic Water Supply and a High Incidence of Leukaemia," *Cancer Immunology and Immunotherapy*, 1988, 27:77–81.

8. Robert G. Feldman, Jeanette Chirico-Post, and Susan P. Proctor, "Blink Reflex Latency after Exposure to Trichloroethylene in Well Water," *Archives of Environmental Health*, March/April 1988, 43(2):143–148.

9. Byers et al., "Association between Clinical Symptoms."

10. The rest of this chapter details our observations from two sets of interviews with the families suffering from leukemia (one family declined to be reinterviewed). The first interview (1985) focused mainly on psychological and psychiatric issues. The second interview (1987) followed up issues raised in the initial interview, though we emphasized the families' overall re-

sponse to the toxic waste contamination and their views of the problem in a larger context.

11. Henry M. Vyner, *Invisible Trauma: The Psychosocial Effects of the Invisible Environmental Contaminants* (Lexington, Mass.: Lexington Books, 1988), pp. 97–98.

12. Lifton, "Psychological Report," p. 44.

13. Vyner, *Invisible Trauma,* pp. 97–98.

14. Lois Marie Gibbs, "Community Response to an Emergency Situation: Psychological Destruction and the Love Canal" (paper presented at the meeting of the American Psychological Association, August 24, 1982).

15. Evelyn J. Bromet et al., "Mental Health of Residents near the Three Mile Island Reactor: A Comparative Study of Selected Groups," *Journal of Preventive Psychiatry,* 1982, 1:225–276.

16. Lifton, "Psychological Report," pp. 41–42.

17. Vyner, *Invisible Trauma,* p. 143.

18. Lifton, "Psychological Report."

19. Robert J. Lifton and Eric Olson, "The Human Meaning of Total Disaster: The Buffalo Creek Experience," *Psychiatry,* 1976, 39:1–18.

20. Bruce P. Dohrenwend et al., "Stress in the Community: A Report to the President's Commission on the Accident at Three Mile Island," *Annals of the New York Academy of Sciences,* 1981, 365:159–174.

21. Ibid.

22. Andrew Baum, Raymond Fleming, and Jerome E. Singer, "Coping with Victimization by Technological Disaster," *Journal of Social Issues,* 1983, 39:117–138.

23. India Fleming and Andrew Baum, "Chronic Stress in Residents near a Toxic Waste Site" (paper presented at the meeting of the Eastern Psychological Association, Baltimore, Maryland, 1984).

24. Kenneth M. Bachrach and Alex J. Zautra, "Coping with a Community Stressor: The Threat of a Hazardous Waste Facility," *Journal of Health and Social Behavior,* 1985, 26:127–141.

25. Mary Amanda Dew et al., "Mental Health Effects of the Three Mile Island Nuclear Reactor Restart," *American Journal of Psychiatry,* 1987, 144:1074–1077.

26. Vyner, *Invisible Trauma,* pp. 171–172.

27. Ibid., p. 173.

28. Jean Comaroff and Peter Maguire, "Ambiguity and the Search for Meaning: Childhood Leukemia in the Modern Clinical Context," *Social Science and Medicine,* 1981, 15B:115–123.

29. Edelstein, *Contaminated Communities,* p. 97.

30. David Ozonoff, interview, Boston, August 1, 1988.

31. Edelstein, *Contaminated Communities,* pp. 93–95.

32. Gibbs, "Community Response to an Emergency," p. 11.

33. Edelstein, *Contaminated Communities,* p. 114.

34. Adeline Levine, *Love Canal: Science, Politics, and People* (Lexington, Mass.: Lexington Books, 1982), p. 185.

35. Elizabeth Smith et al., "Psychosocial Consequences of a Disaster," pp. 50–76 in James H. Shore, ed., *Disaster Stress Studies: New Methods and Findings* (Washington, D.C.: American Psychiatric Press, 1988).

36. Lifton and Olson, "Human Meaning of Total Disaster."

37. Lifton, "Psychological Report," p. 55.

38. Ibid.

39. Edelstein, *Contaminated Communities,* p. 77.

40. Robert Miller, " 'I'm from the Government and I'm Here to Help You': Fieldwork at Times Beach and Other Missouri Dioxin Sites" (paper presented at the annual meeting of the Society for the Study of Social Problems, San Antonio, Texas, August 1984).

41. Karl Reko, "The Psychological Impact of Environmental Disasters," *Bulletin of Environmental Contamination and Toxicology,* 1984, 33:665–671.

42. Beverly Raphael, *When Disaster Strikes: How Individuals and Communities Cope with Catastrophe* (New York: Basic Books, 1986).

43. Baum et al., "Coping with Victimization."

44. Martha Fowlkes and Patricia Y. Miller, "Unnatural Disaster at Love Canal," pp. 23–41 in Michael T. Charles and John Choon K. Kim, eds., *Crisis Management: A Casebook* (Springfield, Ill.: Thomas, 1988).

45. Lifton, "Psychological Report," p. 60.

46. Ibid., p. 56.

47. Robert Hershey, "Grace Study on Federal Spending Called Assault on Social Programs," *New York Times*, August 29, 1985.

48. William A. Gamson, Bruce Fireman, and Steven Rytina, *Encounters with Unjust Authority* (Chicago: Dorsey, 1982), p. 14.

49. Kurt Finsterbusch, "Citizens' Encounters with Unresponsive Authorities in Obtaining Protection from Hazardous Wastes" (paper presented at the annual meeting of the Society for the Study of Social Problems, Atlanta, Georgia, August 1988), p. 7.

50. Celene Krauss, "Community Struggles and the Shaping of Democratic Consensus," *Sociological Forum*, 1989, 4:227–239, 236.

51. Ibid.

Chapter 4

1. Abraham Lillienfeld, *Foundations of Epidemiology*, 2d ed. (New York: Oxford, 1980) p. 4.

2. Sheldon Krimsky, personal communication, Cambridge, Mass., October 11, 1988; Alonzo Plough, personal communication, October 11, 1988.

3. Howard Frumkin and Warren Kantrowitz, "Cancer Clusters in the Workplace: An Approach to Investigation," *Journal of Occupational Medicine*, 1987, 29:949–952.

4. June Nash and Max Kirsch, "Polychlorinated Biphenyls in the Electrical Machinery Industry: An Ethnological Study of Community Action and Corporate Responsibility," *Social Science and Medicine*, 1986, 23:131–138.

5. "'Quiet Triumph' at Hazardous-Waste Site in Jersey," *New York Times*, May 4, 1986.

6. Nicholas Freudenberg, *Not in Our Backyards: Community Action for Health and the Environment* (New York: Monthly Review Press, 1984), p. 112.

7. Richard A. Couto, "Failing Health and New Prescriptions: Community-Based Approaches to Environmental Risks,"

pp. 53–70 in Carole E. Hill, ed., *Current Health Policy Issues and Alternatives: An Applied Social Science Perspective* (Athens: University of Georgia Press, 1986), at p. 55.

8. Adeline Gordon Levine, *Love Canal: Science, Politics, and People* (Lexington, Mass.: Heath, 1982), pp. 14–15.

9. Celene Krauss, "Grass-Root Protests and Toxic Wastes: Developing a Critical Political View" (paper presented at the meeting of the American Sociological Association, New York, August 1986).

10. Claire Safran, "The War on Toxic Waste," *Newsday*, October 4, 1983, p. 49.

11. Ibid.

12. Couto, "Failing Health."

13. Nash and Kirsch, "Polychlorinated Biphenyls."

14. Lonny Shavelson, "Tales of Troubled Waters," *Hippocrates*, March/April 1988, p. 74.

15. Michael R. Reich, "Environmental Politics and Science: The Case of PBB Contamination in Michigan," *American Journal of Public Health*, 1983, 73:302–313.

16. Ibid.; Paula DiPerna, *Cluster Mystery: Epidemic and the Children of Woburn, Mass.* (St. Louis: Mosby, 1985), pp. 93–94.

17. Sam Howe Verhovek, "A Bronx Landfill Raises Concern over Diseases," *New York Times*, June 27, 1988.

18. Martha Fowlkes and Patricia Y. Miller, "Love Canal: The Social Construction of Disaster" (final report for Federal Emergency Management Agency, January, 1983), p. 70.

19. Ibid., pp. 80–81.

20. Helen Rodriguez-Trias, "The Women's Health Movement: Women Take Power," pp. 107–126 in Victor Sidel and Ruth Sidel, eds., *Reforming Medicine: Lessons of the Last Quarter Century* (New York: Pantheon, 1984).

21. Daniel Berman, "Why Work Kills: A Brief History of Occupational Health and Safety in the United States," *International Journal of Health Services*, 1977, 7:63–87.

22. Freudenberg, *Not in Our Backyards.*

23. Steven W. Lagakos, Barbara J. Wessen, and Marvin Zelen, "An Analysis of Contaminated Well Water and Health Ef-

fects in Woburn, Massachusetts," *Journal of the American Statistical Association,* 1986, 81:583–596.

24. Beverly Paigen, "Controversy at Love Canal," *Hastings Center Report,* 1982, 12(3):29–37.

25. David Ozonoff and Leslie I. Boden, "Truth and Consequences: Health Agency Responses to Environmental Health Problems," *Science, Technology, and Human Values,* 1987, 12:70–77.

26. Anders Grimvall and Rolf Ejvegard, "The Dynamics of Scientific Uncertainty and Its Implications for the Use of Conservative Procedures in Risk Analysis," pp. 23–29 in Per Oftedal and Anton Brogger, eds., *Risk and Reason: Risk Assessment in Relation to Environmental Mutagens and Carcinogens* (New York: Liss, 1986).

27. The discussion of Type I and Type II errors in toxic waste contamination has been independently applied by Couto, "Failing Health"; Paigen, "Controversy at Love Canal"; Levine, *Love Canal;* and Michael R. Edelstein, *Contaminated Communities: The Social and Psychological Impacts of Residential Toxic Exposure* (Boulder, Colo.: Westview, 1988).

28. Couto, "Failing Health," p. 216.

29. Fowlkes and Miller, "Love Canal," p. 50.

30. Paigen, "Controversy at Love Canal," p. 32.

31. Ibid.

32. Ibid.

33. Richard Kazis and Richard L. Grossman, *Fear at Work: Job Blackmail, Labor, and the Environment* (New York: Pilgrim Press, 1982).

34. Edelstein, *Contaminated Communities,* p. 129.

35. "Cancer Case Reporting and Surveillance in Massachusetts" (Commonwealth of Massachusetts, Senate Committee on Post Audit and Oversight, Boston, September 1987); Barry S. Levy et al., "Improving the Conduct of Environmental Epidemiology Studies" (Worcester: University of Massachusetts Medical School, Department of Family and Community Medicine, Occupational Health Program, 1986).

36. Richard Clapp, "Cancer Statistics and the Right-to-Know"

(paper presented at the annual meeting of the American Public Health Association, Boston, November 14–16, 1988).

37. Study Commission on Environmental Health Issues, *Final Report* (Boston: Massachusetts Department of Public Health, February 1984), p. 39.

38. Ibid., p. 42.

39. Ozonoff and Boden, "Truth and Consequences."

40. Reich, "Environmental Politics."

41. Paigen, "Controversy at Love Canal."

42. Couto, "Failing Health"; Barry Commoner, *The Closing Circle: Nature, Man and Technology* (New York: Knopf, 1971), pp. 86–87.

43. Malcolm L. Goggin, "Introduction, Governing Science and Technology Democratically: A Conceptual Framework," pp. 3–31 in Malcolm L. Goggin, ed., *Governing Science and Technology in a Democracy* (Knoxville: University of Tennessee Press, 1986).

44. Paigen, "Controversy at Love Canal."

45. Freudenberg, *Not in Our Backyards,* p. 57.

46. Eliot Marshall, "EPA's High-Risk Carcinogen Policy," *Science,* 1982, 218:975–978.

47. Levine, *Love Canal;* Ozonoff and Boden, "Truth and Consequences."

48. Clapp, "Cancer Statistics."

49. Dan Kennedy, "EPA to Say Pollutants Caused Leukemia," *Woburn Daily Times,* May 9, 1988.

50. Paigen, "Controversy at Love Canal."

51. Holly Howe, "Predicting Public Concern Regarding Toxic Substances in the Environment" (paper presented at the annual meeting of the American Public Health Association, Boston, November 14–16, 1988).

52. David L. George and Priscilla L. Southwell, "Opinion on the Diablo Canyon Nuclear Power Plant: The Effects of Situation and Socialization," *Social Science Quarterly,* 1986, 67:722–735.

53. Sheila Jasanoff, "The Misrule of Law at OSHA," pp. 155–178 in Dorothy Nelkin, ed., *The Language of Risk: Conflicting Perspectives on Occupational Health* (Beverly Hills: Sage, 1985).

54. James H. Rubin, "Justices Limit Right of Citizens to Sue

on Water Pollution Violations," *New York Times*, December 2, 1987.

55. Nicholas Freudenberg, "Citizen Action for Environmental Health: Report on a Survey of Community Organizations," *American Journal of Public Health*, 1984, 74:444–448.

56. Kurt Finsterbusch, "Citizens' Encounters with Unresponsive Authorities in Obtaining Protection from Hazardous Wastes" (paper presented at the annual meeting of the Society for the Study of Social Problems, Atlanta, Georgia, August 1988).

57. Philip Shabecoff, "Uncertainties of a Chemical-Filled World Come Home to a Denver Suburb," *New York Times*, April 19, 1987.

58. Ibid.

59. Ibid.

60. Couto, "Failing Health."

61. Levine, *Love Canal*, pp. 103–104.

62. Safran, "War on Toxic Waste."

63. Shavelson, "Tales of Troubled Waters."

64. Ibid.

65. Reich, "Environmental Politics."

66. John Duncan Powell, "A Hazardous Waste Site: The Case of Nyanza," pp. 239–297 in Sheldon Krimsky and Alonzo Plough, *Environmental Hazards: Communicating Risks as a Social Process* (Dover, Mass.: Auburn House, 1988).

67. Frances Irwin, "Integrating Pollution Control to Protect Public Health" (paper presented at the annual meeting of the American Public Health Association, Boston, November 14–16, 1988).

68. Barry Rabe, "The Politics of Alternative Dispute Resolution in American Environmental Policy" (paper presented at the annual meeting of the American Public Health Association, Boston, November 14–16, 1988).

69. Goggin, "Introduction."

70. Barbara Wessen, "Participatory Strategies in Community Health Effects Research" (unpublished manuscript, n.d.).

71. Thomas Kuhn, *The Structure of Scientific Revolutions* (Chicago: University of Chicago Press, 1962).

72. Bruno Latour, *Science in Action: How to Follow Scientists*

and Engineers through Society (Cambridge, Mass.: Harvard University Press, 1987), pp. 99–103.

73. Fowlkes and Miller, "Love Canal," p. 2.

74. Ibid., p. 46.

75. Sheldon Krimsky and Alonzo Plough, *Environmental Hazards: Communicating Risks as a Social Process* (Dover, Mass.: Auburn House, 1988), pp. 107–108, 302.

76. Alonzo Plough, personal communication.

77. Krimsky and Plough, *Environmental Hazards*, p. 6.

78. Robert Miller, " 'I'm from the Government and I'm Here to Help You': Fieldwork at Times Beach and Other Missouri Dioxin Sites" (paper presented at the annual meeting of the Society for the Study of Social Problems, San Antonio, Texas, August 1984).

79. Daniel Wartenberg, "Risk Communication and Perception: A Comparative Study of Temik Pesticide in Groundwater in Three Communities" (paper presented at the annual meeting of the American Public Health Association, Boston, November 14–16, 1988).

80. Krauss, "Grass-Root Protests."

81. Nicholas Ashford, "Communicating Technical Solutions" (paper presented at the annual meeting of the American Public Health Association, Boston, November 15, 1988).

82. Daniel Wartenberg, "Groundwater Contamination by Temik Aldicarb Pesticide: The First Eight Months," *Water Resources Research*, 1988, 24:185–194.

83. Alan F. Chalmers, "Epidemiology and the Scientific Method," *International Journal of Health Services*, 1982, 12:659–666.

84. Dorothy Nelkin, ed., *The Language of Risk: Conflicting Perspectives on Occupational Health* (Beverly Hills: Sage, 1985); Langdon Winner, *The Whale and the Reactor: A Search for Limits in an Age of High Technology* (Chicago: University of Chicago Press, 1986).

85. Bruce Jennings, "Representation and Participation in the Democratic Governance of Science and Technology," pp. 223–243 in Malcolm L. Goggin, ed., *Governing Science and Technology in a Democracy* (Knoxville: University of Tennessee Press, 1986).

86. Stephen Hilgartner, "The Political Language of Risk:

Defining Occupational Health," pp. 25–65 in Dorothy Nelkin, ed., *Language of Risk.*

87. Krimsky and Plough, *Environmental Hazards,* p. 303.

88. Jasanoff, "Misrule of Law."

89. See, in particular, Marvin S. Legator, Barbara L. Harper, and Michael J. Scott, eds., *The Health Detectives' Handbook: A Guide to the Investigation of Environmental Health Hazards by Nonprofessionals* (Baltimore: Johns Hopkins University Press, 1985).

90. Freudenberg, "Citizen Action."

91. Reich, "Environmental Politics."

92. Wessen, "Participatory Strategies," p. 5.

93. Legator, Harper, and Scott, eds., *Health Detectives' Handbook.*

94. Environmental Action Foundation, *Making Polluters Pay: A Citizens' Guide to Legal Action and Organizing* (Washington, D.C.: Environmental Action Foundation, 1987).

95. Commoner, *The Closing Circle,* pp. 197–202.

96. Jan Schlictmann, interview, Boston, May 12, 1987; U.S. Attorney, District of Massachusetts, Press Release, Boston, January 28, 1987.

97. Freudenberg, "Citizen Action."

98. ICF Incorporated, "Analysis of Community Involvement in Hazardous Waste Site Problems," report to the Office of Emergency and Remedial Response, Environmental Protection Agency (Washington, D.C., ICF, 1981), pp. 28–32.

99. Lester Milbrath, *Environmentalists: Vanguard for a New Society* (Albany: State University of New York Press, 1984), pp. 76–78; Howe, "Predicting Public Concern."

100. Stephen Hilgartner and Charles L. Bosk, "The Rise and Fall of Social Problems: A Public Arenas Model," *American Journal of Sociology,* 1988, 94:53–78, p. 67.

101. Ibid.

102. Dorothy Nelkin, "Science and Technology Policy and the Democratic Process," pp. 18–39 in James C. Peterson, ed., *Citizen Participation in Science and Policy* (Amherst: University of Massachusetts Press, 1984).

103. Ibid.

104. Larry Tye, "Critics Say DPH Too Slow to Supply the Crucial Data," *Boston Globe*, October 13, 1986; Ken Cafarell, "Walker Lists Nine Ongoing Studies of Potential Health Problems," *Boston Globe*, November 19, 1986.

105. Freudenberg, "Citizen Action."

106. ICF, "Analysis of Community Involvement," pp. 80–83, 99.

Chapter 5

1. Dorothy Nelkin and Michael S. Brown, *Workers at Risk: Voices from the Workplace* (Chicago: University of Chicago Press, 1984), pp. xv–xvi.

2. Marc Pilisuk, Susan Hillier Parks, and Glenn Hawkes, "Public Perception of Technological Risk," *Social Science Journal*, 1987, 24:403–413.

3. Lawrence C. Hamilton, "Who Cares about Water Pollution? Opinions in a Small-Town Crisis," *Sociological Inquiry*, 1985, 55:170–181.

4. Pilisuk, Parks, and Hawkes, "Public Perception."

5. Ibid.

6. Lawrence C. Hamilton, "Concern about Toxic Wastes: Three Demographic Predictors," *Sociological Perspectives*, 1985, 28:463–486.

7. Craig Calhoun and Henryk Hiller, "Coping with Insidious Injuries: The Case of Johns-Manville Corporation and Asbestos Exposure," *Social Problems*, 1988, 35:162–181, 162.

8. Ibid.

9. Wilbur J. Scott, "Competing Paradigms in the Assessment of Latent Disorders: The Case of Agent Orange," *Social Problems*, 1988, 35:145–161, 145.

10. Leslie I. Boden, J. Raymond Miyares, and David Ozonoff, "Science and Persuasion: Environmental Diseases in U.S. Courts," *Social Science and Medicine*, 1988, 27:1022.

11. Ibid.

12. Calhoun and Hiller, "Coping with Insidious Injuries."

13. Boden, Miyares, and Ozonoff, "Science and Persuasion."

14. Calhoun and Hiller, "Coping with Insidious Injuries."

15. Ibid.

16. Boden, Miyares, and Ozonoff, "Science and Persuasion," p. 1024.

17. Ibid., p. 1025.

18. Calhoun and Hiller, "Coping with Insidious Injuries," p. 171.

19. Sheldon Krimsky, "Beyond Technocracy: New Routes for Citizen Involvement in Social Risk Assessment," pp. 43–61 in James C. Peterson, ed., *Citizen Participation in Science Policy* (Amherst: University of Massachusetts Press, 1984); Rachelle Hollander, "Institutionalizing Public Service Science: Its Perils and Promises," pp. 75–95 in Peterson, *Citizen Participation*.

20. Krimsky, "Beyond Technocracy"; Sheila Jasanoff, "The Misrule of Law at OSHA," pp. 155–178 in Dorothy Nelkin, ed., *The Language of Risk: Conflicting Perspectives on Occupational Health* (Beverly Hills: Sage, 1986).

21. Sheldon Krimsky and Alonzo Plough, *Environmental Hazards: Communicating Risks as a Social Process* (Dover, Mass.: Auburn House, 1988), p. 221.

22. Sheldon Krimsky, "Epistemic Considerations on the Value of Folk-Wisdom in Science and Technology," *Policy Studies Review*, 1984, 3:246–262.

23. Raymond R. Neutra, "Epidemiology for and with a Distrustful Community," *Environmental Health Perspectives*, 1985, 62:393–397.

24. Richard Clapp, interview, March 14, 1987.

25. Gretchen Latowsky, interview, Woburn, Mass., May 26, 1988.

26. David Ozonoff, presentation at conference, "Examining Woburn's Health," Trinity Episcopal Church, Woburn, Massachusetts, April 24, 1988.

27. Latowsky, interview.

28. Ibid.

29. Langdon Winner, *The Whale and the Reactor: A Search for Limits in an Age of High Technology* (Chicago: University of Chicago Press, 1986), p. 142.

30. Ibid., pp. 142–143, 153.

31. Charles Perrow, *Normal Accidents: Living with High Risk*

Systems (New York: Basic, 1984); Charles Perrow, "Risky Systems: Inducing and Avoiding Errors" (paper presented at the annual meeting of the American Sociological Association, New York, August 28, 1986).

32. Nicholas Freudenberg, *Not in Our Backyards: Community Action for Health and the Environment* (New York: Monthly Review Press, 1984), pp. 66–70.

33. "Benzene Exposure Is Curbed by U.S.," *New York Times,* September 2, 1987.

34. Michael R. Edelstein, *Contaminated Communities: The Social and Psychological Impacts of Residential Toxic Exposure* (Boulder, Colo.: Westview, 1988), p. 3.

35. Kurt Finsterbusch, "Citizens' Encounters with Unresponsive Authorities in Obtaining Protection from Hazardous Wastes" (paper presented at the annual meeting of the Society for the Study of Social Problems, Atlanta, Georgia, August 1988).

36. Michael Brown, *Laying Waste: The Poisoning of America by Toxic Chemicals* (New York: Washington Square Press, 1981), pp. 236–249.

37. Philip Shabecoff, "Irate and Afraid, Poor Nations Fight Efforts to Use Them as Toxic Dumps," *New York Times,* January 3, 1988.

38. Freudenberg, *Not in Our Backyards,* pp. 70–72.

39. Ibid., pp. 55–56.

40. Leonard Buder, "Twenty-five Charged in Bribes Tied to Asbestos," *New York Times,* January 6, 1988.

41. Michael deCourcy Hinds, "Slipping through the Cracks: The Filter That Contaminated," *New York Times,* October 8, 1988.

42. Freudenberg, *Not in Our Backyards,* pp. 65–66, 75.

43. Eckard Rehbinder and Richard Stewart, *Environmental Protection Policy* (New York: DeGruyter, 1988), pp. 293, 304, 310.

44. Freudenberg, *Not in Our Backyards,* pp. 76–77.

45. James William Coleman, *The Criminal Elite: The Sociology of White Collar Crime* (New York: St. Martin's, 1979), p. 178.

46. Philip Shabecoff, "Clean Water Bill Passed by Senate, Rebuffing Reagan," *New York Times,* January 22, 1987.

47. Eliot Marshall, "EPA's High-Risk Carcinogen Policy," *Science,* December 3, 1982, 218:975–978, 978.

48. Freudenberg, *Not in Our Backyards,* pp. 75–77.

49. Joseph A. Davis, "Superfund Contaminated by Partisan Politics," *Congressional Quarterly Weekly Report,* March 17, 1984, 42:615–626.

50. Matthew L. Wald, "Clean Air Deadline Is History," *New York Times,* January 3, 1988.

51. Philip Shabecoff, "Bolstering Clean Air Act: Fingers Point in All Directions after Latest Failure," *New York Times,* October 7, 1988.

52. "Ruling Permits Development of Federal Lands," *Boston Globe,* November 5, 1988.

53. Philip Shabecoff, "Reagan Vetoes Bill to Protect 1.4 Million Acres in Montana," *New York Times,* November 4, 1988.

54. Philip Shabecoff, "E.P.A. Says New Toxic Waste Rules for Oil Industry Are Not Needed," *New York Times,* December 30, 1987.

55. Philip Shabecoff, "E.P.A. Declines to Toughen Rule on Sulfur Dioxide," *New York Times,* April 15, 1988.

56. "Study of Drinking Water Assails E.P.A. as Derelict in Monitoring," *New York Times,* January 6, 1988.

57. Philip Shabecoff, "E.P.A. Adopts New Rules on Water Pollution." *New York Times,* October 6, 1988.

58. "Superfund Cleanups Termed Lax," *New York Times,* November 11, 1987.

59. Philip Shabecoff, "Congress Report Faults U.S. Drive on Waste Cleanup," *New York Times,* June 18, 1988.

60. Charles A. Radin, "Scientists Say EPA Needs Shift in Direction," *Boston Globe,* September 12, 1988.

61. Philip Shabecoff, "E.P.A. Is Changing How It Regulates Pesticides in Food," *New York Times,* October 13, 1988.

62. Davis, "Superfund Contaminated."

63. Coleman, *Criminal Elite,* p. 178.

64. Sheila Jasanoff, "The Misrule of Law at OSHA," pp. 155–178 in Dorothy Nelkin, ed., *The Language of Risk: Conflicting Perspectives on Occupational Health* (Beverly Hills: Sage, 1985).

65. Coleman, *Criminal Elite*, p. 178.

66. Stuart Diamond, "Government Is Faulted on Deaths in the Workplace," *New York Times*, July 17, 1988.

67. "Contempt Citations Sought Against Two U.S. Aides," *New York Times*, April 8, 1988.

68. "Clash Looms on a Move to Block Funds to Rid Schools of Asbestos," *New York Times*, January 10, 1986.

69. Siddarth Dube, "Environmental Mismanagement," *Science for the People*, January/February 1987, 19(1):21–23.

70. Freudenberg, p. 81.

71. Andrew Szasz, "The Reversal of Federal Policy toward Worker Safety and Health," *Science and Society*, Spring 1986, 50 (1):25–51.

72. Andrew J. Dabilis, "Eight Families Settle with Firm Over Toxic Lowell Site," *Boston Globe*, June 7, 1989.

73. Jan Schlictmann, interview, Boston, June 3, 1988.

74. Freudenberg, pp. 263–264.

75. Ibid., pp. 265–266.

76. Ibid., pp. 266–269.

Bibliography

Published Sources, Papers, and Reports

Ackerman, Jerry. "Move Widens for Cleaning Water Supply." *Boston Globe,* June 1, 1986.

———. "$2m Settlement in New Bedford Pollution Case." *Boston Globe,* March 5, 1987.

———. "Cost to Combat Toxic Waste Estimated at $250 Million." *Boston Globe,* May 2, 1987.

———. "Woburn Case Families Press Claim with Aid of Ruling." *Boston Globe,* December 14, 1988.

Ackerman, Jerry, and Diego Ribadeneira. "Twelve Families, Grace Settle Woburn Toxic Case." *Boston Globe,* September 23, 1986.

Ashford, Nicholas. "Communicating Technical Solutions." Paper presented at the annual meeting of the American Public Health Association, Boston, November 15, 1988.

Bachrach, Kenneth M., and Alex J. Zautra. "Coping with a Community Stressor: The Threat of a Hazardous Waste Facility." *Journal of Health and Social Behavior,* 1985, 26:127–141.

Barr, Evan T. "Poisoned Well." *New Republic,* March 17, 1986, pp. 18–20.

Baum, Andrew, Raymond Fleming, and Jerome E. Singer. "Coping with Victimization by Technological Disaster." *Journal of Social Issues,* 1983, 39:117–138.

"Beatrice Foods Suit Ruling Is Appealed." *Boston Globe,* February 13, 1988.

225

"Benzene Exposure Is Curbed by U.S." *New York Times,* September 2, 1987.

Berman, Daniel. "Why Work Kills: A Brief History of Occupational Health and Safety in the United States." *International Journal of Health Services,* 1977, 7:63–87.

Boden, Leslie I., J. Raymond Miyares, and David Ozonoff. "Science and Persuasion: Environmental Disease in U.S. Courts." *Social Science and Medicine,* 1988, 27:1019–1029.

Brody, Jane E. "Immunological Defects Found in People in Michigan Who Ate Food Contaminated by PBB." *New York Times,* August 2, 1977.

Bromet, Evelyn J., David K. Parkinson, Herbert C. Schulberg, Leslie O. Dunn, and Paul C. Gondek. "Mental Health of Residents near the Three Mile Island Reactor: A Comparative Study of Selected Groups." *Journal of Preventive Psychiatry,* 1982, 1:225–276.

Brown, Michael. *Laying Waste: The Poisoning of America by Toxic Chemicals.* New York: Washington Square Press, 1981.

Brown, Phil. "Popular Epidemiology: Community Response to Toxic Waste–Induced Disease in Woburn, Massachusetts." *Science, Technology, and Human Values,* 1987, 12:78–85.

Buder, Leonard. "Twenty-five Charged in Bribes Tied to Asbestos." *New York Times,* January 6, 1988.

Burke, William K. "A Double Standard in Toxic-Waste Law." *Boston Globe,* April 5, 1987.

Byers, V. S., A. S. Levin, D. Ozonoff, and R. W. Baldwin. "Association between Clinical Symptoms and Lymphocyte Abnormalities in a Population with Chronic Domestic Exposure to Industrial Solvent–Contaminated Domestic Water Supply and a High Incidence of Leukaemia." *Cancer Immunology and Immunotherapy,* 1988, 27:77–81.

Cafarell, Ken. "Walker Lists Nine Ongoing Studies of Potential Health Problems." *Boston Globe,* November 19, 1986.

Calhoun, Craig, and Henryk Hiller. "Coping with Insidious Injuries: The Case of Johns-Manville Corporation and Asbestos Exposure." *Social Problems,* 1988, 35:162–181.

"Cancer Case Reporting and Surveillance in Massachusetts."

Commonwealth of Massachusetts, Senate Committee on Post Audit and Oversight, Boston, September 1987.

Carbone, A. V. "The Saga of Lake Mishaum." *Woburn Daily Times,* December 2, 1969.

Chalmers, Alan F. "Epidemiology and the Scientific Method." *International Journal of Health Services,* 1982, 12:659–666.

Clapp, Richard. "Cancer Statistics and the Right-to-Know." Paper presented at the annual meeting of the American Public Health Association, Boston, November 14–16, 1988.

———. Presentation at conference, "Examining Woburn's Health," Trinity Episcopal Church, Woburn, Massachusetts, April 24, 1988.

Clarke, Lee. "Explaining Choices among Technological Risks." *Social Problems,* 1988, 35:22–35.

———. "Political Ecology of Local Protest Groups." Paper presented at the annual meeting of the American Sociological Association, Atlanta, Georgia, August 22–26, 1988.

"Clash Looms on a Move to Block Funds to Rid Schools of Asbestos," *New York Times,* January 10, 1986.

Coleman, James William. *The Criminal Elite: The Sociology of White Collar Crime.* New York: St. Martin's, 1979.

Comaroff, Jean, and Peter Maguire. "Ambiguity and the Search for Meaning: Childhood Leukemia in the Modern Clinical Context." *Social Science and Medicine,* 1981, 15B:115–123.

Commoner, Barry. *The Closing Circle: Nature, Man and Technology.* New York: Knopf, 1971.

"Contempt Citations Sought Against Two U.S. Aides," *New York Times,* April 8, 1988.

Couch, Stephen R. and J. Stephen Kroll-Smith. "The Chronic Technical Disaster: Towards a Social Scientific Perspective." *Social Science Quarterly,* 1985, 66:564–575.

Couto, Richard A. "Failing Health and New Prescriptions: Community-Based Approaches to Environmental Risks." Pp. 53–70 in Carol E. Hill, ed., *Current Health Policy Issues and Alternatives: An Applied Social Science Perspective.* Athens: University of Georgia Press, 1986.

Cutler, John L., Gerald S. Parker, Sharon Rosen, Brad Prenney, Richard Healy, and Glyn G. Caldwell. "Childhood Leukemia in Woburn, Massachusetts." *Public Health Reports,* 1986, 101:201–205.

Dabilis, Andrew J. "Eight Families Settle with Firm over Toxic Lowell Site." *Boston Globe,* June 7, 1989.

Davis, Joseph A. "Superfund Contaminated by Partisan Politics." *Congressional Quarterly Weekly Report,* March 17, 1984, 42:615–626.

Dew, Mary Amanda, Evelyn J. Bromet, Herbert C. Schulberg, Leslie O. Dunn, and David K. Parkinson. "Mental Health Effects of the Three Mile Island Nuclear Reactor Restart." *American Journal of Psychiatry,* 1987, 144:1074–1077.

Diamond, Stuart. "Government Is Faulted on Deaths in the Workplace." *New York Times,* July 17, 1988.

Dickson, David. *The New Politics of Science.* New York: Pantheon, 1984.

Diffenderfer, Mark. "The Control of Knowledge as a Factor in Grass Roots Mobilization." Paper presented at the annual meeting of the American Sociological Association, Atlanta, Georgia, August 22–26, 1988.

DiPerna, Paula. *Cluster Mystery: Epidemic and the Children of Woburn, Mass.* St. Louis: Mosby, 1985.

Doherty, William F. "Jury: Firm Fouled Wells in Woburn." *Boston Globe,* July 29, 1986.

Dohrenwend, Bruce P., Barbara Snell Dohrenwend, George J. Warheit, Glenn S. Bartlett, Raymond L. Goldsteen, Karen Goldsteen, and John L. Martin. "Stress in the Community: A Report to the President's Commission on the Accident at Three Mile Island." *Annals of the New York Academy of Sciences,* 1981, 365:159–174.

Dorion, Gary L. "One Chemical Contamination Suit Settled." *Woburn Daily Times,* October 25, 1985.

Douglas, Mary. *Risk Acceptability According to the Social Sciences.* New York: Russell Sage Foundation, 1985.

Dube, Siddarth. "Environmental Mismanagement." *Science for the People,* January/February 1987, 19(1):21–23.

Dumanoski, Diane. "Panel Calls for Action to Slow Rising Earth Temperature." *New York Times,* June 7, 1988.

————. "Because of Environmental Ills, 10 Million Can't Go Home Again." *New York Times,* November 21, 1988.

Edelstein, Michael R. *Contaminated Communities: The Social and Psychological Impacts of Residential Toxic Exposure.* Boulder, Colo.: Westview, 1988.

"Eight Families Seek New Trial Against Beatrice Foods," *Woburn Daily Times,* October 13, 1987.

Environmental Action Foundation. *Making Polluters Pay: A Citizens' Guide to Legal Action and Organizing.* Washington, D.C.: Environmental Action Foundation, 1987.

Environmental Protection Agency. "Status Report of the Ad Hoc 'Woburn Workgroup.' " Washington, D.C.: Environmental Protection Agency, June 2, 1988.

————. "Settlement Reached for Cleanup of Industri-Plex Hazardous Waste Superfund Site." *Environmental News,* January 31, 1989.

————. "EPA Proposes Clean-up Plan for Wells G and H Site." Boston: Environmental Protection Agency Region I Office, February 1989.

Feldman, Robert G., Jeanette Chirico-Post, and Susan P. Proctor. "Blink Reflex Latency After Exposure to Trichloroethylene in Well Water." *Archives of Environmental Health,* March/April 1988, 43(2):143–148.

Finsterbusch, Kurt. "Citizens' Encounters with Unresponsive Authorities in Obtaining Protection from Hazardous Wastes." Paper presented at the annual meeting of the Society for the Study of Social Problems, Atlanta, Georgia, August 1988.

Fischoff, Baruch, Paul Slovic, and S. Lichtenstein. "Lay Foibles and Expert Fables in Judgments about Risk." *American Statistician,* 1982, 36:240–255.

Fleming, India, and Andrew Baum. "Chronic Stress in Residents near a Toxic Waste Site." Paper presented at the meeting of the Eastern Psychological Association, Baltimore, Maryland, 1984.

Fortin, Paul. "The Dump." *Boston Magazine,* April 1981, pp. 98–104.

Fowlkes, Martha, and Patricia Y. Miller. "Love Canal: The Social Construction of Disaster." Final report for Federal

Emergency Management Agency. Washington, D.C.: Federal Emergency Management Agency, January 1983.

———. "Chemicals and Community at Love Canal." Pp. 55–78 in Brandon B. Johnson and Vincent T. Covello, eds., *The Social and Cultural Construction of Risk.* New York: Reidel, 1987.

———. "Unnatural Disaster at Love Canal." Pp. 23–41 in Michael T. Charles and John Choon K. Kim, eds., *Crisis Management: A Casebook.* Springfield, Ill.: Thomas, 1988.

Freudenberg, Nicholas. "Citizen Action for Environmental Health: Report on a Survey of Community Organizations." *American Journal of Public Health,* 1984, 74:444–448.

———. *Not in Our Backyards: Community Action for Health and the Environment.* New York: Monthly Review Press, 1984.

Frumkin, Howard, and Warren Kantrowitz. "Cancer Clusters in the Workplace: An Approach to Investigation." *Journal of Occupational Medicine,* 1987, 29:949–952.

Gamson, William A., Bruce Fireman, and Steven Rytina. *Encounters with Unjust Authority.* Chicago: Dorsey, 1982.

George, David L., and Priscilla L. Southwell. "Opinion on the Diablo Canyon Nuclear Power Plant: The Effects of Situation and Socialization." *Social Science Quarterly,* 1986, 67:722–735.

Gibbs, Lois Marie. "Community Response to an Emergency Situation: Psychological Destruction and the Love Canal." Paper presented at the meeting of the American Psychological Association, August 24, 1982.

Goggin, Malcolm L. "Introduction, Governing Science and Technology Democratically: A Conceptual Framework." Pp. 3–31 in Malcolm L. Goggin, ed., *Governing Science and Technology in a Democracy.* Knoxville: University of Tennessee Press, 1986.

Goodman, Patricia G., and C. Edwin Vaughan. "Prolonged Effects of Natural and Man-Made Disasters on Older and Younger Persons." Paper presented to the annual meeting of the American Sociological Association, 1986.

Greene, Terry, and Kathleen Stanton. "Maryvale Is Not Alone." *New Times* (Phoenix, Ariz.), November 25–December 1, 1987.

Grimvall, Anders, and Rolf Ejvegard. "The Dynamics of Scientific Uncertainty and Its Implications for the Use of Conservative Procedures in Risk Analysis." Pp. 23–29 in Per Oftedal and Anton Brogger, eds., *Risk and Reason: Risk Assessment in Relation to Environmental Mutagens and Carcinogens.* New York: Liss, 1986.

Gruber, Sheila. "Terrible Impact: Residents Suffer Psychologically from Living Near Toxic Site, Study Reveals." *Ann Arbor News,* February 10, 1985.

Gruson, Lindsey. "Town Takes Toxic Wastes in Stride." *New York Times,* March 4, 1987.

Hahns, Susan, and Paul Mindus. "Nobody Wants to Touch It." *Boston Globe,* July 9, 1980.

Hamilton, Lawrence C. "Concern about Toxic Wastes: Three Demographic Predictors." *Sociological Perspectives,* 1985, 28:463–486.

————. "Who Cares about Water Pollution? Opinions in a Small-Town Crisis." *Sociological Inquiry,* 1985, 55:170–181.

Hershey, Robert. "Grace Study on Federal Spending Called Assault on Social Programs." *New York Times,* August 29, 1985.

Hilgartner, Stephen. "The Political Language of Risk: Defining Occupational Health." Pp. 25–65 in Dorothy Nelkin, ed., *The Language of Risk: Conflicting Perspectives on Occupational Health.* Beverly Hills: Sage, 1985.

Hilgartner, Stephen, and Charles L. Bosk. "The Rise and Fall of Social Problems: A Public Arenas Model." *American Journal of Sociology,* 1988, 94:53–78.

Hinds, Michael deCourcy. "Slipping through the Cracks: The Filter That Contaminated." *New York Times,* October 8, 1988.

Hollander, Rachelle. "Institutionalizing Public Service Science: Its Perils and Promise." Pp. 75–95 in James C. Peterson, ed., *Citizen Participation in Science Policy.* Amherst: University of Massachusetts Press, 1984.

Howe, Holly. "Predicting Public Concern Regarding Toxic Substances in the Environment." Paper presented at the annual meeting of the American Public Health Associations, Boston, November 14, 1988.

ICF Incorporated. "Analysis of Community Involvement in Hazardous Waste Site Problems." Report to the Office of

Emergency and Remedial Response, United States Environmental Protection Agency. Washington, D.C.: ICF, 1981.

Irwin, Frances. "Integrating Pollution Control to Protect Public Health." Paper presented at the annual meeting of the American Public Health Association, Boston, November 16, 1988.

Jasanoff, Sheila. "The Misrule of Law at OSHA." Pp. 155–178 in Dorothy Nelkin, ed., *The Language of Risk: Conflicting Perspectives on Occupational Health.* Beverly Hills: Sage, 1985.

Jennings, Bruce. "Representation and Participation in the Democratic Governance of Science and Technology." Pp. 223–243 in Malcolm L. Goggin, ed., *Governing Science and Technology in a Democracy.* Knoxville: University of Tennessee Press, 1986.

Kazis, Richard, and Richard L. Grossman. *Fear at Work: Job Blackmail, Labor, and the Environment.* New York: Pilgrim Press, 1982.

Kennedy, Dan. "Chemical Dumping Charges Leveled at Cryovac." *Woburn Daily Times,* August 28, 1985.

———. W. R. Grace Hits FACE on Tactics." *Woburn Daily Times,* August 29, 1985.

———. "Markey Blasts EPA Delays in Woburn Cleanup." *Woburn Daily Times,* November 26, 1985.

———. "Markey Using Woburn to Push for Superfund." *Woburn Daily Times,* November 27, 1985.

———. "Pump Tests Tie Riley's Land to City's G Well." *Woburn Daily Times,* March 20, 1986.

———. "Witness: Riley Ditch Was Called 'Death Valley.' " *Woburn Daily Times,* April 2, 1986.

———. "Riley Reportedly Complained." *Woburn Daily Times,* April 4, 1986.

———. "Riley Testifies Land Was Never Used as Dump." *Woburn Daily Times,* April 8, 1986.

———. "Riley Admits He Failed to Comply." *Woburn Daily Times,* April 11, 1986.

———. "Cryovac Worker Tells of Barrel-Dumping." *Woburn Daily Times,* April 14, 1986.

————. "Grace Exec. Tells of Barrel-Dumping." *Woburn Daily Times,* April 16, 1986.

————. "Cryovac Knew of TCE Hazards." *Woburn Daily Times,* April 21, 1986.

————. "A Difficult Week for Plaintiff's Scientist in Toxic Trial." *Woburn Daily Times,* May 19, 1986.

————. "Cryovac Manager Requested Barrel Disposal." *Woburn Daily Times,* May 30, 1986.

————. "Judge's Ruling Has Something for All Participants." *Woburn Daily Times,* June 5, 1986.

————. "Beatrice Wins Delay in Answering Appeal." *Woburn Daily Times,* July 17, 1987.

————. "Families' Lawyer Expects Early Hearing." *Woburn Daily Times,* October 14, 1987.

————. "Defense Lawyers Deny Misconduct Charges." *Woburn Daily Times,* November 3, 1987.

————. "Woburn Leukemia Rate Remains High." *Woburn Daily Times,* December 2, 1987.

————. "Citizens Group Angered by Funding Rejection." *Woburn Daily Times,* January 12, 1988.

————. "EPA to Say Pollutants Caused Leukemia." *Woburn Daily Times,* May 9, 1988.

————. "Toxic Trial: Many Questions, Few Answers." Unpublished manuscript. 1989.

Kingson, Jennifer. "$24 Million Accord Reached on Toxic Cleanup." *New York Times,* February 1, 1989.

Knight, Michael. "Pollution Is an Old Neighbor in Massachusetts." *New York Times,* May 16, 1980.

————. "Toxic Wastes Hurriedly Dumped before New Law Goes into Effect." *New York Times,* November 16, 1980.

Knox, Richard A. "Professor Criticizes Woburn Study." *Boston Globe,* June 8, 1984.

Kolbert, Elizabeth. "Upstate Residents' Water Worries Help Move GE to Accord." *New York Times,* May 13, 1986.

Krauss, Celene. "Grass-Root Protests and Toxic Wastes: Developing a Critical Political View." Paper presented at the meeting of the American Sociological Association, New York, 1986.

———. "Community Struggles and the Shaping of Democratic Consensus." *Sociological Forum,* 1989, 4:227–239.

Krimsky, Sheldon. "Epistemic Considerations on the Value of Folk-Wisdom in Science and Technology." *Policy Studies Review,* 1984, 3:246–262.

Krimsky, Sheldon, and Alonzo Plough. *Environmental Hazards: Communicating Risks as a Social Process.* Dover, Mass.: Auburn House, 1988.

Kroll-Smith, J. Stephen, Stephen R. Couch, and Adeline G. Levine. "Research on Technological Hazards and Disasters: Where Are We and Where Do We Go from Here?" Paper presented at the conference on the Study of Science and Technology in the 1990s, Amsterdam, 1988.

Kuhn, Thomas. *The Structure of Scientific Revolutions.* Chicago: University of Chicago Press, 1962.

Lagakos, Steven, Barbara J. Wessen, and Marvin Zelen. *The Woburn Health Study: An Analysis of Reproductive and Childhood Disorders and Their Relation to Environmental Contamination.* Boston: Harvard School of Public Health, Department of Biostatistics, 1984.

———. "An Analysis of Contaminated Well Water and Health Effects in Woburn, Massachusetts." *Journal of the American Statistical Association,* 1986, 81:583–596.

Latour, Bruno. *Science in Action: How to Follow Scientists and Engineers through Society.* Cambridge, Mass.: Harvard University Press, 1987.

Legator, Marvin S., Barbara L. Harper, and Michael J. Schott, eds., *The Health Detectives' Handbook: A Guide to the Investigation of Environmental Health Hazards by Nonprofessionals.* Baltimore: Johns Hopkins University Press, 1985.

Levine, Adeline. *Love Canal: Science, Politics, and People.* Lexington, Mass.: Heath, 1982.

Levine, Adeline G., and Russell Stone. "Threats to People and What They Value: Residents' Perceptions of the Hazards of Love Canal." Unpublished paper, State University of New York at Buffalo, 1985.

Levy, Barry S., David Kreibel, Peter Gann, Jay Himmelstein, and Glenn Pransky. "Improving the Conduct of Environmental Epidemiology Studies." Worcester: University of Massachusetts Medical School, Department of Family and Community Medicine, Occupational Health Program, 1986.

Lewis, Diane E. "W. R. Grace Co. Official Denies Responsibility for Pollution of Wells." *Boston Globe,* March 2, 1986.

Lifton, Robert J. "Psychological Report on Three Mile Island Litigation." Unpublished manuscript.

Lifton, Robert J., and Eric Olson. "The Human Meaning of Total Disaster: The Buffalo Creek Experience." *Psychiatry,* 1976, 39:1–18.

Lillienfeld, Abraham. *Foundations of Epidemiology.* 2nd ed. New York: Oxford, 1980.

Longcope, Kay. "After the Trial—Woburn." *Boston Globe,* October 17, 1986.

Loth, Renee. "Woburn, Science, and the Law." *Boston Globe Magazine,* February 9, 1986.

Lucas, Laurel. "Civil Liberties Union Wants Court 'Gag Order' Removed." *Woburn Daily Times,* October 17, 1985.

Mades, Nancy. "Commissioner Wants FACE-DPH Pact." *Woburn Daily Times,* April 7, 1988.

Marshall, Eliot, "EPA's High-Risk Carcinogen Policy." *Science,* 1982, 218:975–978.

———. "Woburn Case May Spark Explosion of Lawsuits." *Science,* 1986, 234:418–420.

Maynard, Joyce. "The Story of a Town." *New York Times Magazine,* May 11, 1986.

Mazur, Alan. "Placing Hazards on the Public Agenda." Paper presented at annual meeting of American Sociological Association, Atlanta, Georgia, August 1988.

Milbrath, Lester. *Environmentalists: Vanguard for a New Society.* Albany: State University of New York Press, 1984.

Millar, Fred. "Braking the Slide in Chemical Safety." *New York Times,* May 11, 1986.

Miller, Robert. " 'I'm from the Government and I'm Here to Help You': Fieldwork at Times Beach and Other Missouri Dioxin Sites." Paper presented at the annual meeting of the Society for the Study of Social Problems, San Antonio, Texas, August 1984.

Minksy, Terry. "No Way to Predict Leukemia, Woburners Told." *Boston Globe,* February 15, 1984.

Morrison, Allan. Lecture in the Epidemiology Colloquium series, Brown University, Department of Community Health, February 25, 1987.

Nash, Jane, and Max Kirsch. "Polychlorinated Biphenyls in the Electrical Machinery Industry: An Ethnological Study of Community Action and Corporate Responsibility." *Social Science and Medicine,* 1986, 23:131–138.

Nelkin, Dorothy. "Science and Technology Policy and the Democratic Process." Pp. 18–39 in James C. Peterson, ed., *Citizen Participation in Science and Policy.* Amherst: University of Massachusetts Press, 1984.

————, ed. *"The Language of Risk: Conflicting Perspectives on Occupational Health."* Beverly Hills: Sage, 1985.

Nelkin, Dorothy, and Michael S. Brown. *Workers at Risk: Voices from the Workplace.* Chicago: University of Chicago Press, 1984.

Neuffer, Elizabeth. "Court Orders New Hearings in Woburn Pollution Case." *Boston Globe,* December 8, 1988.

————. "EPA Testimony Sought by Eight Woburn Families." *Boston Globe,* February 2, 1989.

————. "Food Giant Accused of Cover-Up." *Boston Globe,* April 7, 1989.

Neutra, Raymond. "Epidemiology for and with a Distrustful Community." *Environmental Health Perspectives,* 1985, 62:393–397.

Ozonoff, David. Presentation at conference, "Examining Woburn's Health," Trinity Episcopal Church, Woburn, Massachusetts, April 24, 1988.

————. "Failed Warnings: Asbestos-Related Disease and Industrial Medicine." Pp. 139–218, in Ronald Bayer, ed., *The Health and Safety of Workers.* New York: Oxford, 1988.

Ozonoff, David, and Leslie I. Boden. "Truth and Consequences: Health Agency Responses to Environmental Health Problems." *Science, Technology and Human Values,* 1987, 12:70–77.

Ozonoff, David, et al. *Final Report of the Study Commission on*

Environmental Health Needs. Boston: Massachusetts Department of Public Health, February 1984.

Pacelle, Mitchell. "Contaminated Verdict." *American Lawyer*, December 1986, pp. 75–80.

Paigen, Beverly. "Controversy at Love Canal." *Hastings Center Reports*, 1982, 12(3):29–37.

Parker, Gerald S., and Sharon L. Rosen. "Woburn: Cancer Incidence and Environmental Hazards, 1969–1978." Boston: Massachusetts Department of Public Health, January 23, 1981.

Perrow, Charles. *Normal Accidents: Living with High Risk Systems.* New York: Basic Books, 1984.

———. "Risky Systems: Inducing and Avoiding Errors." Paper presented at the annual meeting of the American Sociological Association, New York, August 28, 1986.

Pilisuk, Marc, Susan Hillier Parks, and Glenn Hawkes. "Public Perception of Technological Risk." *Social Science Journal*, 1987, 24:403–413.

"Pollution on Top of Pollution in River," *Woburn Daily Times*, February 11, 1972.

Powell, John Duncan. "A Hazardous Waste Site: The Case of Nyanza." Pp. 239–297 in Sheldon Krimsky and Alonzo Plough, *Environmental Hazards: Communicating Risks as a Social Process.* Dover, Mass.: Auburn House, 1988.

Queijo, Jon. "The Middleborough Killer." *Bostonia*, July/August 1987, 61(4):43–45.

" 'Quiet Triumph' at Hazardous-Waste Site in Jersey," *New York Times*, May 4, 1986.

Quill, Ed. "W. R. Grace Admits Lying to EPA." *Boston Globe*, June 1, 1988.

Rabe, Barry. "The Politics of Alternative Dispute Resolution in American Environmental Policy." Paper presented at the annual meeting of the American Public Health Association, Boston, November 16, 1988.

Radin, Charles A. "Scientists Say EPA Needs Shift in Direction." *Boston Globe*, September 12, 1988.

Raloff, J. "Woburn Survey May Become a Model for Low-Cost Epidemiology." *Science News*, February 18, 1984.

Raphael, Beverly. *When Disaster Strikes: How Individuals and Communities Cope with Catastrophe.* New York: Basic Books, 1986.

Rehbinder, Eckard, and Richard Stewart. *Environmental Protection Policy.* New York: DeGruyter, 1988.

"Rehearing of Ruling Reducing Award Sought by Plaintiffs in Sixth Circuit Velsicol Case," *Toxics Law Reporter,* June 22, 1988, pp. 111–112.

Reich, Michael R. "Environmental Politics and Science: The Case of PBB Contamination in Michigan." *American Journal of Public Health,* 1983, 73:302–313.

Reko, Karl. "The Psychological Impact of Environmental Disasters." *Bulletin of Environmental Contamination and Toxicology,* 1984, 33:665–671.

"Remand for Damages Recalculation Clarified by Sixth Circuit Panel in Rehearing Opinion." *Toxics Law Reporter,* September 7, 1988, pp. 448–449.

Restivo, Sal. "Modern Science as a Social Problem." *Social Problems,* 1988, 35:206–225.

Rodriguez-Trias, Helen. "The Women's Health Movement: Women Take Power." Pp. 107–126 in Victor Sidel and Ruth Sidel, eds., *Reforming Medicine: Lessons of the Last Quarter Century.* New York: Pantheon, 1984.

Roisman, Anthony Z. "Proving Cause in Toxic-Tort Litigation: The Threshold of a New Era." *Trial,* October 1986, pp. 59–61.

Rubin, James H. "Justices Limit Right of Citizens to Sue on Water Pollution Violations." *New York Times,* December 2, 1987.

"Ruling Permits Development of Federal Lands." *Boston Globe,* November 5, 1988.

Safran, Claire. "The War on Toxic Waste." *Newsday,* October 4, 1983, p. 49.

Scott, Wilbur J. "Competing Paradigms in the Assessment of Latent Disorders: The Case of Agent Orange." *Social Problems,* 1988, 35:145–161.

Shabecoff, Philip. "Plans to Build Two Waste Plants Upset Many in Poor Section of N. Carolina." *New York Times*, April 1, 1986.

———. "Clean Water Bill Passed by Senate, Rebuffing Reagan." *New York Times*, January 22, 1987.

———. "E.P.A. Says New Toxic Waste Rules for Oil Industry Are Not Needed." *New York Times*, December 30, 1987.

———. "Uncertainties of a Chemical-Filled World Come Home to a Denver Suburb." *New York Times*, April 19, 1987.

———. "Irate and Afraid, Poor Nations Fight Efforts to Use Them as Toxic Dumps." *New York Times*, January 3, 1988.

———. "Toxic Cleanup Plan Moves Slowly amid Criticism from Two Fronts." *New York Times*, January 10, 1988.

———. "Report Sees Hope for Battered Environment." *New York Times*, February 21, 1988.

———. "E.P.A. Declines to Toughen Rule on Sulfur Dioxide." *New York Times*, April 15, 1988.

———. "Congress Report Faults U.S. Drive on Waste Cleanup," *New York Times*, June 18, 1988.

———. "E.P.A. Adopts New Rules on Water Pollution." *New York Times*, October 6, 1988.

———. "Bolstering Clean Air Act: Fingers Point in All Directions after Latest Failure." *New York Times*, October 7, 1988.

———. "E.P.A. Is Changing How It Regulates Pesticides in Food." *New York Times*, October 13, 1988.

———. "Draft Report on Global Warming Foresees Environmental Havoc in U.S." *New York Times*, October 20, 1988.

———. "Reagan Vetoes Bill to Protect 1.4 Million Acres in Montana." *New York Times*, November 4, 1988.

Shavelson, Lonny. "Tales of Troubled Waters." *Hippocrates*, March/April 1988, pp. 70–76.

Shaw, L. Gardner, and Lester W. Milbrath. "Citizen Participation in Governmental Decision Making: The Toxic Waste Threat at Love Canal, Niagara Falls, New York." Rockefeller Institute Working Papers No. 8, Buffalo: State University of New York, 1983.

Simons, Marlise. "Vast Amazon Fires, Man-Made, Linked to Global Warming." *New York Times*, August 12, 1988.

Sinclair, Louis. "Conflict and Policies in Central America Have Resulted in Ecological Devastation." Letter to the editor, *Boston Globe*, April 4, 1988.

"Sixth Circuit Strikes Awards against Velsicol Based on Immune System Injury, Risk of Cancer," *Toxics Law Reporter*, June 8, 1988, pp. 47–49.

Sleeper, Peter. "Dukakis to Fight Ruling on Landfills." *Boston Globe*, May 2, 1985.

Slovic, Paul. "Perceptions of Risk." *Science*, 1987, 236:280–285.

Slovic, Paul, Baruch Fischoff, and S. Lichtenstein. "Weighing the Risks." *Environment*, 1979, 21(3):14–20, 36–39.

Smith, Elizabeth, Lee N. Robins, Thomas R. Przybeck, Evelyn Goldring, and Susan Solomon. "Psychosocial Consequences of a Disaster." Pp. 50–76 in James H. Shore, ed., *Disaster Stress Studies: New Methods and Findings*. Washington, D.C.: American Psychiatric Press, 1988.

Stallones, Reuel A. "Epidemiology and Environmental Hazards." Pp. 3–10 in Leon Gordis, ed., *Epidemiology and Health Risk Assessment*. New York: Oxford, 1988.

Starr, Chauncy, and Chris Whipple. "Risks of Risk Decisions." *Science*, 1980, 208:1114–1119.

Starr, Susan Leigh. "Introduction: The Sociology of Science and Technology." *Social Problems*, 1988, 35:197–205.

Study Commission on Environmental Health Issues. *Final Report*. Boston: Massachusetts Department of Public Health, February 1984.

"Study of Drinking Water Assails E.P.A. as Derelict in Monitoring," *New York Times*, January 6, 1988.

Sullivan, Mark. "Charts, Diagrams Show How Chemicals Reached Water Well." *Woburn Daily Times*, May 9, 1988.

Sullivan, William. "Rabbit Irate over Toxic Trial by Media." *Woburn Daily Times*, February 20, 1986.

"Superfund Cleanups Termed Lax," *New York Times*, November 11, 1987.

Szasz, Andrew. "The Reversal of Federal Policy toward Worker Safety and Health." *Science and Society*, Spring 1986, 50(1):25–51.

Tate, Nick. "Second Woburn Toxic Waste Hearing Set." *Boston Herald*, December 15, 1988.

Therrien, Lois, Jonathan Tasini, and Richard Hoppe. "Why Business Is Watching This Pollution Case." *Business Week*, March 24, 1986.

Thomas, Jack. "Life Forms May Vanish, Report Says." *Boston Globe*, July 23, 1978.

"Toxic Waste Problems Aren't New," *Woburn Daily Times*, June 12, 1980.

Tye, Larry. "Critics Say DPH Too Slow to Supply the Crucial Data." *Boston Globe*, October 13, 1986.

———. "State Health Officials Assailed." *Boston Globe*, October 18, 1986.

———. "State Studies on Cancer Rate Found Lacking." *Boston Globe*, March 23, 1987.

———. "Budget Plan Would Boost State Funds for Local Health Studies." *Boston Globe*, May 9, 1987.

U.S. Attorney, District of Massachusetts. Press Release. Boston, January 28, 1987.

U.S. District Court, District of Massachusetts. C. A. No. 82-1672-S. Anne Anderson et al. v. Beatrice Foods Co. Findings Pursuant to Remand on the Nature of the Defendant's Misconduct. July 7, 1989.

"Velsicol Asks for Full Panel Review of Sixth Circuit Ruling in Sterling Suit." *Toxics Law Reporter*, June 15, 1988.

Verhovek, Sam Howe. "A Bronx Landfill Raises Concern over Diseases." *New York Times*, June 27, 1988.

Vissing, Yvonne. "The Difficulties in Determining Elite Deviance: Dow Chemical Company and the Dioxin Controversy." Paper presented at the annual meeting of the Society for the Study of Social Problems, San Antonio, Texas, August 1984.

Vyner, Henry M. *Invisible Trauma: The Psychosocial Effects of the Invisible Environmental Contaminants*. Lexington, Mass.: Lexington Books, 1988.

"W. R. Grace Misled Public, EPA." *Boston Globe*, February 23, 1983.

Wald, Matthew L. "Clean Air Deadline Is History." *New York Times*, January 3, 1988.

Wartenberg, Daniel. "Groundwater Contamination by Temik Aldicarb Pesticide: The First Eight Months." *Water Resources Research,* 1988, 24:185–194.

———. "Risk Communication and Perception: A Comparative Study for Temik Pesticide in Groundwater in Three Communities." Paper presented at the annual meeting of the American Public Health Association, Boston, Massachusetts, November 14, 1988.

Weinberg, Dinah. "Plan is Penciled in to Clean Industri-Plex." *Boston Globe,* December 6, 1988.

Wessen, Barbara. "Participatory Strategies in Community Health Effects Research." Unpublished manuscript.

Wilford, John Noble. "Ecologists See Warnings in Sea Pollution Incidents." *New York Times,* September 13, 1987.

Winner, Langdon. *The Whale and the Reactor: A Search for Limits in an Age of High Technology.* Chicago: University of Chicago Press, 1986.

Wood, Diane. "Unifirst Countersues for Toxic Allegations." *Woburn Daily Times,* June 3, 1985.

Yeager, Peter C. "Structural Bias in Regulatory Law Enforcement: The Case of the U.S. Environmental Protection Agency." *Social Problems,* 1987, 34:330–344.

Interviews and Personal Communications

As we noted in the text, all unattributed quotes derive from interviews with litigant families, interviews which were central to the research for this book. As these families should remain anonymous, however, their names do not appear below.

Clapp, Richard. Interviews, Boston, March 13 and 14, 1987.

Krimsky, Sheldon. Personal communication, Cambridge, Mass., October 11, 1988.

Lagakos, Steven. Interview, Boston, April 6, 1987.

Latowsky, Gretchen. Interview, Woburn, Mass., May 26, 1988.

Ozonoff, David. Interview, Boston, August 1, 1988.

Plough, Alonzo. Personal communication, Cambridge, Mass. October 11, 1988.

Schlictmann, Jan. Interviews, Boston, May 12, 1987; June 3, 1988; December 13, 1988; June 15, 1989; October 23, 1989; January 10, 1990.

Wessen, Barbara. Interview, Boston, April 3, 1987.

Zelen, Marvin. Interview, Boston, July 1, 1987.

Index

245

Compositor: Maple-Vail Book Manufacturing Group, Inc.
Text: 11/14 Baskerville
Display: Century Bold Condensed
Printer: Maple-Vail Book Manufacturing Group, Inc.
Binder: Maple-Vail Book Manufacturing Group, Inc.